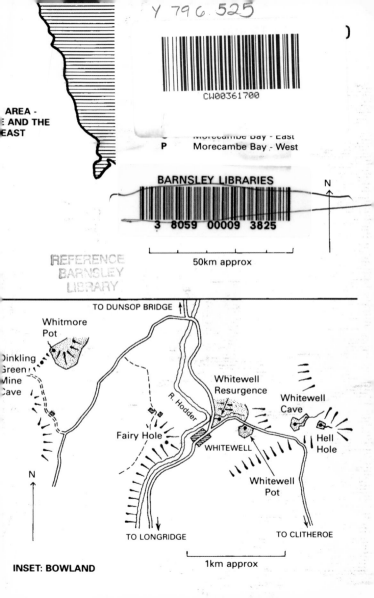

Y 796.525

CW00361700

AREA -
E AND THE
EAST

Morecambe Bay - East
P   Morecambe Bay - West

N

50km approx

TO DUNSOP BRIDGE

Whitmore
Pot

Dinkling
Green
Mine
Cave

R. Hodder

Whitewell
Resurgence

Whitewell
Cave

Fairy Hole

WHITEWELL

Hell
Hole

N

Whitewell
Pot

TO LONGRIDGE

TO CLITHEROE

INSET: BOWLAND

1km approx

Dalesman Publishing Company Limited,
Stable Courtyard, Broughton Hall,
Skipton, North Yorkshire BD23 3AE

First published 1994
© D. Brook, J. Griffiths, M.H. Long, P.F. Ryder, 1994

A British Library Cataloguing in Publication
record is available for this book

ISBN 1 85568 083 1

Volumes in the Northern Caves Series include:

Vol 1   Wharfedale and the North-East

Vol 2   The Three Peaks

Vol 3   The Three Counties System and the North-West

Typeset by Lands Services
Printed by Lavenham Press

CONTENTS

MAPS & SURVEYS

Each area commences with a map. Other maps and surveys are listed below.

Surveys drawn by D. Brook

Cover photo of The Minarets, Lancaster Hole by R. Duffy.

INTRODUCTION

SINCE the last review of the caves covered by this volume, momentous discoveries have taken place. Prodigious feats of diving have linked the master caves of East and West Kingsdale, and have also united the Leck Fell and Ease Gill caves to form the·most extensive cave system in Britain. Other major discoveries in Notts Pot, Rift Pot and Dale Barn Cave are not yet connected to the two super systems, but the eventual link up to form a Three Counties network about 150 kilometres long does not seem far-fetched. Remarkable discoveries have also been made in the thinner limestones of the North – Knock Fell Caverns being nearly 5 kilometres of dense maze cave which defies description.

The guides are now in the form envisaged when we began the series over twenty years ago. There are three volumes with sewn bindings and water resistant covers which should be revised every five years or so, as they go out of print. With the next series we will have to decide how much rigging information to include as bolts and alternative descent routes multiply. A debate on this would be welcome.

Over recent years we have lost three friends whose input to the guides has been invaluable. Roger Sutcliffe, Baz Davies and Derek Crossland were driving forces behind several of the major discoveries described in this volume. They will be sorely missed.

For this volume we have had a record number of people sending us information, and assisting in many ways. Andy Hall supplied much of the new information on Ease Gill and its caverns, Paul Monico provided much data and information for the surveys, and Steven Gale contributed much of the Morecambe Bay area details.

Our thanks also go to Roy Holmes for the DHSS data on Great Knoutberry and to Ian Bretherton, John Cordingley, Colin Davison, Peter Egan, John Holmes, Martin Holroyd, Alan Marshall, Graham Proudlove, Mark Robson, Helen Sergeant, and Alan Speight for all their help.

June 1994.

Caving Club Abbreviations

ACVSU	Ampleforth College Venture Scout Unit
BNFC	Barrow Naturalists' Field Club
BACC	Bishop Auckland Caving Club
BPC	Bradford Pothole Club
BCC	Burnley Caving Club
BSA	British Speleological Association
BSC	Bolton Speleological Club
BRPC	Black Rose Pothole Club
CDG	Cave Diving Group
CNCC	Council of Northern Caving Clubs
CUCC	Cambridge University Caving Club
CPC	Craven Pothole Club
CPG	Cave Projects Group
DHSS	Dent House Speleological Society
EPC	Earby Pothole Club
FMC	Fylde Mountaineering Club
FSWOAG	Friends School, Wigton, Outdoor Activities Group
FSG	Furness Speleological Group
GC	Gritstone Club
HRCG	Heath Rovers Caving Group
HWCPC	Happy Wanderers Cave and Pothole Club
KCC	Kendal Caving Club
LCCC	Lancashire Caving and Climbing Club
LCMRS	Lancaster Cave and Mine Research Society
LUSS	Lancaster University Speleological Society
LUCC	London University Caving Club
MSG	Moldywarps Speleological Group
MUSS	Manchester University Speleological Society
NCC	Northern Cave Club
NCFC	Northern Cavern and Fell Club
NHASA	North Hills Association for Speleological Advancement
NPC	Northern Pennine Club
NSG	Northern Speleological Group
NRCG	North Ribblesdale Caving Group
NSCC	National Scout Caving Centre
OCC	Orpheus Caving Club
PCC	Preston Caving Club
RRCPC	Red Rose Cave and Pothole Club
ULSA	University of Leeds Speleological Association
UWFRA	Upper Wharfedale Fell Rescue Association
VCC	Valley Caving Club
WRPC	White Rose Pothole Club
YRC	Yorkshire Ramblers Club
YSA	Yorkshire Speleological Association
YSS	Yorkshire Subterranean Society
YURT	Yorkshire Underground Research Team

Access and the CNCC

A REFERENCE to a cave or pothole in this guidebook does not imply any right of access or that permission to visit can be obtained. Ask the appropriate person before going to any of them; most people are reasonable and will allow access if you have the courtesy to ask.

Some caving areas require advance application for permits and it is not always possible to include all necessary details in this guidebook. Where indicated it is essential to refer to the Northern Caving Handbook, published by the Council of Northern Caving Clubs and available from caving shops in the Dales. This Handbook also gives full details about CNCC, its membership requirements and club addresses, as well as the background to specific access agreements negotiated with landowners who imposed restrictions. Under the terms of these agreements the Council has the thankless task of controlling access by prior booking for member clubs. In case of difficulty obtaining the CNCC Handbook contact: Council of Northern Caving Clubs, c/o The Sports Council (NW Region), Byrom House, Quay Street, Manchester M3 5FJ.

The Caving Code

ALWAYS tell a responsible person where you are going and when you expect to return. Use your common sense before calling the cave rescue to an overdue party.

Practise the Country Code – close gates, cover up digs, and don't knock walls or fences down. Take any litter home.

Ensure that all equipment is sound and that the party is properly equipped with safety helmets, adequate clothing, good lamps with reserves, and food if necessary. For ladder pitches everyone must have a whistle and use the standard code – one blast, stop; two blasts, haul in; three blasts, pay out. Keep lifelines taut and only use appropriate knots.

Treat caves with care – their great interest and scientific value depend on them staying as unspoilt as possible. Preserve all underground phenomena, such as calcite formations, and protect cave life, particularly by not polluting water or cave deposits. Spent carbide must always be taken out. In known or potential archaeological sites don't do any digging; any accidental find of archaeological material must not be touched and should be reported immediately to a museum or similar authority.

If you want to go caving, join a club and gain experience with reliable companions and equipment.

ACCIDENT PROCEDURE – SEE OUTSIDE BACK COVER

Access and English Nature

Through consultation with the Council of Northern Caving Clubs, landowners and occupiers, English Nature hopes to maintain the caves both on its own land, and within Sites of Special Scientific Importance (S.S.S.I.'s). Access restrictions would only be warranted if the caves were being damaged irresponsibly, or similar damage was being inflicted on vegetation and wildlife. Restrictions will not be necessary as long as the tradition of care and concern for the caves and their surroundings is maintained. English Nature is constantly reviewing its access policies, and any requirements will be posted on the land. All cavers are urged not to carry out works such as digging, and diverting streams within the S.S.S.I.'s without first consulting them so as to prevent unwitting damage. It is likely they will usually have no objections.

For access, consent and other advice write to:
English Nature
N.E. Regional Office,
Archbold House,
Archbold Terrace,
Newcastle-upon-Tyne
NE2 1EG
(Tel: 091-2816316)

Geological Information

AT the beginning of many descriptions in volumes 1 and 3 in particular is a note of the bed in which the cave lies. The names of Carboniferous limestones are abbreviated in accordance with the conventions used by the British Geological Survey and, if no bed is listed, the cave is in Great Scar Limestone – which is here taken to include the lower beds of the Yoredale Series in those places where they are, for caving purposes, effectively part of the Great Scar; and which incorporates the Hawes Limestone in much of the Three Peaks area.

The names of similar beds vary from place to place, as do the beds themselves. A simplified correlation of the Carboniferous limestones of interest to cavers is given below for the main part of the caving area covered in this series of guides. The vertical sequence is correctly shown, and beds on the same line are equivalents. Caves are not known in every bed and the intervening sandstones, shales, etc., including some thin limestones, have been ignored. Beds other than limestones are named in full where possible. The Askrigg Block names apply in the areas up to and including Gretadale, and the Alston Block names apply in the Teesdale, Weardale and Alston areas.

MORECAMBE BAY AND FURNESS	ASKRIGG BLOCK	ALSTON BLOCK
	Grassington Grit	
RM Roosecote Mudstones	Upper Bowland Shales	Hensingham Group
	ML Main Limestone	**GL** Great Limestone
	UnL Underset Limestone	**4FL** Four Fathom Limestone
	3YL Three Yard Limestone	**3YL** Three Yard Limestone
	5YL Five Yard Limestone	**5YL** Five Yard Limestone
GF Gleaston Formation	**MdL** Middle Limestone	**ScL** Scar Limestone
	SiL Simonstone Limestone	**TBL** Tynebottom Limestone
	HScL Hardraw Scar Limestone	**JL** Jew Limestone
	HwL Hawes Limestone	**SmL** Smiddy Limestone
		PgL Peghorn Limestone
UL Urswick Limestone	**GScl** Great Scar Limestone	**RnL** Robinson Limestone
		MSL Melmerby Scar Limestone
PL Park Limestone		
DB Dalton Beds		
RHB Red Hills Beds		
MaL Martin Limestone		
BB Basement Beds		

Using this Guide

THIS book is intended as guidance for the wise, not the obedience of fools.

LOCATIONS

The national grid reference (NGR) gives the location of the south-west corner of the 100m square in which the entrance lies, in accordance with convention. Altitudes are given to help in locating entrances on maps and in relation to one another; it should be noted that relatively few entrances have been precisely located by levelling and altitudes are generally approximations, although they should be sufficiently accurate for most purposes.

The maps are sketch maps, to show the locations of entrances in relation to nearby features, and should not be regarded as accurate over longer distances.

The inclusion of a track or footpath does not infer a public right of way, and this should always be checked from other sources.

GRADING

The grades usually apply only to the normal route to the deepest or furthest point of a cave. In complex systems they can only be a rough guide; where convenient some sections of caves may have their own grade, which also includes the easiest route from the surface to that section. Alternatively the cave is given a varying grade and the comparative difficulties of different routes should be apparent from the text. The grades only apply to those caves or parts of caves which are accessible to non-divers.

When planning trips think of the return journey and remember that the grades only apply to fit, competent and properly equipped parties; novices in particular will find the caves harder than indicated and for most systems there must be sufficient experienced and competent cavers in the party.

Grade I	Easy cave; no pitches or difficulties.
Grade II	Moderate caves and small potholes.
Grade III	Caves and potholes without any particularly hazardous, difficult or strenuous sections.
Grade IV	Caves and potholes which present some hazard, difficulty or large underground pitch.
Grade V	Caves and potholes which include very strenuous sections or large and wet underground pitches.

SUMPS

The descriptions of underwater passages given in this guide are intended to act merely as a record of their existence. They are not adequate for anyone contemplating diving. No warnings on sumps are given as it is assumed that all sites should be approached with extreme care. For details on specific hazards and line configurations the reader is referred to the publications of the Cave

Diving Group, in particular the Northern Sump Index and the quarterly Newsletter.

Free dives are always a hazard – conditions in sumps alter, lines may snag or break, air in airbells may be foul, and route finding can be a difficulty. Only go with a competent diver who knows the sump well.

FLOODING

Any stream cave or pothole can flood rapidly and unpredictably; so can many which are usually dry. The warnings are for guidance and cannot cover all circumstances – no warning does not mean no hazard. If in doubt – stay out.

OTHER HAZARDS

Minimise objective dangers by using fail-safe techniques in which the party is competent. Safety should be uppermost in the thoughts of all cavers. Lifelines should be used on ladder pitches, and secondary belays should be used as necessary.

Potential hazards for the careless or unwary caver are too numerous to mention and are present in any cave or pothole, whatever its grade. Route finding in complex systems also defies adequate description and there is no substitute for an experienced leader.

ARTIFICIAL AIDS

References in these guidebooks to artificial aids such as bolt belays, iron ladders, fixed lines in sumps, shoring in digs, etc., does not imply that such aids are safe. All artificial aids should be regarded with suspicion; they have usually been provided only for the short-term convenience of the persons who originally placed them. The use of small bolts to facilitate exploration or single rope techniques has increased to such a degree that it would be impossible for a guide of this sort to be up-to-date on their placing. For that reason, and the more important one that small bolts are likely to be relatively impermanent, they have generally not been mentioned. Deterioration of all artificial aids is inevitable and it is up to every individual potholer or group leader to decide whether or not to rely upon any such fixtures.

SINGLE ROPE TECHNIQUES

The descriptions and tackle lists in this guide generally refer to the traditional route down a pitch – usually the most direct – and may not be appropriate for SRT descents. Early SRT routes followed the traditional routes and encountered problems such as volume of water, rope abrasion and sharpness of rock, making rope protection essential. Modern SRT routes are attempts to avoid such hazards: they may vary greatly in route and rope needs from the traditional way. For example, a pitch might involve a traverse with six or seven bolts, a Y hang, two re-belays, a deviation belay, and could need a rope two or three times as long as the vertical drop. SRT routes and rope lengths will alter depending on the whims of the rigger; as bolts rust and are replaced; and as better routes are found. By contrast, the details of a traditional route will usually remain unchanged – save that alternative belays may be used. It is consequently impractical to describe SRT routes and keep the guide to a reasonable length. SRT cavers, while using the general description of a pothole, must be sufficiently competent to establish their own routes and tackle requirements for pitches as the descent progresses.

WARNING
Many threaded anchor sleeves are now unsafe, and failures have occurred. Always inspect carefully, and use back up belays. If in doubt don't use it!

IMPORTANT
While every reasonable effort has been made to ensure the information in this guidebook is accurate, neither the authors nor the publisher can accept responsibility for any errors, inaccuracies or omissions.

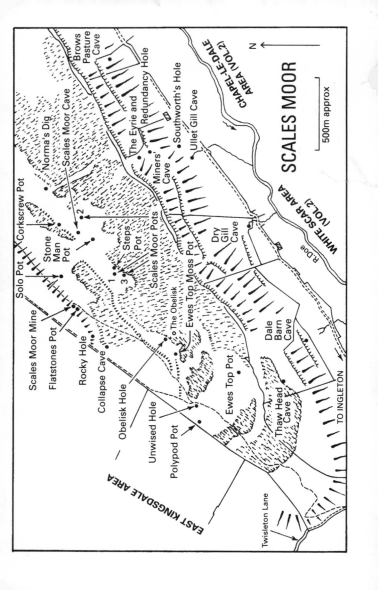

SCALES MOOR

N

500m approx

CHAPEL-LE-DALE AREA (VOL.2)

WHITE SCAR AREA (VOL.2)

EAST KINGSDALE AREA

Brows Pasture Cave

Norma's Dig

Scales Moor Cave

The Eyrie and Redundancy Hole

Southworth's Hole

Miners' Cave

Ullet Gill Cave

Corkscrew Pot

Solo Pot

Stone Man Pot

2

Steps Pot

Scales Moor Pots

3

1

Scales Moor Mine

Flatstones Pot

Rocky Hole

Collapse Cave

The Obelisk

Ewes Top Moss Pot

Dry Gill Cave

R.Doe

Obelisk Hole

Unwised Hole

Polypod Pot

Ewes Top Pot

Dale Barn Cave

Thaw Head Cave

TO INGLETON

Twisleton Lane

SCALES MOOR

BROWS PASTURE CAVE NGR SD 730769 Grade II
Alt. 267m   **Length 37m**
Explored 1969, BSA.

 Insignificant entrance covered by rocks at foot of small outcrop about 30m from boundary wall. Low crawl leads to small, mud-floored phreatic tube. After crawling through pool, passage gradually enlarges at bend to the right, and walking for a short distance enters a small breakdown chamber. From far side of this an extremely tight crawl leads past several bends to where way on is choked completely.

COLLAPSE CAVE NGR SD 710769 Grade I
Alt. 390m   **Length 4.5m**
Situated 46m S of Rocky Hole and 50m from wall in shakehole where roof of a shallow cave has collapsed. Passage can be followed in a northerly direction as a low streamway for 4,5m to where the continuation becomes too low.

CORKSCREW POT NGR SD 719772 Grade II
Alt. 389m   **Depth 14.6m**
Explored 1970, BSA.

 Entrance in steep sided shakehole 90m S of ruined building on the clints, and is at present covered by boulders. The rift pitch enlarges considerably 4.5m down, then spirals round on itself to end in a choke. It is possible to free climb to the bottom but is easier with a ladder.

Tackle – 15m ladder; stake & sling belay; 18m lifeline.

DALE BARN CAVE NGR SD 711755 Grade IV-V
Alt. 259m   **Length 4.1km**
Explored 1956, NSG; extended 1967, HWCPC; 1973-1976, NCC; 1989-1993 CDG.

WARNING – Neopolitan Pool in the new entrance and parts of Anathema Crawl sump in wet weather.

Entrance Series
 Old entrance, now blocked, is in field near spring. Use new entrance in boulders below first prominent scar. A fascinating cave of considerable significance for this area of Scales Moor. Descending muddy crawl for 30m leads to two chambers and a crawl in pools, ending at Neapolitan Pool. This

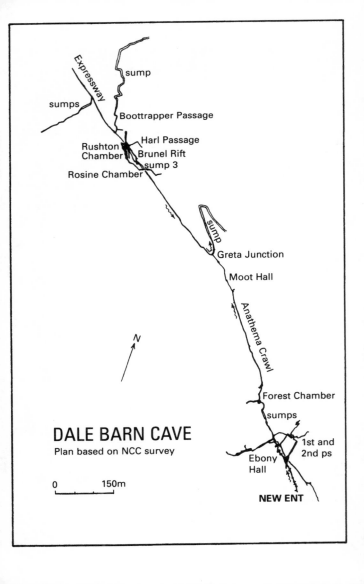

DALE BARN CAVE

Plan based on NCC survey

0   150m

was a tight, technical free-dive which had to be treated with great respect, even though only 2m long, but has been improved by blasting.

Low varied passage leads to the 12m high Ebony Hall. Down slope on right and across hall leads for 61m up steep boulder slope in rift. At top after 9m is a 17m pitch and a further 3m drop to a pool. Other side from drop is 9m pitch to boulder choke and sink. Over top of main pitch on left is small passage which ends in a draughting dig after 91m.

From Ebony Hall slope below opposite wall leads to several chambers via low arches and to another large chamber. Left leads for 137m through rifts and low sandy crawls past small oxbow to a choked sandy dig. Straight on and down from large chamber for 15m, still in main system, leads to stream and low passage on right. This is end of way in from old entrance and may be followed for 46m of wet crawling to junction. Stream comes from right out of rifts which have been blasted but get too tight. Off left leads through low canals for 213m and emerges below old entrance which is usually blocked.

Back in main system way leads on via stream through phreatic chambers to low canal and chamber before first sump. Normally this is low airspace to an enlargement and short dive to an airbell. Easy 13m dive to another airbell and then 6m dive through to large chamber.

Dale Barn 2

From large chamber is 18m of passage to Forest Chamber. Inlet off left leads after 30m to sand choke in tight crawl. Main way on is down right, past aven, to arduous 317m long Anathema Crawl. Halfway along this is Ogden's Inlet, a short ascent to the base of a 50m high rift climbed in two sections. At the top a low bedding leads off ending after 30m at a collapsed boulder. Anathema continues to Moot Hall and a further 91m crawl emerges through boulders at Greta Junction in large stream passage. Downstream passes under an 8m aven, which becomes tight at the top, to sump after 46m. This has been dived for 280m to where the way on was lost. Upstream 317m of easy cave, with canals, leads to another sump.

Dale Barn 3

This sump is 46m long with airbells and emerges in cross rift with steep mud slope on right. Continuing sump is too low. At top of slope is rift passage for 61m to where false floor ends at formations. An exposed traverse, Brunel Rift, is made via a rocking boulder (care) to climb up into Rushton Chamber, with straw formations. To right is calcite-floored crawl which becomes extremely low before emerging in a very large passage, the Expressway. In one direction this leads back to Rushton Chamber via a sandy, sloping crawl. The other way passes under a huge aven, the Missile Silo, climbed for 25m and continuing above, and another aven 15m high, to a section of well decorated passage which closes down. Just before the Missile Silo a passage leads off on the left. After 15m is a sump. This is 20m long to a short section of muddy passage and another 3m sump. Beyond is 150m of passage, mainly crawling, to low silted bedding. Two inlets on left become impassable.

Back in Rushton Chamber on left side are two low crawls, the lower one ending after about 24m. The upper passage, at roof level, starts 4.5m wide and 1m high and is floored with boulders. After 30m is a 15m long boulder choked passage on right. Generally unappealing caving follows for several hundred metres punctuated by two chambers, the first, Rosine Chamber, with magnificent 1m long red stalactite hanging from the centre. Passage ends in a low draughting bedding.

Above the far end of Brunel Rift is Harl Passage, gained by a short climb from the bottom of Rushton Chamber. This begins 1m high and 1.5m wide, but soon intersects a slightly larger passage at a 'T' junction. Right leads to a window overlooking Brunel Rift, while left degenerates into a squalid crawl that has been followed for 76m before commonsense prevailed.

At the bottom of Brunel Rift is small complex of passages on left ending in a sump which closes down to an impenetrable bedding. This is not far from the upstream continuation of the sump leading into Dale Barn 3. Straight on at the base of Brunel Rift a climb up a flake enters Boottrapper Passage. After 61m is 6m climb up into bedding plane. Ahead is a low inlet, but passage turns left to reach a sump after a further 61m. This heads down dip and up valley and has been dived for 360m.

Tackle

Pitch	Ladder	Belay	Lifeline
1st	17m	3m	21m
2nd	9m	1m	12m

Permission – Twisleton Dale House.

DRY GILL CAVE   NGR SD 718759   Grade III
Alt. 236m   Length 1070m
Extended 1969, BSA and GC; 1970-1991, CDG; 1988, NCC.

WARNING – In wet weather the whole system is extremely flood prone and large lengths fill completely in a very short space of time. If any water is flowing from the entrance the cave should not be entered.

Obvious entrance at head of normally dry watercourse to W of road, just up-valley from Twisleton Dale House. Short sideways crawl and climb into roof bedding enters wide collapse chamber and further awkward crawl to a 'T' junction. To the left a tight crawl can be followed through two squeezes to where it splits and becomes impassable. To the right the passage ends in a pool alongside a boulder wall but a climb up through blocks on the right at the start of the pool emerges in a wide, low, boulder-floored passage – The Obstacle Course.

Crawling over fallen slabs reaches a lower section with a solid floor. A short sloping bedding up to the right becomes too tight. Main way continues as a flat-out crawl to more collapsed blocks; a crawl over one of these beneath a hanging slab reaches The Arch, a low horizontal slot. From here a confusing crawl at two different levels with several tight squeezes finally enlarges and after 30m reaches a ledge 1m above the floor of the main stream passage.

Upstream Series

From junction with entrance passage the initially small streamway enlarges rapidly but then lowers to a short duck, with adequate airspace in good conditions. An impassable aven on the right here connects with the high level Disappointment Passage. Beyond, the roof lifts into a fine passage 4.5m wide and 3m high with a sloping cascade, and odd boulders littering the floor. The roof lowers at the start of a long pool with a 1m long low airspace duck at the far end. Short canal crawl leads over a cobble bank to a large passage and only a few yards further is the upstream sump. This has been dived for 320m, past an underwater boulder choke, to emerge in 35m of passage with an aven inlet which becomes too tight. This passage ends at a second sump in a low bedding. A dive of 40m leads to a further 15m of dry cave with a 21m aven blocked by boulders. The continuing sump has been dived for 100m to where it gets too low.

On the right just before the sump is an inspill of boulders, and a cautious climb up through these enters an aven with numerous unstable hanging blocks. A climb to the right leads to a further passage which quickly descends a steep shingle slope to a static sump. This has also been dived through a tight squeeze into a small submerged chamber after 6m, the apparent way on being an unexplored, constricted slot.

Downstream Series

Streamway narrows rapidly from junction with the entrance passage, to deep water and a long duck which emerges in a low, wide chamber with mud banks around the walls. On the left a slope leads into the Upper Series. From far side of the chamber the roof drops to a low airspace 6m duck into a large passage. Ahead is a steep mud and boulder slope, whilst the stream flows off down impassable slots in the left wall. Water can be regained by climbing part way up the slope to a rift in the left wall. On up the slope leads to two chambers, both with unstable boulders everywhere, and no obvious route on. Following the water enters a low, wet crawl which after about 24m, including a bad duck, reaches a drop to an impassable passage.

Beyond the drop a low crawl ends at a junction, both ways off soon closing down. In the roof though a tight rift climb of 3m emerges in a bedding plane. 150m of varied going, past a short sumped inlet, leads to a calcite choke.

Upper Series

From the top of the slope referred to above a large passage is entered. Right ends at a beautiful stalagmite cascade whilst left ascends a steep mud slope to a small circular chamber with a bedding passage running across it at roof level. Left here quickly becomes too low, whilst in the opposite direction a flat-out crawl along the left wall enlarges considerably into a small chamber. Under the left wall is a crawl to the top of the impassable aven seen in the Upstream Series, whilst ahead lies a crawl alongside a large stalagmite bank, past several squeezes to where the way enlarges dramatically at the start of Disappointment Passage.

The next stretch is very pretty, the walls, roof and floor being covered with a powdery stal deposit, and odd pools have a film of cave ice. Walking continues for 46m to where the passage becomes a tall rift. Just beyond a pile of boulders the route divides. Left climbs up a stalagmite-covered boulder pile to a small choked grotto and right is an extremely tight crawl for 6m to a narrow, impassable slot down against the right wall. Through this blows a strong draught and the main stream can be heard below, as this point is in the wall of the unstable aven just down from the upstream sump.

Permission – Twisleton Dale House.

EWES TOP POT   NGR SD 709761   Grade II
Alt. 396m   Depth 8m

Rather obscure shaft at SW corner of Scales Moor, not far from valley edge. A straight descent in small rift to solid boulder-choked floor.

Tackle – 8m ladder; stake & sling belay; 12m lifeline.

EWES TOP MOSS POT   NGR SD 710764   Grade II
Alt. 392m   Depth 8m
Explored 1981, BSC.

Situated in small grassy depression 150m W of The Obelisk (see Obelisk Hole) is a narrow, convoluted shaft. At a depth of 6m the shaft ends at slope to a complete choke of boulders.

Tackle – 6m ladder; sling belay; 9m lifeline.

THE EYRIE   NGR SD 723767   Grade I
Alt. 350m   **Length 6m**

Rift entrance situated high up in the left hand gulley of Ullet Gill just above the broken down wall. Small, phreatically enlarged rift passage slopes upwards and gradually narrows until it becomes impassable. Immediately above this point on the surface is a small hole down through large boulders, although there is no physical connection.
Permission – Springcote Farm.

FLATSTONES POT   NGR SD 713770   Grade II
Alt. 396m   Depth 18m

Midway along line of shakeholes at foot of final slope up to top boundary wall dividing Scales Moor from East Kingsdale, and recognisable by the large flat limestone slabs bridged across the entrance pitch. A straight descent of 9.4m lands in a slight enlargement of the rift on top of a debris cone. To the NE a boulder slope can be followed down for 4.5m to where the way on is choked, whilst in the opposite direction a small slope and further vertical drop of 4.5m lands in a rift passage. In front the passage enlarges at an aven, and then immediately closes into a narrow fissure which can only be followed for a few metres to an unstable choke.

Tackle

Pitch	Ladder	Belay	Lifeline
1st and 2nd	17m	2m	23m

MINERS' CAVE   NGR SD 724766   Grade I
Alt. 328m   **Length 76m**   Depth 18m – dived to 38m
Explored 1974, LUSS.

Entrance part way up the Ullet Gill gulley below old mine workings. Beware of loose boulder at entrance. Descending rift passage with boulders is formed in a fault and ends in a small sump pool.

Sump has been dived for 30m to 20m depth. Cave was used to drain a mine level above, which has collapsed.

NORMA'S DIG NGR SD 721 772 Grade I
Alt. 390m **Depth 20m**
Explored 1989, NCC.

Narrow rift entrance in featureless area of Scales Moor E of old ruined building on raised clint area. 3m climb leads to boulder floor and hole leading to a further 8m descent to severe restriction. Below this is further 8m drop to complete boulder choke.

There is a 4m deep shaft with a tight entrance in the clints 50m SSE of Norma's Dig.

Tackle – 20m ladder; stake & sling belay; 25m lifeline.

OBELISK HOLE NGR SD 711765 Grade II
Alt. 392m **Depth 4.5m**
Explored 1981, BSC.

230m E of the footpath crossing Ewes Top Moss is a large isolated limestone erratic block – The Obelisk. 73m to the NW and just off the limestone pavement, is a constricted shaft covered with small slabs. Tight entrance opens out slightly to end at an organic choke!

Tackle – 4.5m ladder; 9m belay; 8m lifeline.

POLYPOD POT NGR SD 705762 Grade II
Alt. 396m **Depth 8m**
Explored 1973, BSA.

Small shaft 20m from top boundary wall at S end of Scales Moor. A descent to a boulder floor leads to excavated section into small chamber with further slot in the floor too narrow to enter.

Tackle – 8m ladder; stake & sling belay; 9m lifeline.

REDUNDANCY HOLE NGR SD 723766 Grade I
Alt. 311m **Length 18m**
Explored 1975, NCC.

In Ullet Gill slightly lower than and to the right of The Eyrie. A 1m diameter tube gradually decreases to body size. It becomes even smaller and there is no draught.

ROCKY HOLE NGR SD 710769 Grade II
Alt. 396m **Depth 6m**

Entrance is in small shakehole at S end of row leading to Flatstones Pot. Climbable descent through boulders, some quite loose, to a complete choke.

SCALES MOOR CAVE NGR SD 718770 Grade II
Alt. 389m **Length 15m** **Depth 14m**
Entrance in large shakehole just below final step up on to clint area with old ruin on it. A scramble down over a boulder leads into a large rift passage sloping downwards, and lit by daylight entering through a narrow hole from an adjoining shakehole. The slope ends at a tight slot in the floor, but it is

possible to traverse forward on ledges to where the passage widens and a showerbath enters from the roof ahead. Again daylight enters from an open shaft. The floor and final choke can be reached by climbing down into the slot just before the traverse ends.

There is a short cave in the next shakehole NE from Scales Moor Cave. It is a 10m crawl, tight in places.

SCALES MOOR MINE   NGR SD 713771   Grade II
Alt. 396m   **Length 36m**   **Depth 23m**

Explored 1971, BSA; extended 1983, NCC.

Entrance in row of shakeholes 30m NE of Flatstones Pot, and on ridge between two adjacent hollows. Small shaft leads to artificially enlarged crawl, 18m long, ending at short slope down to head of 12m pitch with bolt belay.

At foot upstream passage can only be followed for 4 metres to a constriction, whilst downstream a crawl leads to a short drop into a chamber. The outlet passage becomes too tight almost immediately.

Tackle

Pitch	Ladder	Belay	Lifeline
Entrance	free climbable, 8m rope useful		
2nd	12m	Spreader	15m

SCALES MOOR POTS   Grade II
Alt. 389m

These shafts are very hard to locate on the almost featureless limestone wastes of Scales Moor, but 1 is almost straight out onto the bench from Flatstones Pot, 2 is nearly 400m NW of the head of Ullet Gill, and 3 is about 90m S of 1.

1. NGR SD 715768   Length 22m   Depth 21m

In a long rift shakehole with the entrance at the end. A 11m pitch lands in a small chamber with an inlet stream cascading out of a very narrow passage up one wall. To the side of the chamber is a further 5.5m pitch to a boulder floor, and a few metres along the rift is a small climb down to an enlarged passage which becomes too tight after 15m.

Tackle

Pitch	Ladder	Belay	Lifeline
1st and 2nd	18m	Sling	21m

2. NGR SD 719770   Depth 12m

The entrance is surrounded by an almost smooth circle of exposed limestone to one side of a large rocky shakehole. An awkward free climb, or 8m ladder climb leads to a window to one side, and a further 4.5m descent down an off-vertical pitch reaches a choke. In wet weather a small stream enters part way down first pitch to sink in choke.

There is a 4m deep rift 20m N of 2.

Tackle

Pitch	Ladder	Belay	Lifeline
1st and 2nd	12m	Sling	18m

3. NGR SD 715767 **Depth 18m**
Explored 1973, BCC.

Excavated entrance to fine, free-hanging ladder climb. At foot is passage which narrows very quickly in both directions. 10m E of 3 is a small cave, 8m long and 5m deep ending in a choke.

Tackle – 20m ladder; stake & sling belay; 23m lifeline.

SOLO POT
NGR SD 715771
Grade II
Alt. 396m
Depth 6m

In shallow shakehole 80m SW of first small stream sink at foot of Rigg Side and 20m from path. A straight descent into rift, with narrow passage leading off. This gradually closes in to become impassable after about 6m.

Tackle – 8m ladder; stake & sling belay; 12m lifeline.

SOUTHWORTH'S HOLE
NGR SD 724764
Grade I
Alt. 251m   **Length 8m**
Explored 1969, HWCPC.

On up-hill side of wire fence, and just to S of Ullet Gill. A small gully entrance covered with large boulders, which must be replaced, leads into a short, sloping passage and a chamber. All possible ways on are choked, but in wet weather a small stream entering in wall of chamber sinks in floor.
Permission – Springcote Farm.

STEPS POT
NGR SD 715768
Grade III
Alt. 389m
Depth 15m
Explored 1967, BSA.

Entrance is in centre of clint outcrop in shakehole some 46m E of Scales Moor Pot 1. A very tight section opens out into a large shaft, and care should be taken passing a huge boulder bridged across part way down. At the foot of pitch is small chamber with a choked floor, and an impassable slot to one end through which can be heard the noise of flowing water.

Tackle – 15m ladder; bar & sling belay; 18m lifeline.

STONE MAN POT
NGR SD 717770
Grade III
Alt. 389m
Depth 14m
Explored 1949, CPC.

The entrance is situated in the more northerly of a pair of adjacent shakeholes some 37m from a large isolated limestone boulder. A cautious descent past unstable boulders can be made to a landing on a loose pile of rocks. To one side a further precarious descent over debris can be made for 6m to a choke, whilst on the opposite side, and now covered by collapse debris, was a further shaft plumbed to 27m but which got too tight 8m down.

Tackle

Pitch	Ladder	Belay	Lifeline
1st and 2nd	14m	Stake & sling	18m

THAW HEAD CAVE   NGR SD 708757   Grade I
Alt. 375m   **Length 10m**

Rock shelter above spoil heap. Excavated and recorded by John Thorp (NCC). Do not disturb the deposits.

ULLET GILL CAVE   NGR SD 723763   Grade II
Alt. 241m   **Length 75m**

At head of normally dry stream bed at foot of small scar. In wet weather is an important flood rising, issuing a very large stream. A small step down at right hand end of scar leads into a low, but wide bedding cave. Excavated crawl for 34m leads to junction. To left becomes too low after 20m while passage on right needs diving gear to progress without drowning. It has been pushed for 20m.

UNWISED HOLE   NGR SD 706762   Grade I
Alt. 396m   **Length 6m**   **Depth 6m**
Explored 1983, NCC.

Entrance is in small shakehole beside path on Ewes Top, 200m from gap through clints. A slide down small tube leads to drop into small chamber. Hole in floor gains boulder floored bedding which chokes immediately.

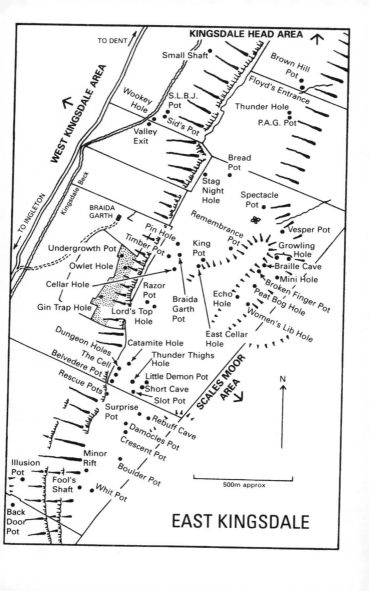

EAST KINGSDALE

BACK DOOR POT NGR SD 699761 Grade III
Alt. 294m **Depth 27m**
Explored 1977, NCC.

In small valley to N of Wackenburgh Hill, and near northern boundary wall. Steep-sided shakehole has narrow cleft in floor between limestone outcrops, and 3m climb down leads to awkward squeeze and further 3m drop. At foot a tight rift quickly reaches yet another 3m climb, possibly best dealt with by ladder or handline. From bottom an inclined fissure descends to head of a 14m pitch, tight at top, but opening out lower down. Only possible outlet at foot quickly narrows to impassable dimensions.

Tackle

Pitch	Ladder	Belay	Lifeline
3m Climb	6m handline or sling & 4.5m ladder		
14m Pitch	15m	3m	21m

BELVEDERE POT NGR SD 704768 Grade II
Alt. 366m **Depth 8.2m**
Explored 1956, FMC.

The most southerly of the group of holes which are located in the SW corner of Lord's Lot Top. A narrow rift with sharp projections on the walls leads to a boulder choked floor. The pitch is rather awkward to climb.

Tackle – 8m ladder; stake & sling belay; 12m lifeline.
Permission – Braida Garth Farm.

BOULDER POT NGR SD 705764 Grade II
Alt. 396m **Depth 8m**

At head of shallow gully in shakehole with large boulder along one side. Slide down mud slope under boulder leads into small chamber with short climb down muddy rift to choke.

Close by are two further unnamed holes; one being a scramble down a mud and boulder slope into a choked chamber and the other a small rift passage which can be followed for a few metres to where it becomes too low.
Permission – Braida Garth Farm.

BRAIDA GARTH POT NGR SD 707775 Grade II
Alt. 372m **Depth 12m**

Fenced shaft directly above Braida Garth Farm. An easy ladder climb down leads to a choked floor which slopes down into what may be the start of a passage at the SE corner.

Tackle – 12m ladder; stake & sling belay; 15m lifeline.
Permission – Braida Garth Farm.

BRAILLE CAVE   NGR SD 712775   Grade I
Alt. 383m   **Length 21m**   Depth 3m
Explored 1981, NCC.

Situated in a shallow valley between Growling Hole and Broken Finger Pot. Climb down at entrance to crawl heading N which ends where large block bisects passage. Left of block is choked, while right of block the passage becomes too narrow to follow but emits a strong draught, probably indicating a connection with Growling Hole in the vicinity of the big pitch.

At opposite end of entrance shakehole a low cave, used as a fox lair, can be followed for 9m.
Permission – Braida Garth Farm.

BREAD POT   NGR SD 710779   Grade II
Alt. 373m   Depth 12m

The most northerly of the fenced shafts on Lord's Lot Top, and close to the tumbledown N boundary wall. A slope of boulder clay leads to the edge of the wide hole, and an easy ladder pitch reaches a sloping choked floor which drops to a complete choke at the N side.

Tackle – 12m ladder; stake & sling belay; 18m lifeline.
Permission – Braida Garth Farm.

BROKEN FINGER POT   NGR SD 711774   Grade IV
Alt. 383m   **Length 61m**   Depth 27m
Explored 1964, HWCPC.

Follow the dry side valley by the pile of gritstone boulders to enter the Growling Hole basin. If the row of shakeholes along the W side is followed, the last to be reached is a large rock-sided one. The entrance to the pot is behind boulders at the foot of the drainage gully. From the entrance a small drop leads to the start of a very narrow passage only passable in the roof bedding, and after 12m of hard going the head of the only pitch is reached. This is extremely awkward both to ladder and to climb at the top. The wood beam and a rock flake on the right are both rather dubious belay points.

The shaft bells out to large dimensions and the landing is in a roomy chamber. To one side is a short upstream crawl to an aven chamber with two inlets splashing down, whilst downstream another short crawl quickly enlarges into a high but narrow fissure. Traversing is necessary, and three further aven inlets are passed before the way on becomes too narrow. Just before this point is reached it is possible to descend from the traverse to floor level but again the way forward is impassable.

Tackle – 15m ladder; stake & sling belay; 18m lifeline.
Permission – Braida Garth Farm.

BROWN HILL POT   NGR SD 714784   Grade IV
Alt. 370m   Length 1010m   Depth 112m
Explored 1980, NCC.

WARNING – Entrance passage and bottom of big pitch become impassable in wet weather.

Excavated entrance near gate in S boundary wall of Heron Pot field is recognisable by scaffold shoring. Climb down entrance leads to Velcro Pot, which can be free-climbed. Directly below is Le Boyau a flat-out crawl in water for 30m to two avens and squeeze to a third aven. A washed-out shale bed in the roof of a narrow rift is then followed for 21m to a 4.5m climb down to the head of a blind 8m pot. Step over hole in floor to crawl over loose blocks, ending at squeeze below jammed boulder. Through squeeze the 1st pitch is met, and Floyd's Entrance enters on the left.

At foot of pitch is roomy chamber, but passage out is a hands and knees crawl to the large Galerie pas Mur, where a spectacular waterfall enters from left. This has been bolted for 18m to enter 190m of streamway, ending under large surface sink.

From Galerie pas Mur, traverse along rift at ledge level leads to climb down to stream and a boulder fall, where a traverse on good ledges above stream leads to a widening of the passage and choice of two climbs back down to floor level. Easy going follows to a 9m pitch with narrow outlet. However, traverse over pitch and short crawl lead to the magnificent Puits Ian Plant. This pitch of 50m is split by a large ledge at 29m, and the 21m pitch from the ledge is right in the stream and can become impassable. The easy Marmite Passage follows to the last pitch, at foot of which the passage swings sharp right and ends in a large sump pool. The sump has been dived for 400m to a depth of 6m and continues.

Tackle

Pitch	Ladder	Belay	Lifeline
Entrance			9m
1st	8m	3m	15m
Puits Ian Plant	{ 30m	Short spreader	36m
	{ 21m	Short spreader	27m
Last	8m	3m	9m

BOLT BELAYS – see Warning, page 13.
Permission – Braida Garth Farm.

CATAMITE HOLE   NGR SD 705769   Grade II
Alt. 375m   Depth 14m
Explored 1968, KCC; extended 1975, NSG & PCC.

At foot of stream gully NE of Dungeon Hole in SW corner of Lord's Lot Top. Entrance pitch over and through dangerously poised boulders leads to further 3.7m climb and short length of rift passage. Wedged blocks end this and over them is further short climb down to mud floor in a low, undercut area.

Tackle – 8m ladder; stake & sling belay; 12m lifeline.
Permission – Braida Garth Farm.

THE CELL   NGR SD 704768   Grade I
Alt. 366m   **Depth 4.5m**
Explored 1975, NCC.

Tight shaft situated between Belvedere Pot and Dungeon Hole. It is possible to climb down to the choked floor without needing any tackle.
Permission – Braida Garth Farm.

CELLAR HOLE   NGR SD 707774   Grade I
Alt. 372m   **Depth 9m**

Entrance in steep rock sided shakehole almost on the line between the two shafts of Lord's Top Hole and Braida Garth Pot. A descent of the slope at the S end leads to a climb down over boulders into a small chamber, the walls and roof of which are of highly shattered rock. There is no sign of any way on.
Permission – Braida Garth Farm.

CRESCENT POT   NGR SD 705766   Grade V
Alt. 394m   **Length 1146m**   **Depth 122m**
Explored 1956, FMC; main explorations 1974-9, PCC.

WARNING – Many of the crawls flood to the roof in wet weather. The Parba belay bolts were fixed in 1974-9; only the anchors are in place and they should be treated as potentially unsound.

Entrance lies in rift shakehole approximately 183m SSE of tree at boundary wall of Lord's Lot Top. A mud slope leads down to entrance at N end, and a steep climb down leads to head of first pitch, the landing from which is on a small ledge. A small inlet passage enters here, and can be followed for 12m to a chamber with no passable way on. The second pitch descends from the ledge and a reasonable sized shaft brings one to a further ledge. From here a short climb and traverse reach the head of the short third pitch into a large chamber with floor of stacked boulders and an excavated hole into a low crawl. On left is 21m long inlet terminating at an aven and the main stream then cuts down, necessitating crawling at roof level. On rejoining the water the passage is a tortuous fissure until the struggle eases and an aven is reached with an impassable inlet passage. The main route continues pleasantly passing Tonal Aven on the left and a major inlet on the right. The inlet is 122m of roomy passage to a duck and a choked rift discharging the stream.

On downstream prominent roof tube leads to short fourth pitch followed quickly by the 17m fifth pitch. The stream now runs in a tall fissure to the next pitch, a series of four cascades and on the left another inlet. This tributary is 37m long to two avens and a very tight passage. The main cave however lowers to a crawl until relieved by the seventh pitch and easier passage, lowering once more to a 3m climb and a long canal to a very awkward duck in deep water. The last pitch follows but the worst is yet to come since all the remaining 800m of cave is crawling.

Monotonous crawling for 366m reaches the junction with the Passage of Slime on the left and 61m forward is another passage on the same side which

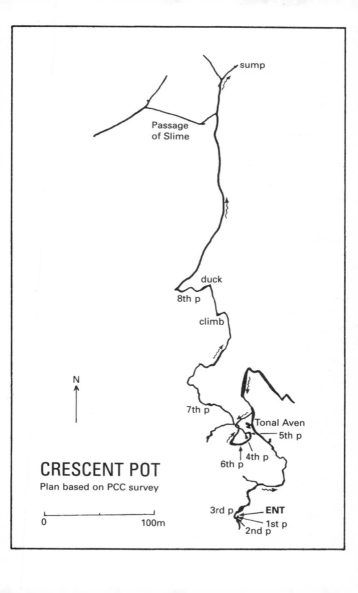

sump

Passage of Slime

duck

8th p

climb

7th p

Tonal Aven

5th p

6th p 4th p

N

CRESCENT POT

Plan based on PCC survey

0   100m

3rd p   ENT

1st p

2nd p

becomes a low inlet after 46m. The main stream finally slides away into a miserable bedding plane sump.

The Passage of Slime is well named for all of the 91m until it reaches a 'T' junction. Here the inlet passage to the left lowers after 76m and the other branch is the unspeakable Passage of Outer Slime, which is a flood outlet and ends in a dig after a struggle over mudbanks.

Tackle

Pitch	Ladder	Belay	Lifeline
1st	9m	1m	12m
2nd	9m	First ladder	12m
Climb		An 8m handline is useful	
3rd	4.5m	1m	8m
4th	4.5m	Bolt & spreader	8m
5th	18m	Bolt & spreader	24m
6th	21m	3m	27m
7th	4.5m	1m	8m
8th	12m	Bolt & spreader	15m

BOLT BELAYS – see Warning, page 13.
Permission – Braida Garth Farm.

DAMOCLES POT   NGR SD 705766   Grade II
Alt. 389m   **Depth 18m**

A deep shakehole 37m N of Crescent Pot, with rock outcrop to one side. A short drop leads into a narrow boulder floored rift sloping down at a steep angle. Just beyond a squeeze an awkward slot gives onto a 3m vertical step into a chamber with just one magnificent stalactite decorating it. The floor of the chamber slopes down to the edge of a further vertical drop, and the same ladder can be used to negotiate them both. At foot the way on is a tight meandering fissure which can only be followed for a few metres before becoming too tight.

Tackle – 9m ladder; 3m belay; 15m lifeline.
Permission – Braida Garth Farm.

DUNGEON HOLES   NGR SD 704768   Grade II
Alt. 366m

1.   **Depth 6m**
In the most northerly shakehole in group of holes lying in SW corner of Lord's Lot Top. Climb down rock into shakehole leads to crawl at N end. Two small steps lead to 3m rift in floor, best laddered, and below is further climb down into small aven chamber with several stunted stalactites in roof. Slot in floor is choked, as also is small inlet in far wall.

Tackle – 4.5m ladder; sling belay; 8m lifeline.

2. Explored 1976, NCC.   **Depth 4.5m**
At SW end of shakehole containing the more obvious large entrance to Dungeon Hole is tight rift pitch which can be descended by slim cavers for 4.5m – foot stirrup useful on return. At bottom is further pitch estimated as

12m deep, with enigmatic noise of running water floating up, but top of shaft is far too tight.

Tackle – 8m ladder; short bar & sling belay; 8m rope as foot loop.
Permission – Braida Garth Farm.

EAST CELLAR HOLE
Alt. 381m

NGR SD 707774
Length 9m

Grade I
Depth 6m

At toe of bank in the next shakehole S from King Pot. A small passage leads off under a rock face as a crawl. The way on enlarges into a narrow rift, and after passing round two right angled bends ends at narrow slot down in the floor.

Permission – Braida Garth Farm.

ECHO HOLE
Alt. 390m

NGR SD 710772

Grade II
Depth 9m

Explored 1964, HWCPC.

In steep mud-sided shakehole at southern end of the Growling Hole basin. An awkward entrance leads onto a 6m shaft, broken a few metres down by a ledge. The bottom section opens out into a spacious rift, and the landing is on a choked floor of mud and boulders. The small stream sinks into a minute slot at one end.

Tackle – 9m ladder; stake & sling belay; 12m lifeline.
Permission – Braida Garth Farm.

FLOYD'S ENTRANCE
Alt. 374m

NGR SD 714784
Length 1010m

Grade IV
Depth 115m

(Grade, length and depth include Brown Hill Pot)
Explored 1980, NCC.

WARNING – Entrance can sump completely in wet weather.

Entrance is 46m SE of Brown Hill Pot at end of shallow gully in obvious flood sink. Climb down of 3.7m in oil drum leads to squeeze and short length of narrow rift passage to a small chamber with inlet on left. Main way is a traverse in roof to a squeeze round a calcite mass into another chamber. An inlet on the right is too tight. Route continues in roof to next bend where climb down to stream leads to narrow, awkward stretch. Easier going follows to a short traverse and two squeezes down to head of a pitch which leads to the junction with Brown Hill Pot upstream of the first pitch. For rest of description see entry for Brown Hill Pot.

Tackle – 8m ladder; 1,5m belay; 15m lifeline.
          Rest of tackle as for Brown Hill Pot.
Permission – Braida Garth Farm.

FOOLS' SHAFT
Alt. 366m

NGR SD 702762

Grade II
Depth 6m

Explored 1975, NCC.

Shaft is on valley side S of George's Scar, opposite Whit Pot. Very tight climbable descent which opens out slightly after initial constriction. Floor is choked but there is a noticeable draught. Rope or foot loop useful for ascent.

Tackle – 9m rope.

GIN TRAP HOLE   NGR SD 704773   Grade I
Alt. 282m   **Length 9m**   **Depth 6m**
Explored 1976, NCC.

Inconspicuous entrance close to bottom wall in centre of Braida Garth Wood. Two short, unstable climbs lead down to a roomy chamber with much flood debris scattered everywhere. A short crawl below entance climb leads to a blockfall where the noise of flowing water can be heard.
Permission – Braida Garth Farm.

GROWLING HOLE   NGR SD 712774   Grade V
Alt. 383m   **Length 290m**   **Depth 111m**
Explored 1968, BSA; extended 1971, LUSS.

WARNING – The tight bedding crawl from the New Entrance floods badly, and some of the pitches quickly become impassable with much water flowing.

Following up the dry side valley with the large pile of gritstone boulders, and continuing round the toe of the bank to the right, the original entrance is to be found in the far corner of a double shakehole marked by signs of excavation and pieces of corrugated iron. The new entrance lies in a large shakehole 41m to the E in the centre of the basin. The original entrance has now collapsed and access can only be gained by the more flood-prone New Entrance.

New Entance pitch is down one of two avens, from where the upstream passage continues to a duck and sump which is by-passed via a constricted crawl in a muddy tube to rejoin the stream. Not far on the main flow enters from an insignificant sump passage on the right, while the low bedding plane ahead becomes too low after 6m.

Downstream from the New Entrance is a canal, ending where a dry oxbow commences on the right. The streamway is a flat-out, wet crawl, becoming easier to a junction where the oxbow re-enters and the way on becomes a hands and knees crawl. Pool Chamber follows after a 1.5m climb down; an inlet to the chamber is a rough crawl for 24m, passing two short, choked inlets on the right before becoming too low.

On downstream a crawl enlarges to a narrow rift which ends at Waterfall Pitch. Beyond, the passage becomes smaller after two avens and a crawl to one side enters the foot of the pitch from the old entrance. Back in the main passage, the water flows in a narrow slot and an awkward traverse leads to a widening at Scimitar Aven, where a short pitch descends to the stream. A tight slot and wet crawl follow to where the passage enlarges somewhat; then two small climbs, best negotiated by traversing out into the wider part of the fissure, lead to the head of Stemple Pitch which has a bolt belay. From the foot a crawl in thick shale bed emerges at a small climb down into a chamber. To the right a steep gully descends to the top of a 9m pitch, whilst along the left wall an easy traverse reaches some large stalagmite bosses and columns, and beyond is The Fault, a magnificent shaft 76m deep.

The best belay is one of the stal bosses with the ladder down the narrow slot. This opens out a short way down and lands on a sloping ledge at 38m. From here it is possible to ascend a steep boulder slope and obtain a splendid view of people climbing the shaft. The next part of the shaft can either be laddered straight on down in a gully against the left wall, or by traversing along a shale bed. Bolts in the wall allow a dry descent of 8m to a further small ledge. Again, the next part can either be laddered straight through as one, or bolts on the right will keep the ladder out of the water for the first part of the climb. A landing is reached on a wide ledge containing a pool, and an easy traverse to the left offers a dry route for the last part of the pitch, a comfortable climb of 9m with adequate natural belay points. The final floor consists of a steep boulder slope through which the stream sinks, and at the opposite end a climb up leads to a very tight crawl and small chamber. Beyond this the fissure is completely choked.

Tackle

Pitch	Ladder	Belay	Lifeline
New Entrance	4.5m	2m	8m
Waterfall Inlet	9m	Sling	15m
Scimitar Pitch	3m	Sling	
Stemple Pitch	6m	Short spreader	12m
The Fault	69m	3m	76m
	and 9m	and sling	and 12m

Or alternatively the top part can be split:

(A)	38m	3m	43m
(B)	21m	Short spreader	24m
(C)	9m	Sling	12m

All the bolts are the small Parba type, fixed in 1971. They should be treated with caution and alternative belays sought if they appear unsound.
Permission – Braida Garth Farm.

ILLUSION POT   NGR SD 700762   Grade II
Alt. 285m   **Length 30m**   **Depth 23m**

In small valley to N of Wackenburgh Hill about 100m from wall. Entrance pitch of 14m in excavated shaft. From base three ways lead off. The first is an unstable, 4m descent to a squeeze into a low crawl ending after 10m in a boulder choke. The second is a series of rifts which leads back towards the surface. The main way on is down slope to free-climbable 8m pitch. Base of this is being excavated.

Tackle – 15m ladder; 1m belay; 18m lifeline.

KING POT   NGR SD 708774   Grade V
Alt. 378m   **Length 5km**   **Depth 125m – dived to 169m**
Explored 1954, RRCPC; extended 1965/6, HWCPC; main exploration 1978, NCC.

WARNING – Areas of loose boulders in vicinity of second pitch, beginning of Queensway and King Henry Hall. Grasshopper Series is liable to serious flooding and must only be entered in dry settled weather.

Located in steep shakehole at foot of bank almost due E of Braida Garth Pot. Entrance is narrow 6m deep climbable rift followed immediately by a

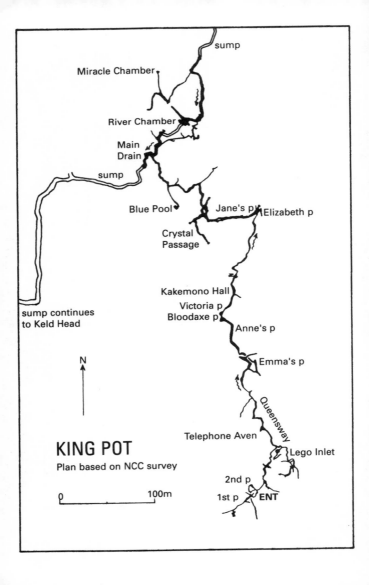

sump

Miracle Chamber

River Chamber

Main
Drain

sump

Blue Pool

Jane's p

Elizabeth p

Crystal
Passage

sump continues
to Keld Head

Kakemono Hall

Victoria p
Bloodaxe p

Anne's p

Emma's p

Queensway

Telephone Aven

Lego Inlet

2nd p

1st p   ENT

N

KING POT

Plan based on NCC survey

0   100m

slot which is top of a 9m rope climb down onto a roomy ledge above the first pitch. Landing is in a chamber with several ways out. Up the wall to left of ladder quickly chokes while opposite the ladder a rift passage soon reaches a junction. To the left is a small chamber with impassable inlets, or straight ahead a muddy tube can be followed for 34m to where a rock projection prevents progress.

The way forward is a short crawl over blocks and scramble up and along a narrow rift to pit in floor which can be traversed by the long-legged or over-come by a 4.5m descent and ascent (rope or ladder). A further crawl enters top of chamber sloping down to hole in dubious boulders (care!) at head of second pitch. Climb up and crawl through boulders to block-strewn canyon and two small climbs to old terminal chamber.

Down slope is flat out bedding plane with 37m long inlet to a small aven and roof chambers. The downstream crawl soon enlarges and beyond a fault chamber develops into a tortuous traverse. Inlet at fault chamber splits into two branches which narrow down. Traverse is strenuous for 37m to awkward exit over hole in boulders at start of Queensway, which is very loose at first (care!) until a 4.5m climb down marks the start of a fine canyon.

43m ahead on the right is Lego Inlet, a large passage which is followed past a choke to a junction. Up to the right is Lego Chamber and 46m of roomy passage to a high chamber. To the left is a crawl beneath avens to a series of climbs up to Black Chamber on the right and 24m of passage straight ahead which becomes too tight. Difficult 8m climb in Black Chamber gains 30m of passage. Step across from top of climb enters another crawl above loose blocks into a larger section which is close to the surface.

Queensway continues in great style beneath Telephone Aven to the Squashed Chihuahua Passage on the left. This is a 79m long inlet to a sump. Eventually beyond a boulder choke the high level section of Queensway closes down and the water must be followed into the hands and knees crawl of Canutes Canal to Emma's Pitch, below which more canyon passage marches on to a sizeable rock fall. The way through the fall involves a short pitch (Anne's) and a steep loose slope ascends into the breakdown cavern of King Henry Hall.

Bloodaxe Pitch, belayed to the right drops into another boulder floored chamber and Victoria Pitch leads back to the stream in a canal occupying a tall rift. The way on opens out into Kakemono Hall – 6m wide and 20m high – but the only exit is a low crawl in the stream. A dry crawl up a rift on the right ends after 21m in a choke but pressing on downstream a 152m crawl eases off at the top of Elizabeth Shaft – a superb 21m shaft which can be laddered direct or over a rock bridge to give a drier hang.

From the cavern below Elizabeth Shaft the obvious outlet soon sumps and the way forward is up and over a rib of rock via a 3m climb and Jane's Pitch into a mud floored chamber. The stream is rejoined in a low, wet, muddy crawl but the roof rises into a fine domed passage with formations. An inlet emerges from boulders on the left and 61m further on is a junction with large passages on either hand. To the right a gour floored passage becomes too low while up a mud slope to the left a large passage leads to a 4.5m climb into the fine Crystal Passage, which ends after 61m in a calcite-encrusted chamber.

Once again the way ahead is a low crawl in the stream for 122m to a depressing inlet on the right which can be forced for 61m to a sump. The downstream crawl enlarges at a short inlet, again on the right, and a short distance forward on the left a muddy rift drops 4.5m down a mud cliff into Blue Pool. A swim across the pool ends at a draughting choke. Pressing on downstream 152m of crawling suddenly ends 3m above East Kingsdale Main Drain.

Downstream a 6m wide passage soon ends in a deep sump pool linking to Kingsdale Master Cave and Keld Head 2km and 3km distant respectively (see description of Keld Head). Upstream 131m is another sump which has been dived for 76m to River Chamber but 'dry' cavers must proceed up bypass on right going upstream and through low duck and up calcite slope to a junction with boulder-strewn passage. To right beyond a shattered chamber is a stal blockage but along the fault to the left is a squeeze into a series of decorated chambers dropping to the river.

Downstream the river cascades beneath the great rift of Geoff's Fault into a deep lake covering half of the floor of River Chamber. Up steep slope ends in calcite choke after 30m but upstream the meandering arched streamway reaches a sump after 230m with the entrance to Grasshopper Series on the left. The sump has been dived for 91m to 91m of canal and another 415m of sump with occasional airbells which is continuing.

Grasshopper Series is entered via a 61m wet crawl which becomes impassable with only a slight water rise. Easier going in a larger tube divides and to the right an easy crawl degenerates into a struggle through ooze into Miracle Chamber. To the left a wide wet bedding plane has been forced to rifts having a vocal connection with Wookey Hole and a dry chamber was forced to the surface by digging through a plug of glacial debris (see Valley Exit for a fuller description of this series).

Tackle

Pitch	Ladder	Belay	Lifeline
Rope			12m
1st	9m	1m	12m
Traverse	4.5m	1.2m	
2nd	9m	0.6m	15m
Emma's	11m	1.5m	15m
Anne's	4.5m	3m	
Bloodaxe	12m	1.3m	18m
Victoria	9m	0.6m	15m
Elizabeth	21m	2.4m	30m
Jane's	9m	Sling	

BOLT BELAYS – see Warning, page 13.

Permission – Braida Garth Farm.

LITTLE DEMON POT   NGR SD 706768   Grade I
Alt. 390m   **Length 4.5m**   **Depth 4.5m**
Explored 1981, NCC.

Entrance is in shakehole where small stream sinks 46m N of Slot Pot. Awkward free-climbable descent with window into parallel shaft. Fist-sized

hole in wall of parallel shaft emits a powerful draught, but is far too tight.
    Entrance may be blocked by run-in of bank above.
Permission – Braida Garth Farm.

LORD'S TOP HOLE   NGR SD 706772   Grade II
Alt. 378m   Depth 12m

    Isolated fenced shaft on Lord's Top, approximately 3.7m square at the top.
A straight ladder climb to a solidly choked floor with no sign of a possible
way on.

Tackle – 12m ladder; stake & sling belay; 15m lifeline.
Permission – Braida Garth Farm.

MINI HOLE   NGR SD 712774   Grade I
Alt. 384m   Depth 3m
Explored 1972, LUSS.

    Situated in the centre bank of a double shakehole some 75m SE of Growling
Hole. A tight drop down through boulder clay leads to an impossibly tight
choked fissure.
Permission – Braida Garth Farm.

MINOR RIFT   NGR SD 703763   Grade I
Alt. 381m   Depth 6m
Explored 1980, NCC.

    Situated near Whit Pot, close to edge of plateau. Straight-forward free-
climbable descent of rift. Shaft continues below too tight.
Permission – Braida Garth Farm.

OWLET HOLE   NGR SD 704774   Grade II
Alt. 290m   Length 4.5m

    High in scar in Braida Garth Wood. Tricky climb into a short cave which
quickly closes down to an earth choke.
Permission – Braida Garth Farm.

P.A.G. POT   NGR SD 712782   Grade III
Alt. 372m   Depth 18m
Explored 1969, BSA.

    Situated in a deep rock walled shakehole, with corrugated iron sheet
covering entrance. A free-climbable pitch of 8.2m in a small elliptical shaft
leads to a sloping floor where the pot steps sideways. The head of the second
pitch is extremely tight and awkward, but opens out into a larger rift after
a few metres. A small inlet stream enters part way down and cascades to the
floor of small rocks. The only way on is a narrow meandering fissure which
rapidly becomes too tight.

Tackle

Pitch	Ladder	Belay	Lifeline
1st	Free climb but 9m handline may be useful		
2nd	9m	Short bar and sling	15m

Permission – Braida Garth Farm.

PEAT BOG HOLE   NGR SD 712773   Grade II
Alt. 387m   **Length 6m**   Depth 4.5m
Explored 1981, NCC.

Entrance situated at top of shallow shakehole taking bog drainage, 91m SE of Broken Finger Pot. Crawl down slope leads to 1.5m drop and further slope to overtight crawl. Cave is extremely tight and should only be attempted feet first. Water probably drains to Broken Finger Pot.
Permission – Braida Garth Farm.

PIN HOLE   NGR SD 707775   Grade II
Alt. 361m   Depth 11m

Shaft above and behind the farm, recognisable by the abandoned agricultural implement over the top. Narrow rift with bridge across; care should be taken on the pitch as the E wall has a number of shattered slabs. At the foot of a short length of passage can be followed to a choke.

Tackle – 9m ladder; stake & sling belay; 15m lifeline.
Permission – Braida Garth Farm.

RAZOR POT   NGR SD 706772   Grade II
Alt. 372m   Depth 6.4m
Explored 1972, BSA.

In shallow shakehole 55m NW of Lord's Top Hole, covered by slabs which must be replaced. A tight rift pitch in extremely jagged rock which becomes too tight before the floor can be reached. To one side is an impassable slot which descends further than the main shaft.

Tackle – 8m ladder; stake & sling belay; 9m lifeline.
Permission – Braida Garth Farm.

REBUFF CAVE   NGR SD 706766   Grade II
Alt. 396m   **Length 12m**
Explored 1972, BSA.

Excavated entrance in deep rocky shakehole near boundary wall. Short climb down leads to an undercut into low bedding cave which can only be entered feet first. The passage narrows in, and tight crawl leads past an awkward squeeze to an acute bend. Beyond this the passage gets too small.
Permission – Braida Garth Farm.

REMEMBRANCE POT   NGR SD 710775   Grade III
Alt. 378m   Depth 29m
Explored 1964, BSA.

The entrance lies in a deep circular shakehole with no sign of any bed rock, approximately 185m SW of the large pile of gritstone boulders at the mouth of the shallow side valley. The entrance itself is subject to collapse of the unstable boulder clay bank above, and care should be exercised. The first pitch of 16m lands on a sloping boulder floor with an impassable inlet entering from a narrow slot to one side, and the stream flows via a small oxbow to the lip of the second pitch a few metres away. A further descent of 6.4m, best laddered right through from the surface, reaches a chamber with a boulder floor sloping steeply down to a sump. This has been dived and is only passable at floor level 6m down. A short dive and ascent leads to a mud bank completely choking the way on.

Tackle – 27m ladder; stake & sling belay; 37m lifeline.
Permission – Braida Garth Farm.

RESCUE POTS   NGR SD 703767   Grade I
Alt. 366m
Explored 1981, NPC.

1.   Length 6m. At foot of George's Scar in field S of Braida Garth Farm is opening into small chamber.

2.   Length 6m. About 9m to right of 1 is small entrance to excavated bedding plane blocked by mud and calcite.
Permission – Braida Garth Farm.

SHORT CAVE   NGR SD 706768   Grade I
Alt. 390m   Length 4.5m
Explored 1981, NCC.

   Small cave situated between Slot Pot and Little Demon Pot. Entrance is in N end of small shakehole, and leads to a 4.5m long crawl over boulders to a complete choke – most likely a surface run in. The small stream entering the cave filters away through the choke, but backs up in times of wet weather.
Permission – Braida Garth Farm.

SID'S POT   NGR SD 707783   Grade II
Alt. 335m   Depth 6m
Explored 1980, NCC.

   Extremely tight shaft 20m S of S.L.B.J. Pot. Awkward descent leads to a choke. Foot loop is useful for return.

Tackle – 8m rope.

Permission – Braida Garth Farm.

S.L.B.J. POT   NGR SD 708783   Grade I
Alt. 335m   Depth 6m
Explored 1979, NCC.

   Narrow shaft 61m NE of Wookey Hole above a prominent scar. Narrow descent in cross joint can be free-climbed to a completely choked floor.
Permission – Braida Garth Farm.

SLOT POT   NGR SD 705767   Grade II
Alt. 387m   Depth 6m
Explored 1972, BSA.

   Entrance in double shakehole a few metres N of boundary wall of Lord's

Lot Top. A small rift choked at bottom which can be free-climbed, but easier with a ladder.

Tackle – 8m ladder; stake & sling belay; 9m lifeline.
Permission – Braida Garth Farm.

SMALL SHAFT   NGR SD 709784   Grade I
Alt. 323m   **Depth 4.5m**
Explored 1980, NCC.

Small shaft at foot of pronounced gully to right of stone pile is 4.5m rope climb to choked floor which emits a cool draught.

Tackle – 6m rope.
Permission – Braida Garth Farm.

SPECTACLE POT   NGR SD 711777   Grade V
Alt. 369m   **Length 244m**   **Depth 102m**
Explored 1936, YRC; extended 1960, Black Rose PC and 1971, LUSS.

WARNING – Splutter Crawl will become impassable in wet weather, and the looseness of Dodd's Pitch demands extreme caution. Rescue of an injured person would be almost impossible under certain conditions.

Tight initial crawls leading to a spectacular big pitch. The entrance shakehole is best found by walking from Braida Garth onto the moor, and across to the large pile of gritstone boulders at the entrance to the dry side valley. From here if one makes for the large obvious shakehole at the toe of the bank on up-valley, Spectacle Pot will be found in a small elongated depression out from the bank about 60m before this is reached, and is recognisable by the roll of wire netting. The entrance pitch is split by a ledge halfway down, and from the foot an awkward 2m climb leads to the floor of a narrow rift. A further climb down of 2.4m quickly follows, to emerge in a small aven. From here a short crawl and squeeze lead to the Letterbox and the start of Splutter Crawl. This is a flat out crawl, possibly best dealt with by crawling on one's back, the rift above being far too narrow to be of use. At the far end is a further 2.4m drop and approaching this head first is awkward, although the short fixed ladder is a help. The chamber at the foot gives directly onto the second pitch with a bolt belay, the take-off being rather tight. Below, two bends lead to the junction with Onion Passage, a tight inlet 76m long, passing squeezes to two avens and a choke.

Easy going from junction leads to Moorhouse Aven, 11m high, with small stream entering. The fault which controls this part of the pot can be seen clearly where a shale bed has been displaced. The passage on is a low, wet crawl, and in wet weather can become a long duck although normally has plenty of airspace. At the far end of the crawl Dryden Chamber is entered, being fairly spacious with boulders littering the floor. Dodd's Pitch follows immediately, and there are two routes which can be used for the descent. The first, and original one followed the water down a tight slot to two eyeholes, and is tight and awkward. This way has become partly blocked by excavation of an upper bedding reached via a climb up at the end of the chamber. A short crawl enters a small chamber suitable for the lifeliner, whilst the pitch is reached feet first through the continuing bedding. A descent of 18m lands on a ledge, from which an exposed traverse leads to a piton and bolt which serve as the belay points for the next drop of 23m.

At the foot of this pitch are a number of blind holes in the floor, and to one side are the twin eyeholes giving onto the pitch at the head of The Great Rubble Heap. The lower eyehole is the safer, and a long belay and at least 8m of ladder lead onto the top of the extremely unstable boulder slope. Great care must be exercised here, and only one person should move at a time. The final pitch of 9m is reached at the foot of the slope, and is very tight and awkward at the top. Below the pitch is a final small boulder chamber and an excavated route down to a sump which was dived for 6m, and to a similar depth only to end in an underwater boulder choke.

The final pitch of Vesper Pot enters near the foot of The Great Rubble Heap.

Tackle

Pitch	Ladder	Belay	Lifeline
Entrance	11m	0.6m	15m
2nd	6m	Short spreader	9m
Dodd's Pitch	18m	Short spreader	24m
	and 23m	and short spreader	and 30m
4th	8m	6m	12m
5th	9m	0.6m	12m

Note – All the bolts are of the Parba type and were installed early in 1971. They should be treated with caution and alternative belays sought if they appear unsound.

Permission – Braida Garth Farm.

STAG NIGHT HOLE

NGR SD 709780   **Grade II**

Alt. 351m   Length 6m   Depth 8m

Explored 1971, LUSS.

Entrance lies within a few metres of the scar top wall NE of Braida Garth Farm. An easy descent leads to a tight loose squeeze down into a small passage. Crawling over a soft silt floor quickly leads to a complete choke.

Permission – Braida Garth Farm.

SURPRISE POT

NGR SD 706766   **Grade I**

Alt. 390m   Length 6m   Depth 8m

Explored 1981, NCC.

Entrance is in reasonably large shakehole between Slot Pot and Rebuff Cave, S of the boundary wall, and taking a small stream. Shaft opened up after heavy rains, and is free-climbable with a constriction half way down. At foot the way on ends quickly in a very restricted sump.

Permission – Braida Garth Farm.

THUNDER HOLE

NGR SD 712782   **Grade I**

Alt. 372m   Depth 6m

Explored 1969, BSA.

Excavated shaft a few metres N of P.A.G. Pot covered with corrugated

iron sheets, and recognisable by the pile of debris to one side. An easy free climb leads down to where the rift narrows to a very tight slot.
Permission – Braida Garth Farm.

THUNDER THIGHS HOLE   NGR SD 705768   Grade I
Alt. 387m   **Length 6m**   **Depth 8m**
Explored 1981, NCC.

In large shakehole 30m N of Slot Pot on Lord's Lot Top. Crawl below entrance shoring, best tackled feet first, to climb down into small chamber with cobble slope. Passage closes down, but stones dropped down hole in floor land in water.
Permission – Braida Garth Farm.

TIMBER POT   NGR SD 707774   Grade II
Alt. 366m   **Depth 11m**
Explored 1972, BSA.

Situated in shallow shakehole immediately to the W of Braida Garth Pot, and covered over with boards, which must be replaced. A small circular shaft gradually enlarges into a rift, the foot of which is severely choked, as is the continuation to the N.

Tackle – 12m ladder; stake & sling belay; 15m lifeline.
Permission – Braida Garth Farm.

UNDERGROWTH POT   NGR SD 704774   Grade I
Alt. 283m   **Length 11m**   **Depth 6m**
Explored 1976, NCC.

To left of Owlet Hole low down in thick undergrowth near wall, and in the only noticeable shakehole in the area. At upper left of shakehole is excavated flooded bedding where stream can be heard, but pot is at lower end of shakehole. A 3.6m descent through boulders leads to a junction. Opposite is 1m drop into chamber 4.5m long, 3m wide and 1.5m high, sloping down to far wall of flood debris.

Two other short passages from foot of entrance climb enter unstable boulder area; one is 3m long to a cross rift where sound of stream is very noticeable.
Permission – Braida Garth Farm.

VALLEY EXIT   NGR SD 706782   Grade IV
Alt. 274m   **Length as for King Pot**   **Depth 21m to sump**
                                                                   level in King Pot
Explored 1980, NCC.

WARNING – Extremely flood liable. Should not be attempted if Kingsdale Beck is flowing past entrance.

Entrance lies on S side of wall near Wookey Hole, close to Kingsdale Beck. A 4.5m shaft lined with oil drums, where a ladder is a help, enters inclined passage down to low stream passage. A low airspace section after 15m soon opens up to a comfortable hands and knees crawl for 76m ending where the passage enlarges to 3.7m square, and a junction is reached.

Passage on left at junction is Miracle Passage. 45m of easy crawling leads to a further 46m of flat out crawling in a mud slurry, ending in the roomy Miracle Chamber. The only route out of the chamber involves bailing a sump, which can take up to an hour. Beyond sump is flat out crawl up to a large cross passage. Left branch ends after 21m in a draughting calcited choke, while right branch quickly reaches a second bailable sump. Through sump a calcite slope enters a large passage and spacious chamber, with three short side passages all choking quickly. A strong draught is noticeable in this section of the cave, but the sumps should be treated with the utmost caution as they fill up, and can only be bailed from the entrance sides.

Back at the first main junction, Miracle Junction, the large passage to the right leads on for 21m to the beginning of the 61m Grasshopper Crawl, with a tight squeeze at the start, and a long wet section at the far end. Grasshopper Crawl enters the East Kingsdale Main Drain 46m below the upstream sump. (See King Pot description.)

Tackle – 8m ladder for oil drum entrance descent.

Permission – Braida Garth Farm.

VESPER POT

VESPER POT	**NGR SD 712776**	**Grade IV**
Alt. 381m	Length 274m	Depth 114m
Explored 1978, NPC.		

Manhole entrance in shakehole near small sinks. Short crawl to constricted bend into low passage, then hands and knees crawling reaches enlarging streamway. Main inlet on right is low, twisting passage to a decorated chamber with climb up to a degenerating crawl. Downstream, first pitch enters a chamber followed by a tall rift and twisting canyon to second pitch. Another short drop follows and cave widens but stream cuts down in steps and through a constriction into a climbable rift. Dry alternative is by laddering from boulders on broad ledge above. Through a narrow slot, fourth pitch is broken by two ledges in widening shaft opening into the side of the big fault rift of Spectacle Pot. Final pitch hangs free in lower half and lands near the foot of the Great Rubble Heap.

Tackle

Pitch	Ladder	Belay	Lifeline
First	8m	3m	9m
Second	8m	3m	12m
Rift Climb			12m
Dry alternative	11m	4.5m	15m
Fourth Pitch	27m	Short spreader to bolt	37m
Final pitch	46m	4.5m	61m

BOLT BELAYS – **see Warning, page 13.**

Permission – Braida Garth Farm.

WACKENBURGH POT   NGR SD 698757   Grade I
Alt. 296m   **Length 15m**   **Depth 15m**

For location see key map on back endpaper.

Isolated shaft above Twistleton Lane on S flank of Wackenburgh Hill. Large entrance covered by railway sleepers and tin sheets which must be replaced. Pitch lands on a boulder slope, and rift on right enters chamber 6m by 3m and 9m tall. Crawl at bottom of boulder slope closes down after 9m.

Tackle – 9m ladder; 1.2m belay; 15m lifeline.

WHIT POT   NGR SD 703762   Grade II
Alt. 381m   **Depth 11m**

Explored 1950 and 1972, BSA.

Entrance is in rift shakehole containing a small tree well out towards edge of bench. A tight shaft leads to a cross joint, and a squeeze at floor level to the N opens out into two small aven chambers. There is no passable way on, although the boulder floor in the end chamber may be worth a dig.

Tackle – 9m ladder; stake & sling belay; 12m lifeline.
Permission – Braida Garth Farm.

WOMEN'S LIB HOLE   NGR SD 711772   Grade I
Alt. 390m   **Length 6m**   **Depth 4.5m**

Explored 1981, NCC.

Situated at S end of Growling Hole basin, 46m E of Echo Hole, in shallow shakehole. Entrance is crawl past unstable boulders to slope down into a breakdown chamber with no way on.
Permission – Braida Garth Farm.

WOOKEY HOLE   NGR SD 706782   Grade I
Alt. 274m   **Depth 11m**

Explored 1980, NCC.

Entrance lies on N side of wall, a few metres from Kingsdale Beck where it crosses from E to W side of the valley above Braida Garth. Descent of 4.5m down oil drums leads to rift and tight squeeze into small chamber with a trench in floor. Squeeze follows to top of 3.7m drop, which can be free-climbed, and below is sumped bedding passage.

Entrance has been blocked at the request of the farmer.
Permission – Braida Garth Farm.

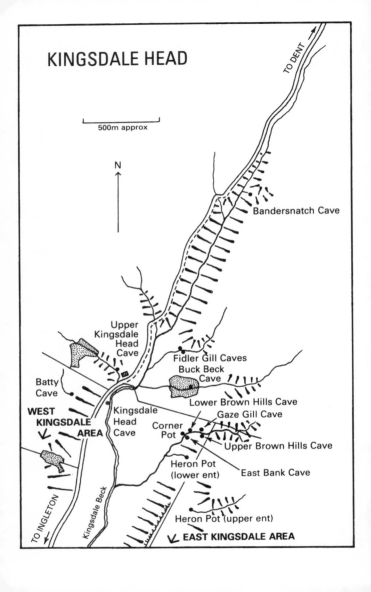

KINGSDALE HEAD

BANDERSNATCH CAVE   NGR SD 717809   Grade III
Alt. 387m   **Length 46m**
Extended 1978, DHSS.

WARNING – Most of cave floods severely in wet weather.

Small entrance just above the obvious resurgence visible from the gate on the Ingleton-Dent road on the opposite side of Long Gill. Tight passage and very awkward right-angled bend leads to hands and knees crawl in stream passage. Easy going round several acute corners in deep water, and a climb over large fallen blocks encounters better going, with several short side passages, to where the roof drops suddenly. Flat out crawl in stream with only 150mm airspace leads to small chamber with roof pendants. Duck under flake on far side gives access to two passages, one containing the main stream, which have yet to be forced to a conclusion.

BATTY CAVE   NGR SD 706795   Grade III
Alt. 344m   **Length 396m**   **Depth 43m**
Explored YRC; extended 1949, NPC.

Prominent stream sink surrounded by fence. Way in is dry hole to E of sinkhole but water is joined just inside entrance and falls over a short pitch. Outlet from chamber soon lowers to a crawl over cobbles until solid floor appears and the going eases as small rapids are encountered. Calcite creates a squeeze into a high passage to a decorated chamber and series of climbs into a low wet bedding plane. Traverse over climb leads to a dry cavern choked by calcite.

Wet downstream bedding is 61m long to a strong inlet on the left but the continuing higher passage soon becomes almost choked with gravel in the floor and calcite in the roof. Beyond this obstacle is a 6m long, extremely tight crawl to a very small sump.

Tackle – 6m ladder; 2.4m belay; 12m lifeline.
Permission – Braida Garth, Westhouse, via Carnforth.

BUCK BECK CAVE   NGR SD 714796   Grade II
Alt. 335m   **Length 37m**
Extended 1978, DHSS.

Small, insignificant entrance on N bank of Buck Beck in plantation. Sideways crawling for few metres into small chamber with two possible ways on. A climb up to the right leads to bedding crawl where daylight enters through impassable holes on right. Beyond these the passage enlarges somewhat to junction with small stream passage. Right chokes almost immediately, while left continues as a low wet crawl with glutinous mud. This has been followed for at least 12m and it may be possible to push it further.

To the left in first small chamber a 2m climb up reaches a body-sized tube and awkward going round tight bend and through constriction, to short length of tight and unpleasant rift passage with several choked branches.
Permission – Kingsdale Head Farm.

CORNER POT   NGR SD 713793   Grade II
(West Bank Cave)
Alt. 320m   Length 15m
Explored 1966, RRCPC.

Fissure entrance just upstream of main resurgence in Gaze Gill. Inside the stream drops into a sumped pool and upstream is a wet crawl past solution tubes until the way becomes too small.
Permission – Kingsdale Head Farm.

EAST BANK CAVE   NGR SD 713793   Grade I
Alt. 320m   Length 21m
Explored 1966, RRCPC.

Small cave entrance into wide crawl and tight passage down with the water. Up the stream are a series of small chambers to a choke near a large shakehole.
Permission – Kingsdale Head Farm.

FIDLER GILL CAVES   NGR SD 713798   Grade I
Alt. 328m

1.   Length 18m
Furthest upstream cave in left bank of small gorge in Fidler Gill. Short narrow through cave of stooping height with one small inlet which quickly chokes with stalagmite.

2.   Length 4.5m
At downstream entrance to 1 is further small cave entrance. Small passage can be followed to a junction where both ways on are too tight.

3.   Length 3m
A few metres downstream of 2, also on left bank of gill is low crawl heading towards 2.

4.   Length 18m   Depth 6m
In right bank of gill where majority of stream usually sinks. Large cave entrance onto boulder slope leading down past a series of choked fissures on the left to a large fissure at bottom. Routes to either side soon choke.

5.   Length 37m
Entrance at rising in right bank of gill at foot of gorge. Crawl leads into wide passage with route to right past unstable boulders to a choke, while straight on splits into a number of different passages which all quickly become too tight.
Permission – Kingsdale Head Farm.

GAZE GILL CAVE   NGR SD 714793   Grade II-III
Alt. 335m   **Length 244m**
Vertical range 15m
Explored 1948, NPC; extended 1966, RRCPC.

An intricate oxbow cave which has been cut through by Gaze Gill. One of four entrances is in the right bank downstream of waterfall. Crawl through small pool into a network of passages and an upstream chamber with another entrance. Ahead is traverse into Red Pool Passage which is a crawl to avens with pools and ends in a narrow inlet. Main upstream route is easy going to a choke. Back from end high level route emerges on surface just above waterfall. Downstream is a canal to Daylight Chamber and very small entrance. Lower Stream Passage continues over roof fall to a narrow stream slot bypassed by an upper level. Roof descends to water at flat out short sump into Lower Brown Hills Cave.

Permission – Kingsdale Head Farm.

HERON POT   NGR SD 714787   Grade III
Alt. 360m   **Length 1097m**   **Depth 40m**
Explored 1955, FMC and NPC.

WARNING – Pitches and Lower Entrance become impassable in flood.

Top entrance is near sink of Thack Pot Gill and is to the left of the stream bed. Drop into small chamber with way on back under climb as a twisting passage to junction with the streamway. Upstream through chamber to a crawl until water emerges from a boulder choke. Downstream a fine canyon with formations passes a 76m long inlet on the left; this sub-divides and chokes close to the flood sink. The stream canyon continues until cascades drop to two pitches, following in rapid succession.

From the pitch chamber a fine passage provides easy going to a sharp right bend where a 3m climb leads to the Phreatic Inlet.

This ascends through an aven chamber to fine formations and an awkward 3.7m climb into a narrow fissure passage splitting into two tortuous inlets. The main inlet gets too low after about 60m and the right branch rises past an extremely tight squeeze into a bedding crawl terminating in two choked rifts.

Downstream continues large to deep pools and a calcite slope up to the Fossil Roof Series which trends back upstream. The water enters a long pebble crawl and a damp exit is made into daylight at the bottom entrance on the slope above Gaze Gill.

Tackle

Pitch	Ladder	Belay	Lifeline
1st	6m	1m	9m
2nd	9m	1m	12m

BOLT BELAYS – see Warning, page 13.

Permission – Braida Garth Farm.

KINGSDALE HEAD CAVE   NGR SD 708795   Grade III
Alt. 302m   Length 76m
Explored 1969, RRCPC.

WARNING – Floods suddenly after rain.

In scar by main beck just below Kingsdale Head Farm and 12m from rising. Low wet crawl for a few metres into hands and knees crawl with stalagmites until passage becomes too low. Water comes from Batty Cave.
Permission – Kingsdale Head Farm.

LOWER BROWN HILLS CAVE   NGR SD 713793
Grade II

Alt. 320m   Length 46m

Two holes in right bank of Gaze Gill 122m below waterfall. Downstream is too narrow but upstream is a canal and a shingle crawl to a low bedding plane and nasty low sump to link with Gaze Gill Cave.
Permission – Kingsdale Head Farm.

UPPER BROWN HILLS CAVE   NGR SD 714793
Grade I

Alt. 335m   Length 18m

Resurgence cave by the waterfalls in Gaze Gill. Slit entrance lowers to a sharp left bend and the cave divides beneath the surface streambed.
Permission – Kingsdale Head Farm.

UPPER KINGSDALE HEAD CAVE   NGR SD 797707
Grade II

Alt. 320m   Length 24m

On N bank of Backstone Gill upstream of Kingsdale Head Farm. Resurgence cave is a wet crawl becoming too low.
Permission – Kingsdale Head Farm.

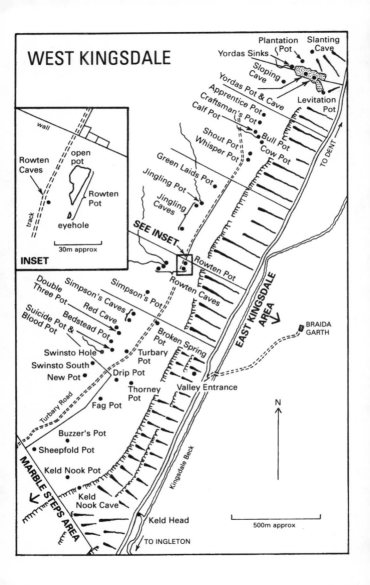

WEST KINGSDALE

INSET

Rowten Caves
wall
open pot
Rowten Pot
track
eyehole
30m approx

Plantation Pot
Slanting Cave
Yordas Sinks
Sloping Cave
Yordas Pot & Cave
Apprentice Pot
Craftsman's Pot
Calf Pot
Shout Pot
Whisper Pot
Bull Pot
Cow Pot
Levitation Pot
TO DENT
Green Laids Pot
Jingling Pot
Jingling Caves
SEE INSET
Rowten Pot
Rowten Caves
EAST KINGSDALE AREA
BRAIDA GARTH
Double Three Pot
Simpson's Caves
Simpson's Pot
Red Cave
Bedstead Pot
Suicide Pot & Blood Pot
Swinsto Hole
Swinsto South
New Pot
Drip Pot
Broken Spring
Broken Pot
Turbary Pot
Valley Entrance
Turbary Road
Thorney Pot
Fag Pot
Buzzer's Pot
Sheepfold Pot
MARBLE STEPS AREA
Keld Nook Pot
Keld Nook Cave
Kingsdale Beck
Keld Head
TO INGLETON
N
500m approx

WEST KINGSDALE

APPRENTICE POT
NGR SD 703788
Grade I
Alt. 351m
Depth 6m
Explored 1972, BSA.

Entrance in small rock face in line of shakeholes from Bull Pot, approximately 50m from next wall up valley. A small climb down leads after a few metres to a sharp corner to the right and further climb down of 3m. At foot is a rift which rapidly closes in and becomes an over-tight meandering fissure.

BEDSTEAD POT
NGR SD 694776
Grade III
Alt. 384m
Length 52m
Depth 9m
Explored 1962, ULSA.

Shaft covered by bedstead in small shakehole 90m NE of Swinsto Hole. Straight pitch to crawl which can be forced to Swinsto South in upstream direction. Downstream the hands and knees crawl becomes lower and wetter until the way is blocked by a mudbank only 6m from Double Three Pot.

Tackle – 9m ladder; 2m belay; 12m lifeline.
Permission – Thornton Hall, Westhouse, via Carnforth.

BLOOD POT
NGR SD 694775
Grade II
Alt. 381m
Depth 8m
Explored 1970, University of Hull Speleological Society.

Open shaft covered by corrugated iron sheets, in same shakehole as Suicide Pot, approximately half way between Swinsto Hole and Turbary Pot. At foot of shaft is a narrow rift on down, with small stream seen at foot of Suicide Pot. Way on is too tight to follow.

Tackle – 8m ladder; stake & sling belay; 12m lifeline.

BROKEN SPRING POT
NGR SD 697777
Grade II
Alt. 378m
Length 20m
Depth 6m

In same field as Simpsons Caves, a few metres S of gate on Turbary Road (at NE end) is small shakehole with covered hole. Climbable descent to blasted crawl ending at descent into cross rift which is too narrow.

BULL POT
NGR SD 702787
Grade III
Alt. 358m
Length 216m
Depth 79m
Explored 1899 and 1934, YRC; extended 1948, CPC.

WARNING – Lower pitches become impassable in flood.

Most notable sink between Jingling Pot and Yordas. Traditional entrance is a boulder covered rift just beyond end of stream channel. Belay to block for shaft into long fissure. Proceeding S the stream is found emerging from a small passage, and it may be followed back up two climbs into a bedding plane leading to daylight at the sink. Across the surface stream channel a very tortuous route drops awkwardly to a 9m pitch into a chamber. A climb up onto a shelf reveals two high level passages above fissures. The N branch leads to another chamber and a low crawl, whilst the S passage connects with Bull Pot entrance rift.

Downstream is the second pitch where the fall is descended partway and a crossing made to a ledge. Dry short passage to the third pitch where the water is rejoined and the last 4m from a large ledge may be laddered separately. Fourth pitch is broken and lands in a pinnacle chamber where the rift doubles back and drops quickly into another chamber with the stream sinking in the floor. The narrow floor fissure leads to the final pitch (which can be awkward for larger cavers) and a small cavern with a duck through to a rift which gets too tight. From the sink chamber a fossil route passes through a deep pool to a succession of climbs ending at a static sump, which has been dived for 18m to a mudbank. A rope will be found useful in reversing two of the climbs.

Tackle

Pitch	Ladder	Belay	Lifeline
1st	11m	2m	15m
2nd	6m	3m	12m
3rd	17m	1m	21m
4th	17m	3m	21m
5th	11m	3m	15m

BOLT BELAYS – see Warning, page 13.

Permission – Westgate, Westhouse, via Carnforth.

BUZZER'S POT   NGR SD 692771   Grade I
Alt. 387m   Depth 6m
Explored 1938, BSA.

On High Plain 183m NE of Sheepfold Pot. Narrow climbable rift to floor of boulders. Stream can be heard but it flows in a deep impassable crack.
Permission – Thornton Hall, Westhouse, via Carnforth.

CALF POT   NGR SD 702787   Grade I
Alt. 360m   Depth 12m
Explored 1964, NCC.

Deep shakehole upstream of Bull Pot on right bank. Rift with steep slope of boulders. Choked by mud and rocks.
Permission – Westgate, Westhouse, via Carnforth.

COW POT   NGR SD 702787   Grade II
Alt. 357m   Depth 12m

Immediately below scar at Bull Pot. Open pot onto boulder slope which chokes the rift.

Tackle – 6m ladder; 3m belay; 12m lifeline.
Permission – Westgate, Westhouse, via Carnforth.

CRAFTMAN'S POT   NGR SD 702788   Grade III-IV
Alt. 366m   **Length 387m**   **Depth 76m**

Explored 1986, DCC.

WARNING – The section between Hickory and Dickory pitches is an inclined face of glacial fill 30m high and prone to collapse.

Entrance at S end of shakehole 100m N of Calf Pot. Short climb of 4m leads to flat out crawl with boulder run in to the left (care!). A short squeeze is followed by a narrow rift to the head of a tight vertical slot of 4m landing on a ledge above Hickory Pitch.

Below is a spacious rift with two ways on. Under far wall is descending boulder slope to head of Dickory Pitch (great care needed). The main rift from Hickory Pitch leads to Mouse Pitch down glacial fill and on to a complete blockage. Parallel ramp climbs back to 3m above the head of Hickory Pitch.

From the bolt belay above Dickory Pitch drop 5m to a wide but easy traverse for 7m (bolts) to Jack Horner's Corner. Here an echoing rift is too tight, but below is Dock Pitch which lands in a magnificent fault controlled rift with a stream.

Upstream is a low bedding and downstream is also low into a tight rift.

A bolt traverse from the head of Dock Pitch leads to a phreatic tube and hence to a breakdown chamber 'Bequest to the Brave' where a black void beckons above an extremely unstable boulder ruckle.

Tackle

Pitch	Ladder	Belay	Lifeline
Hickory	14m	1m	20m
Dickory	8m	1m	20m
Dock	19m	1m	25m
Mouse	9m	1m	15m

BOLT BELAYS – see Warning, page 13.

DOUBLE THREE POT   NGR SD 694776   Grade II
Alt. 384m   **Depth 10m**

Explored 1908, YRC.

137m NE of Swinsto and 183m S of the wall. Straight shaft into a small chamber with a fissure inlet high in the W wall. Waterlogged inlet and outlet passages at floor level are choked by mud, but tortuous upstream crawl leads to Red Cave.

Tackle – 11m ladder; 3m belay; 15m lifeline.
Permission – Thornton Hall, Westhouse, via Carnforth.

DRIP POT   NGR SD 694774   Grade III
Alt. 381m   **Length 25m**   **Depth 24m**

Explored 1978, CPG.

Entrance in small shakehole between Thorney Pot and wall corner S of Swinsto Hole.

Short free climb leads immediately to excavated boulder choke. Through highly unstable boulders (care!) and down into tight descending rift passage. Floor of jammed boulders leads to pitch with no natural belay point. After tight take-off pitch bells out into impressive rift chamber. Landing on silt floor with trickle flowing through impenetrable fissure to E. No open way on.

Tackle – 15m ladder; 0.6m bar belay; 30m lifeline.
Permission – Braida Garth,

FAG POT   NGR SD 693772   Grade I
Alt. 384m   Depth 4.5m

Small shaft 61m E of wall. May be climbed (but beware of sharp rock) and is choked by earth and rocks.
Permission – Thornton Hall, Westhouse, via Carnforth.

GREEN LAIDS POT   NGR SD 700784   Grade II
(McShea's Mine)
Alt. 366m   **Length 15m**   Depth 12m
Explored 1967, HWCPC.
First small stream sink N of Jingling Pot. Entrance is abandoned sink with a narrow fissure passage to a pitch. Continuing rift is too tight.

Tackle – 8m ladder; 3m belay; 15m lifeline.
Permission – Ireby Hall Farm, Cowan Bridge, via Carnforth.

JINGLING CAVES NGR SD 698782 and 699784 Grade II
Alt. 378m   **Length 375m**

Cave opening by Jingling Pot. Downstream is crawl past unroofed section and another entrance. Passage slowly increases in height and passes under window in bottom of deep shakehole after 183m. Beyond a damp 3m climb easy walking leads of Rowten Cave.
Permission – Ireby Hall Farm, Cowan Bridge, via Carnforth.

JINGLING POT   NGR SD 699784   Grade III
Alt. 378m   **Length 61m**   Depth 67m
Explored 1926, YRC; extended 1969, BSA.

A superb daylight shaft. Next sink N of Rowten above the Turbary Road. Water may be diverted into Jingling Cave and the shaft laddered from the tree 43m or as two pitches at the S end of the rift. The first short pitch can be climbed with care, but ladder the main shaft. From the bottom a separate series of shafts ascends to 9m below the surface; this point is difficult to reach from above.

At foot of main shaft a fine cleft continues to a 8m climb but it quickly chokes with shingle. On the left is a blind pot 4.5m deep but to the right at the base of the 8m climb is a small drop and window to a chimney. Below is a complex of crawls and choked rifts; one 8m deep.

Tackle

Pitch	Ladder	Belay	Lifeline
Main shaft	$\left\{\begin{array}{l} 8m \\ 37m \end{array}\right.$	3m 6m	49m

BOLT BELAYS – see Warning, page 13.

Permission – Ireby Hall, Cowan Bridge, via Carnforth.

KELD HEAD

NGR SD 696766

Alt. 253m   **Length 6.7km**   **Depth 34m**

Explored 1945-1992, CDG.

A major resurgence, forming the outlet for most of the water sinking in east and west Kingsdale. There is no passage accessible for non-divers. For a full description with information necessary for diving the CDG's Northern Sump Index must be consulted as the following description is only a brief outline of the complexities of the cave. The length and depth given refer only to flooded passages downstream of the West Kingsdale Master Cave sump and King Pot's final sump.

Entrance Series

Two routes diverge at the entrance. Crossland's Passage starts as a descent of a 3m pot to a passage which heads up valley and then curves southwards to join the start of the main Kingsdale Passage at the '100m' airbell.

The other route from diving base at the entrance pool enters a large passage. An airbell at 46m is the start of a loop, one passage heading N to the '100m' airbell with a route off to one side linking back to Crossland's Passage close to the entrance. The other passage forming the loop continues to an airbell at 76m before swinging N to the '100m' airbell.

The 76m airbell is also the start of Wooding's Passage, a 454m dive which rejoins the main Kingsdale Passage 295m from the entrance.

Kingsdale Passage

From the '100m' airbell a large tunnel continues generally W past two airbells to a junction with the Marble Steps Branch 335m from base. The passage then swings N gradually deepening and increasing in size until 580m forward Dead Mans Handshake is reached. This is a very low bedding forming the link between two high joints. Beyond the passage is large and complex and a junction at 960m marks the re-entry of the Dark Side, a passage 587m long that runs parallel to the main Kingsdale Passage from a point not far past the Marble Steps Branch. At 1097m a shaft leads upwards to shallower waters and Kingsdale Master Cave downstream sump (see below).

Marble Steps Branch

From its junction with Kingsdale Passage the inlet continues to an airbell and aven after 327m. Beyond the passage descends into Great Western which ends at a junction. To the W the Osmotic Palpitator quickly becomes too low, to the N is another junction 997m from entrance. To the W again the Scissorhands Series becomes too small after 90m with another branch also too low. To the E the Tubular Bore heads gradually down dip, past a low muddy inlet after 110m, to a squeeze up into a more comfortably proportioned passage. One way this chokes, the other soon degenerates and has been explored to a silty chamber 1372m from base.

Kingsdale Master Cave Sump

From the top of the shaft is 61m of passage to the Yorrurt Revisited airbell from which a complex of passages lead off. 39m past this the passage splits. The Original Route continuing past the Muddyways Loop to a junction with

Cobble Inlet where the Loop rejoins. Beyond the passage passes the Useless Yorrurt airbell to meet the Main Route, the other branch from the junction. This is a 452m dive to where it links again with the Original Route and there is a further passage linking the two routes which runs from a shaft 180m into the Main Route to just upstream of the Useless Yorrurt airbell. The combined passages lead to the downstream sump in Kingsdale Master Cave after 168m, 1.9km from Keld Head entrance.

King Pot Branch
There are two entrances to this, one via Cobble Inlet the other a passage just downstream of Useless Yorrurt airbell. These join within 100m and a large tunnel continues E deepening as it goes. 200m forward is the start of a long meander which ends as the passage turns to head towards King Pot. The Sea of Tranquility follows, 350m long averaging over 25m depth. Beyond the passage briefly turns E and then resumes its course for King Pot. Eventually it lowers and becomes silty before ascending to the sump pool in King Pot, 1.5km from Cobble Inlet and 3km from the entrance to Keld Head.
Permission – Braida Garth Farm.

KELD NOOK CAVE   NGR SD 693767   Grade II
(Scar Cave)
Alt. 366m   Length 9m   Depth 4.5m
Low entrance below cliff in escarpment overlooking Keld Head. Crawl descends to a muddy squeeze into a chamber whose floor is choked by mud and boulders.
Permission – Thornton Hall, Westhouse, via Carnforth.

KELD NOOK POT   NGR SD 692768   Grade II
(Black Pot)
Alt. 372m   Depth 8m
Explored 1972, LUCC.
Rift in shallow shakehole 91m W of Keld Nook Cave and 274m E of Sheepfold Pot. Deepest part is at E end where an easy chimney leads to a horizontal squeeze into an open rift dropping into a small chamber with a boulder floor.
Permission – Thornton Hall, Westhouse, via Carnforth.

LEVITATION POT   NGR SD 705790   Grade II
Alt. 308m   Length 27m   Depth 11m
Explored 1981-3, ULSA.
WARNING – The whole system is a boulder choke of dubious stability.
Entrance is covered slot just over wall from Yordas Back Door. 5m crawl and 3m climb down to awkward corner into a rift. Way on is down under Amazing Levitated Boulder to a tight squeeze into a 'chamber', which floods in wet weather. The Yordas stream is running in boulders beneath this point.

NEW POT
Alt. 381m

NGR SD 692775

Grade II
Depth 11m

Inconspicuous shakehole 91m from wall. Simple ladder descent into joint chamber with a choked floor. Entrance now buried beneath heap of rubbish, which may fill the shaft completely.

Tackle – 11m ladder; 1.5m belay; 15m lifeline.
Permission – Thornton Hall, Westhouse, via Carnforth.

PLANTATION POT
Alt. 355m

NGR SD 704792
Length 8m

Grade II
Depth 9m

Explored 1972, BSA.

In steep, grass-sided shakehole just up-valley from wall round head of Yordas Plantation. A rift pitch with very unstable excavated entrance leads to chamber with mud floor. At one end is slope down into start of bedding passage, leading to a choke, but now blocked.

Tackle – 9m ladder; stake & sling belay; 15m lifeline.

RED CAVE
Alt. 384m

NGR SD 694776
Length 37m

Grade II

Long shakehole 18m N of Double Three. Entrance is a shallow canyon with inlet and outlet passages. The inlet is a square crawl and very tight passage emerging at the nearby sink. Downstream a very tortuous crawl above a deep floor slot connects with Double Three Pot.
Permission – Thornton Hall, Westhouse, via Carnforth.

ROWTEN CAVES   NGR SD 697780 and 698780   Grade II
Alt. 372m

Length 290m

Large entrance at the sink of Rowting Beck. Tributary passage connects with another entrance where a crawl continues but splits and becomes too low. Main downstream passage is easy going for 61m to where a tight rift passage enters to the right. The roof of the main streamway suddenly lowers to a flat-out crawl before rising again into a walking passage. The Jingling Cave inlet enters on a sharp right bend 91m before the trench passes under a slippery chimney out to the surface. Continuing, the water cascades into a wide pool and a bedding plane emerges in Rowten Pot above the gulley.
Permission – Fore Dales, Ingleton, via Carnforth.

ROWTEN POT
Alt. 363m

NGR SD 698780
Length 259m

Grade IV
Depth 105m

Bottomed 1897, YRC.

A tremendous chasm which provides a memorable trip. Great open pot by gate on the Turbary Road. Climb down onto boulder floor and either cross stream to ladder gully if dry, or scramble down a buttress onto jammed blocks and ladder a short pitch over chockstones onto the traverse which follows the gully pitch. From a large bridge the main shaft may be laddered to the left or right and the last section below a wet ledge can be hung separately. The cavern at the base of the main shaft may be reached by a direct pitch of 67m from the surface eyehole by the open pot.

A dry bypass and series of climbs cuts out the next waterfall and a dry pitch down a chimney (climbable with care) gains the top of the last waterfall. The fall is usually laddered to the right but a traverse and climb (or short pitch) drop into a dry passage leading to the waterfall chamber. The stream runs into two sumps and from the larger one it is possible to dive into the West Kingsdale Master Cave (see Valley Entrance).

Tackle

Pitch	Ladder	Belay	Lifeline
Gully	12m	2m	18m
Traverse	4.5m	6m	12m
Main	{ 30m	3m	46m
Shaft	{ 14m	0.6m	18m
3rd	8m	1.2m	12m
4th	12m	1m	18m

Calcite Inlet

Part way along dry bypass below main shaft is a steep inlet on the right. Passage with pools ends in two avens.

Leak Inlet.

Explored 1969, HWCPC.

Cross above 3rd pitch to 4.5m cascade and 6m shaft requiring a maypole. Next 9m shaft can be climbed using a convenient axle to a chamber with two inlets. One is too tight but the other is a 3m climb into Straw Chamber which has two narrow avens.

Frake's Series. Explored 1965, 1973-76, 1980, 1992 and 1993, CDG.
Length 1790m

From Rowten sump pool climb up into short roof passage or dive into a complex of canals ending at an upstream sump. Although there is a 1.5m dive into the canals it is not the obvious route; the present line follows a 4m long sump into the canals. On the left at the end of the canals is a 15m sump to a canal, followed by a 46m sump through into Frake's Passage. After 213m is a small inlet on the right, with a sump dived for 46m of very low passage. On the left at the junction with the small inlet is a deep canal and the start of a 168m sump which emerges in a low airspace canal. After 30m this is crossed by a very high rift – Aquamole Aven.

Scaling in this area has resulted in the discovery of more than 305m of passage. To the right (NE) of the canal is a low opening into a blind 10m aven. A climb before the aven gained a false floor, from which a 6m waterfall was scaled to reach a steeply rising inlet fissure, which became tight after 20m. On the opposite (SW) side of the canal is the massive Aquamole Aven, at least 46m high. The rift extends past the aven and climbs of 11m and 26m were overcome with scaling gear to reach a passage ascending to a bedding plane and junction. Left is a crawl 30m long to a mud choke beyond a boulder-filled aven. Right is a muddy bedding plane into a hands and knees crawl, lowering again and having been explored to a point very close to the bottom of Jingling Pot. A deserted passage from the top of the 26m climb passes over the pitch to reach a 5m pitch down, to emerge 39m up Aquamole Aven at an undescended pitch.

The canal below the Aquamole Aven ends at a 46m sump, emerging in a canal. On the left is a sump and ahead is a canal which forms part of a loop. The sump is 15m long to 76m of canal and another sump. This is 46m long to an airbell where a sump on the right goes back to the canal at the start of the loop.

The main way upstream is left from the airbell where the underwater passage continues its journey up valley, passing under Bull Pot, to the current limit of exploration 600m from base at 11m depth.

BOLT BELAYS – see Warning, page 13.

Permission – Fore Dales, Ingleton, via Carnforth.

SHEEPFOLD POT   NGR SD 690769   Grade I
Alt. 387m   **Length 9m**   **Depth 11m**
Explored 1908, YRC.

Large shakehole approached by gate below Turbary Road. Walk down grass and boulders into tall fissure and scramble over rocks until the way forward narrows. Beyond a tight section the passage continues but it seems to be an inlet.

Permission – Thornton Hall, Westhouse, via Carnforth.

SHOUT POT   NGR SD 702787   Grade II
Alt. 361m   **Length 96m**   **Depth 26m**
Extended 1987, DCC and NCC.

Entrance 100m S of Bull Pot in line of shakeholes above Shout Scar. Irregular rift passage drops to pitch and streamway which is impassable upstream but can be followed downstream for 60m where it is tight. Water emerges in Bull Pot.

Tackle

Pitch	Ladder	Belay	Lifeline
First	10m	2m	15m

Permission – Westgate, Westhouse, via Carnforth.

SIMPSON'S CAVES   NGR SD 695777 and 696778
    Grade II-III

Alt. 378m   **Length 317m**
Explored 1940, BSA; extended 1949, Bradford Tech. Coll. PC; and 1964, ULSA.

A shallow cave system with many points of entry in the bench between Swinsto Hole and Simpson's Pot. Dug out entrance is 61m NE of Double Three Pot and may be blocked by earth. It drops into the main crawl which soon becomes very low upstream. Downstream passes beneath two other entrances and through long pools to an inlet where daylight can be glimpsed. The passage now enlarges but quickly sumps, although a bypass is provided by Birthday Passage on the left. This abandoned crawl ends at a 'T' junction 76m forward. Left is a wet crawl into Simpson's Pot shakehole while right is a muddy, wet passage back to the streamway. The water falls down cascades into a pool and waterlogged bedding plane. Upstream passes beneath another entrance as a walking passage which suddenly sumps.

Permission – Fore Dales, Ingleton, via Carnforth.

SIMPSON'S POT   NGR SD 696779   Grade IV

Alt. 376m   **Length 884m**   **Depth 112m**

Explored 1940, BSA; extended 1962, ULSA.

A justly popular pot which provides a fascinating and sporting trip. Entrance in small shakehole at back of bench 91m from wall. Clean crawl with short inlet to left and two short drops to a further crawl becoming wet where a chink of daylight is seen to the left. Passage becomes higher and Simpson's Cave water enters from an impassable inlet before the stream falls down the Five Steps (rope useful for novices). Now the water plunges into the Pit (on its way to Storm Pot) but it is easier to traverse across and climb Chandelier and Camel Pots to Stake Pot. Traverse over next hole and clamber down to Storm Pot where stream falls through roof. Deep pool is blind but back towards the ladder is a short duck into a fine passage and traverse to Carol Pot. Squeeze forward to Shuffle Pot where route enlarges and wide ledges above stream channel lead to Lake Pot. Outlet from pool is a decorated streamway to Aven Pot followed by a squeeze and climb into the chamber at the top of Slit Pot. Even large people can pass this obstacle by going through upright (on a line). This fine ladder climb lands in Swinsto Hole just above the last pitch.

A roof traverse upstream of Aven Pot leads to a false floor and climbable bypass to Aven Pot. Above the false floor is a climb up into a decorated chamber, high level passage and traverse way above Slit Pot to a choke. In the corner of the decorated chamber is the magnificent Great Aven pitch onto the boulder pile overhanging Swinsto Final Chamber.

At SE end of Great Aven a hole in boulders drops into a crawl of 24m to window overlooking Swinsto Final Chamber.

Strike Series

Explored 1978, NCC.

Ascent of 21m at SE end of Great Aven leads to a junction of routes at the Conference Chamber. Water emerges from narrow rift 3.7m up wall and 61m of passage and a series of climbs rise to boulders and a tight bend. Beyond bend is the 3m wide Marvel Chamber and 9m bolt route gains another 15m of nasty passage to yet another squeeze requiring enlargement.

Straight ahead from the Conference Chamber steps up into a short crawl to another junction. Left is a fault passage which chokes after 24m, but ahead a low crawl enters the impressive Bear Chamber. A 9m pitch gains the floor of the cavern and further downward progress is possible (care!) for 15m to a choke. To the N a 3.7m climb up enters 40m of passage ending with no hope of further progress and a rift to the S chokes after 18m. An aven in the cavern roof is estimated at 14m high.

Tackle

Pitch	Ladder	Belay	Lifeline
Stake Pot	6m	Spreader	12m
Storm Pot	9m	3m	15m
Carol Pot	11m	1m	15m
Shuffle Pot	4.5m	1.2m	12m
Lake Pot	4.5m	9m	12m
Aven Pot	8m	1.2m	15m
Slit Pot	24m	3m	30m
Great Aven	40m	2m	46m
Boulder Pitch	8m	6m	12m

BOLT BELAYS – see Warning, page 13.

Permission – Fore Dales, Ingleton, via Carnforth.

SLANTING CAVE   NGR SD 705792   Grade IV
Alt. 344m   **Length 372m**   **Depth 64m**
Explored 1956, FMC; extended 1972, CPC.

WARNING – Short sections flood to roof in wet weather and crawls may silt up.

One in a line of shakeholes – 137m NE of the top of Yordas Wood. Climb down into a steep little streamway which divides upstream and soon becomes too small for progress. Downstream is a small chamber where flood inlet enters on right and passage descends steeply to a short wet crawl. Fine twisting trench to cascade and lower passage before a traverse provides the easiest route in a passage 8m high. Flowstone almost blocks the way before a chamber and aven full of boulders is gained. Bedding plane crawl enters a canal and small rift passage to a duck and well decorated section. Roof descends to the Trap (a low airspace canal) and easier going to the two terminal pitches. Continuing passage is large but soon leads to the final sump.

Tackle

Pitch	Ladder	Belay	Lifeline
1st	6m }	3m	17m
2nd	21m }		

Permission – Braida Garth, Westhouse, via Carnforth.

SLOPING CAVE   NGR SD 704791   Grade II
Alt. 351m   **Length 18m**   **Depth 6m**
Explored and extended 1972, HWCPC, BSA and ULSA.

Collapsed sinkhole S of Yordas Gill. Loose entrance squeeze into small chamber and tortuous inlet passage, which becomes too tight although a wider section can be seen above. Blocked with earth at present.

Permission – Braida Garth, Westhouse, via Carnforth.

SUICIDE POT NGR SD 694775 Grade IV
Alt. 381m   Depth 6m
Explored 1969, BSA.

WARNING – The whole of this pot is in unstable boulders and demands the greatest caution.

Entrance down under boulders immediately adjacent to Blood Pot (approximately mid-way between Swinsto Hole and Turbary Pot). A short climb leads to a very tight squeeze through loose rocks, and an awkward climb down on insecure blocks to a choked floor. A small stream enters part way down final climb, and this is seen in Blood Pot.

SWINSTO HOLE NGR SD 694775 Grade IV
Alt. 384m   Length 914m   Depth 131m
Entered YRC; extended 1930, GC and 1962, ULSA.

A tremendous sporting pot – very popular as a through route into the West Kingsdale Master Cave (see Valley Entrance). Follow up Swinsto Beck from the Turbary Road. Entrance is in shakehole to right of top sink, where a manhole enters a small streamway leading quickly to the first pitch into a chamber with an inlet passage to two avens. Outlet is Swinsto Long Crawl, 274m of stooping and crawling in water to a 4m climb into a deep pool (rope useful). First Inlet in Long Crawl is 61m long and the second 15m. Both become too tight.

Curtain Pitch follows and is succeeded by Pool Pitch, which is laddered dry by climbing into the roof. Exit from Pool Chamber by crawling over or under blocks to the top of the Main Pitch, which is conveniently split by a spray-lashed ledge. A wide passage gains in height and Turbary Inlet cascades in high on the right. It provides good going with odd squeezes for 152m and ends in a boulder choke under Turbary Pot.

Traverse on downstream into easy passage until water sinks into a crack. Deserted route drops into a chamber with a deep pool and a 6m climb over a parapet (rope useful). Next pitch into Spout Chamber where water is rejoined and followed down sporting cascades until the passage enlarges and Simpson's Pot water enters from Slit Pot aven. Cascade into Final Chamber is climbable on the left but should be lined since rock is shattered. Final Chamber is overhung by boulder chaos flooring the Great Aven (see Simpson's Pot). Two ways forward are possible. Left is Philosopher's Crawl and right is East Entrance Passage (see Valley Entrance).

Tackle

Pitch	Ladder	Belay	Lifeline
1st	6m	3m	12m
Curtain	8m	3m	12m
Pool Pitch	9m	2.7m	12m
Main Pitch {	15m	3m	24m
	14m	1m	21m
Spout	8m	3m	12m
Final	6m	3m	12m

BOLT BELAYS – see Warning, page 13.
Permission – Thornton Hall, Westhouse, via Carnforth.

SWINSTO SOUTH   NGR SD 693775   Grade III
Alt. 393m   **Length 198m**   **Depth 6m**
Extended 1982, Bentham & Ingleton Caving Club.
WARNING – Floods to roof along entire length.

   Stream sink by wall S of Swinsto Beck. Scramble down into low, boulder-strewn passage and drop into small chamber. Crawl to right through Expansion Chamber into Hydrophile Highway, 183m of arduous crawling past Nipple Squeezer and very tight bedding plane to emerge at bottom of Bedstead Pot.
Permission – Thornton Hall, Westhouse, via Carnforth.

THORNEY POT   NGR SD 695773   Grade I
(Hut Pot)
Alt. 372m
                                                               Depth 11m
   Large open pot surrounded by a low wall. May be climbed at S end to a floor which slopes down to choke the N end of the rift.
Permission – Thornton Hall, Westhouse, via Carnforth.

TURBARY POT   NGR SD 695775   Grade III
Alt. 378m   **Length 37m**   **Depth 40m**
Explored 1964, HWCPC.

   In small shakehole by Turbary Road just N of Swinsto Beck flood sink. Steep slope to low entrance and bedding plane crawl to first pitch onto a large ledge. Second pitch follows at once, down a rift with some loose rock, into McShea Chamber. Water sinks into formidable choke and climb up inlet rift ends in tight passage.

Tackle

Pitch	Ladder	Belay	Lifeline
1st	18m ⎫		
2nd	15m ⎭	8m	46m

Permission – Thornton Hall, Westhouse, via Carnforth.

VALLEY ENTRANCE   NGR SD 698774   Grade III-IV
(West Kingsdale Master Cave)
Alt. 268m   **Length 4.2km**
Explored 1966, ULSA and CDG.

   Obvious orange oil drum in field across road from Braida Garth track. Please close field gate and replace drum cover. Crawl forward into stooping tunnel and three waist deep pools, the first having limited airspace (sumps in wet weather). The Roof Tunnel continues easily past the low entrance to the Milky Way on the left and a 15m long sink passage in the floor. 183m forward is a short inlet on the right to a very loose aven, and after passing under Window Aven the Roof Tunnel emerges above the downstream sump in the West Kingsdale Master Cave.

   Inlet below Window Aven is horrible sludge crawl through serious duck into further small passage and, after 24m, an independent streamway – too tight downstream and calcite choked 6m upstream.

Window Aven
Explored 1977, NCC.
37m climb up aven (aids needed) leads to squeeze and 2m climb into tubular passage. Beyond boulders is 3m pitch into canyon opening out into Charolais Chamber. To right is rift passage which climbs to a chamber roofed by boulders and an aven which has been bolted for 15m to a boulder choke.

Much of Charolais Chamber is occupied by a monumental boulder and beneath it a way down through boulders is possible for 15m. This point is very close to a horrible boulder filled rift reached in an inlet in the Roof Tunnel.

West Kingsdale Master Cave
Serious climb from Roof Tunnel to floor of Master Cave is best laddered. The downstream sump is at the foot of the ladder and has been dived through to Keld Head – see that entry for description. Upstream is a classic canyon with cascades. At roof level on the right 15m upstream from the pitch is Black Rose Tunnel, an 18m long dig entering Union Aven, 6m high. On the left 61m from the pitch is a rope climb up to a muddy passage ending in a choke after 12m. Further upstream the canyon becomes shallower until the Master Junction is reached. On the left at roof level 46m before the Junction is a short, shingly passage which soon chokes.

The Master Junction is a complex of branching tunnels. Left through a wet crawl opens out into East Entrance Passage, which is walking and crawling to an aven on the left and a route up boulders into Swinsto Final Chamber straight ahead. The most obvious tunnel from the Master Junction joins the Swinsto water which runs into a sump and may be followed up the wide passage of Philosopher's Crawl to a short well watered thrutch into Swinsto Final Chamber.

Bearing right at the Master Junction opens out to a chest deep canal as far as the River Junction where the Mud River water rises from a sump to the right. Left continues under a series of avens to a wet passage below rock curtains and passing the Linking Crawl to the right shortly before the Rowten Sump. This may be passed by dives of 2m, 3.7m and 8.2m. (See Rowten Pot.)

Mud River Series
Linking Crawl meets a passage carrying a strong stream flowing into a sump. Upstream is another sump and a very low crawl to the right. Force Passage is on the left where a small tube intersects a larger tunnel terminating in a sand choke and a static sump. The main stream sump has been dived for 61m to a streamway (Ogden's Passage) with a short choked side passage and a further sump which has been dived to a flooded pot, (Deep Rising) at the foot of which exploration was continued along 91m of large, silty passage.

Milky Way and Carrot Passage
The Milky Way is a long crawl to a choked sink and the Cascade Inlet beyond a series of gour pools. Climb up slot onto chockstone (ladder useful) and forward into Toyland – a cavern 15m in diameter with good formations (care). Upstream are fine pools to a strenuous climb up a rope into a high chamber with three avens. The water emerges from a boulder choke, and a 9m climb up on the right leads through choke to rift chamber, succeeded by

squeeze and decorated chamber from which Axehead Passage, with more formations (care!), leads to junction. Right is inlet becoming too low. Left is muddy crawl to chamber with stalagmite, and squeeze on right into large choked chamber.

Back at the high chamber, the boulder choke may be passed with care to a boulder chamber and a passage which becomes too low. Main inlet part way along on right meanders to choked oxbow where an excavated route leads on into fissure ending at draughting choke. Just back from choke on right is remarkable straight rift; this leads to climb up to traverse and ends at left bend, where more traversing changes to a crawl which becomes too tight. Aven on right near end is close to Thorney Pot but is tight at top.

The Milky Way opens out beyond the Cascade Inlet but the main tunnel is choked with sand and the route is a low level crawl to Tri Junction. To the right the West Stream Passage is an 82m struggle until it becomes too low, straight ahead is a canal which leads to a duck in a low bedding. A flat out crawl for 30m past small inlet on right from West Stream ends at 9m free climb to sump (ladder useful as foothold on return!). At top of pitch small stream issues from passage in far wall and is presumably from Carrot Passage since a vocal connection has been made.

To left at Tri Junction is Shingle Crawl with another way off to left into Compost Series and 20m of crawling to a 10m aven. Above is passage running across top of aven. To N it soon becomes too tight but to S is a junction. Continuation to S becomes low over silt but crossover to left enters parallel passage running NW. Pit in floor is 10m deep and blind and continuation above ends too low over shingle.

Shingle Crawl itself soon shelves down to a stream and now begins the lengthy crawl of Carrot Passage. All side passages quickly close down except the last one which becomes low after 21m. Eventually the passage dives into a revolting tube with mud banks, to easier going and a junction. Stream emerges from passage to wide mud-choked bedding with sump. Right from junction leads to choke.

Tackle

Pitch	Ladder	Belay	Lifeline
Roof Tunnel	6m	12m	12m
Cascade Inlet	6m	1m	12m

BOLT BELAYS – see Warning, page 13.

Permission – Thornton Hall, Westhouse, via Carnforth.

THE WEST KINGSDALE SYSTEM
Length 9km   **Vertical range 131m**

This unique example of integrated underground drainage provides good instruction for the novice and a great diversity of entertaining through trips for the sporting caver. The description of the system falls into natural sections. The inlet passages of Swinsto, Simpson's Pot and Caves, Rowten Pot and Caves, and Jingling Cave are described from their respective entrances until they unite with a larger tributary or reach the Master Cave level. The West Kingsdale Master Cave is described from the Valley Entrance except Frakes'

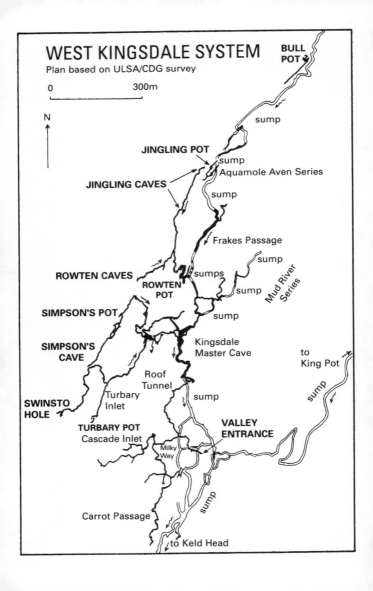

Series, which is guarded by the Upstream Rowten Sump and so is included in the Rowten Pot account.

Keld Head description includes the flooded passages downstream of the Master Cave sump and the link across to King Pot in East Kingsdale. Its length and depth are not included above.

WHISPER POT   NGR SD 702786   Grade II
Alt. 366m   Depth 6m

In next shakehole to S of Shout Pot. Entrance, at top of shakehole, is a cave in glacial drift with a shaft in the floor. Climb is narrow at first and widens to a choked floor. Rope or foot stirrup useful. Vocal connection with Shout Pot. Permission – Westgate, Westhouse, via Carnforth.

YORDAS CAVE   NGR SD 705791   Grade II
Alt. 312m   Length 213m   Vertical range 43m

A former show cave, deriving its name from the Norse 'Jord aas' – literally 'earth stream'. Main entrance with steps is at the bottom of Yordas Gill in plantation. Down the steps and across mudbank into Main Chamber – 55m long and 15m wide. Stream may be followed into crawl which is liable to be choked by flood debris. An oxbow provides a partial bypass on the left via Yordas Bedchamber. Water sinks into shingle but daylight can be seen up a shale slope at the Back Door entrance in a circular shakehole. Another passage from the Back Door (now blocked) led to a small stream passage and sump. Stream has been tested to Frakes' Passage in Rowten Pot.

At top end of the Main Chamber are avens above the Bishop's Throne on the right, and the Chapter House waterfall straight ahead. Top entrances further up the gill swallow the stream in normal weather and twin climbs unite above the first pitch (climbable via a convenient tree trunk) to a cascade and short passage opening out at a 'T' junction. Upstream is a bedding plane crawl to Yordas Pot but downstream easy going in an enlarging passage leads to the top of the Chapter House waterfall – sporting when wet.

Tackle

Pitch	Ladder	Belay	Lifeline
1st	6m	2m	12m
Chapter House	9m	6m	18m

BOLT BELAYS – see Warning, page 13.

Permission – Braida Garth, Westhouse, via Carnforth.

YORDAS POT   NGR SD 705791   Grade III
Alt. 347m

Descended 1964, GC.

Beneath fallen tree on bank above Yordas top entrances. Daylight pitch into fine wet aven with floor pinnacle and low crawl through to Yordas Cave.

Tackle – 24m ladder; 6m belay; 30m lifeline.

Permission – Braida Garth, Westhouse, via Carnforth.

YORDAS SINKS   NGR SD 704792   Grade I
Alt. 351m   **Length 9m**
Explored 1972, BSA.

   Entrance in left bank of gill above wall at top of Yordas plantation is covered by large rocks. Short drop into tight rift passage which closes to crawl and can be followed for only 9m to where the way on is too tight. The Girvanella bed is visible at the foot of the entrance drop.

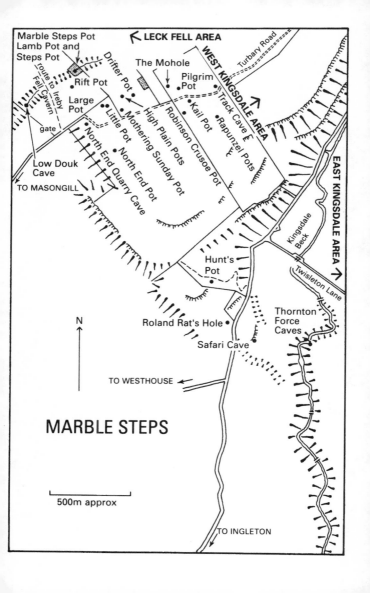

MARBLE STEPS

DRIFTER POT
Alt. 415m

NGR SD 683768
Length 60m

Grade III
Depth 10m

Explored 1986, NCC.

Entrance in shallow shakehole midway between cluster of trees and Large Pot.

Climb down 3m into chamber and low crawl for 12m to tight squeeze and bend. Small drop is climbable and leads to a streamway. Upstream has been forced for 20m and downstream ends in a wallow in silt which has been forced for 10m.

HIGH PLAIN POTS
Alt. 415m

NGR SD 683769

Explored 1956, NPC.

Entrances in shakeholes in middle of pasture NE of Little Pot.

1. Depth 10m **Grade II**

Pitch with constriction partway down lands in chamber with rock bridge and low choked crawl leading off. Liable to be blocked at bottleneck on pitch. Entrance blocked at present.

Tackle – 12m ladder; stake & sling belay; 15m lifeline.

2. Depth 10m **Grade I**

Small opening in nearby shakehole to 1 is excavated and shored shaft descending 6m to choke. Shaft is free-climbable.

HUNTS POT
Alt. 325m

NGR SD 688757
Length 10m

Grade I
Depth 8m

On left of track just before bend in wall. Shaft becoming too narrow with muddy passage part way down ending in choke. Partially collapsed.

KAIL POT
Alt. 396m

NGR SD 687769

Grade II
Depth 17m

Impressive fenced hole in shallow valley below Turbary Road. With care climb down gully (rope advisable) into open pot. Only outlet is a fissure and scramble down onto a steep slope running back towards the open pot. The passage quickly chokes. There is also a choked 4m shaft 80m SE of Kail Pot, between Kail and Rapunzel Pots.

Permission – Thornton Hall, Westhouse, via Carnforth.

LAMB POT   NGR SD 680771   Grade II
Alt. 372m   Length 12m   Depth 17m
Explored 1968, ULSA.

Second opening on right down boulders leading to gully of Marble Steps Pot. Best tackled first to a small drop. A series of steps descend to a pitch with a dry mud floor. Short passage becomes very narrow.

Tackle – 8m ladder; 1.2m belay; 12m lifeline.
Permission – Masongill Hall, Westhouse, vua Carnforth.

LARGE POT   NGR SD 682768   Grade IV
Alt. 402m   Length 1440m   Depth 122m
Explored 1982, NPC; extended 1983, Eldon P.C.

WARNING – Great care should be taken throughout the pot as the awkward entrance would make rescue very difficult. An accident in the far reaches of Arcadia would be extremely serious.

A very interesting pot which may prove to be a key to part of the Three Counties System. Entrance in first shakehole W of Little Pot, 6m away, is 12m shaft which is broken into 8m and 4.5m sections. A ladder is advisable on the 8m section. Small hole at bottom opens out, but is followed by awkward short section – best tackled feet first on the left side – opening directly onto restricted top of 2nd pitch. Ladder is belayed in crack in floor but the awkward approach means that lifelining by normal methods is not possible. Lower down, the pitch opens into a high chamber. Left is a climb up to a cross rift and blind 8m pit. The main way continues down a 3m climb to the top of the 3rd pitch, which enters Thornton Hall – a sizeable chamber.

On the right is an inlet which becomes too tight just short of Little Pot. The obvious way on is large, passing an over-tight inlet on the left to reach a junction with a large, partially silted passage on the left– the start of Secret Seven Passage, leading to Arcadia. The continuing downstream route is Red Herring Series.

Red Herring Series
Downstream the top of the 4th pitch is soon met. On the right just before the pitch a passage leads off from a muddy chamber to an aven and squeeze into a large rift – North Inlet. A hole in the floor leads to a partially excavated crawl with vocal connection to the top of the 4th pitch. A 3m climb above the hole is followed by a hard climb of 9m to a blocked passage.

The 4th pitch – 24m – is immediately followed by the 4.5m 5th pitch into a round chamber, To the left is a short bedding plane reaching the head of the Flake Aven Route, a succession of pitches dropping into the passage between the 8th and 9th pitches. The main way on is to the right down a straight rift to the 6th pitch, landing on a ledge above the 7th pitch – a 7m climb down into a chamber.

High up on the right is a passage which can only be reached by combined tactics and a large nut to jam in a crack. This passage, Occult Series, contains fine formations and flowstone and becomes hands and knees size before a canal is reached. After an awkward squeeze at the far end of the canal, an enlargement is followed by a 4.5m climb down to a chamber with mud sump.

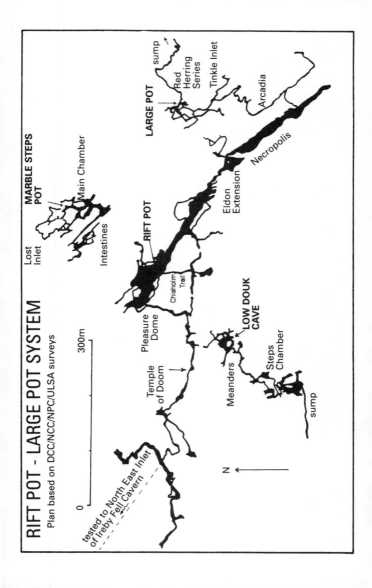

RIFT POT - LARGE POT SYSTEM

Plan based on DCC/NCC/NPC/ULSA surveys

0   300m

N

tested to North East Inlet
of Ireby Fell Cavern

MARBLE STEPS POT

Lost Inlet

Main Chamber

Intestines

RIFT POT

Pleasure Dome

Temple of Doom

Chisholm Trail

LOW DOUK CAVE

Meanders

Steps Chamber

sump

Eldon Extension

Necropolis

LARGE POT

sump

Red Herring Series

Tinkle Inlet

Arcadia

From the chamber below the 7th pitch a small, meandering passage leads to the 8th pitch, a 3.4m climb down into a high rift passage. Flake Aven Route joins down a high aven before the 9th pitch, which drops into a chamber; foam has been noted 4.5m up the walls here after exceptional rainfall. The succeeding crawl is finely decorated and varies in size between flat-out and stooping height until a calcite barrier is encountered. This forces a wriggle between sharp flakes to the head of the 10th pitch, which lands on a ledge with the 11th and Last pitches following immediately. Last pitch lands in large chamber from which a short wet crawl enters a passage to the sump, dived for 9m to an impenetrable slot beyond an airbell.

Arcadia

The silted passage just below Thornton Hall encounters The Pit almost immediately. A 4.5m climb down is followed by an awkward 5m climb up (fixed rope). A few metres ahead on the right is an inlet crawl to a blind aven with stream entering halfway up; the passage beyond the aven splits into three small inlets after some wet wallowing. Main way from The Pit, Secret Seven Passage, continues as a pleasant, sandy hands and knees crawl which enlarges to a narrow rift, leading to a 'T' junction with a stream passage. Upstream, to the left, is Tinkle Inlet, a crawl past fine formations to a sump. Sump is 0.7m long, but awkward and leads to 61m of passage which divides and lowers. Downstream, crawling changes to a fine rift and some zig-zags to an aven where the stream falls into a slot in the floor.

The way on is either an awkward squeeze in the roof or a more difficult route at floor level, into a short section of narrow passage to a right-angled left bend. People with long legs may find it easier to drop down to floor level before the chockstone at the corner. Easier going follows with the passage enlarging until the 9m long Calcite Inlet is met straight ahead. The main way is a flat-out crawl to the right around some awkward double bends to an enlargement, from which a fine, though muddy, passage continues to the junction with Pumpkin Passage – 91m of rift, passing a fine calcite formation, to a boulder choke.

On downstream the main passage widens and suddenly opens out at the top of an impressive 46m pitch – Colossus. Belay to peg or high stal boss on left – 2.4m belay needed – or to spike back on right – 3.7m belay needed. The circular shaft drops straight into the side of a large chamber – Necropolis – 91m in length. A bedding plane to the SE of the pitch closes down after 61m, but at NW end is way through boulders into a cross passage at start of the Eldon Extension. To N is crawl through boulders to Mystical Way leading to a streamway. Upstream is close to the sump in Occult Series and downstream needs enlarging to descend a pitch.

To S in Eldon Extension is a triangular chamber and way out to NW is crawl which can sump in wet weather and 3m ascent to the Mousehole in Rift Pot.

Tackle

Pitch	Ladder	Belay	Lifeline
Entrance	8m	1m	15m
2nd	12m	1.5m	30m
3rd	8m	1m	9m

Tackle

Pitch	Ladder	Belay	Lifeline
4th	24m	2m	30m
5th	4.5m	1.2m	6m
6th	12m	Spreader	15m
7th	9m handline for climb		
8th	Climbable but 4.5m rope useful		
9th	8m	2m	9m
10th	6m	1.5m	8m
11th	6m	1m	8m
Last	Climbable but 4.5m rope useful		
Flake Aven	30m	1.2m	37m
Colossus	46m	2.4m	52m
		or 3.7m	

BOLT BELAYS – see Warning, page 13.

Permission – Thornton Hall, Westhouse, via Carnforth.

LITTLE POT   NGR SD 682768   Grade III
Alt. 403m   **Length 30m**   **Depth 27m**
Extended 1964, NPC; 1979, NCC.

South of Marble Steps Pot over wall is prominent entrance in field bordering Turbary Road. Scramble down onto ledge and climb devious route to floor of pot 6m below. From here are two possible routes.

East Route

At E end of rift is short boulder slope leading to narrow fissure and 6m pitch. At foot is small chamber followed immediately by a 4.5m pitch. Landing is in another small chamber with no passable way on.

West Route

From opposite end of entrance rift a small climb and awkward short section of passage lead to head of pitch with narrow take-off. At foot, 4.5m of tight passage leads to a junction. Left closes down almost immediately, while right is a difficult crawl over the top of a narrow rift which is too tight to descend. After only 6m further progress becomes impossible.

Tackle

Pitch	Ladder	Belay	Lifeline
Entrance			12m
East Route			
1st	6m	3m	12m
2nd	4.5m	1.2m	8m
West Route			
1st	14m	1.2m	21m

Permission – Thornton Hall, Westhouse, via Carnforth.

LOW DOUK CAVE   NGR SD 677768   Grade III
Alt. 335m   **Length 540m**   **Depth 82m**

Explored 1963, NPC; extended 1965, British Aircraft Corp. C.C.; 1971, ULSA and BUSS; 1987, NCC.

Prominent shakehole in dry valley below Marble Steps Pot. Original entrance was by scrambling down into daylight series. This is now choked. New entrance is off to one side and is a drop down between boulders to a traverse over a 6m pitch and into a low crawl. A squeeze up leads to the first pitch of 6m and thrutch through to second pitch, 8m deep. At foot a further squeeze down and 1.5m drop emerges at the head of the third pitch.

From base two ways lead off. The obvious route forward terminates in a choke close to the Kendal Extension in Rift Pot. The other, a muddy pool continues as a low crawl until it breaks out into a small chamber. From here a wide bedding plane joins way in from original entrance and bedding plane inlet to waterlogged rising. Downstream is drop into a twisting canyon.

Tributary on left may be entered at roof level and followed to a choke. Violent meanders continue to a procession of cascades into Steps Chamber. Above the cascades a fine roof passage leads to a climb and 9m pitch back into the streamway. A tube before the climb connects with Mud Chamber and another link to the streamway just after the short crawl succeeding Steps Chamber. The downstream route leads to a waterfall into the small sump chamber and a steep inlet choked by fill and calcite. Above the fall a deserted passage and mud slope end in a static sump. Downstream sump has been dived for 107m and continues small and silty. Water emerges at Keld Head.

Between the sumps a wet crawl emerges in the BAC Rift which ascends to a boulder choke. High in the roof is Straw Chamber and a series of passages and chambers while straight ahead is a crawl to a deep pool and a muddy aven.

Tackle

Pitch	Ladder	Belay	Lifeline
1st	6m	3m	10m
2nd	8m	Bolt	12m
3rd	6m	3m	10m

BOLT BELAYS – see Warning, page 13.

Permission – Masongill Hall, Westhouse, via Carnforth.

MARBLE STEPS POT   NGR SD 680771   Grade III-IV
Alt. 384m   **Length 1273m**   **Depth 131m**

Extended 1976, Grampian Spel. Group; 1978, NCC.

WARNING – Avoid the area below the main chamber in wet conditions, as almost instant flooding occurs in places, without warning.

This classic entrance is located in an isolated plantation above Masongill. The impressive dry rift near the stream sink is a scramble down to the head of a gully, which is best laddered for the inexperienced. At the foot of the gully is the Upper Main Chamber. An exposed traverse round the Chamber, followed by a 6m bolt route, reaches a ledge with a window into a chamber with animal bones on the floor. The bolt route continues for 4.5m to reach

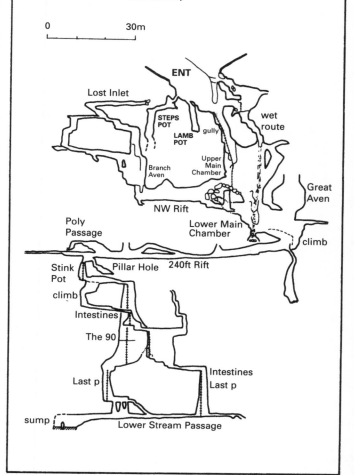

MARBLE STEPS POT

Section based on ULSA survey

0   30m

ENT

Lost Inlet

wet route

STEPS POT

gully

LAMB POT

Upper Main Chamber

Branch Aven

Great Aven

NW Rift

Lower Main Chamber

climb

Poly Passage

240ft Rift

Pillar Hole

Stink Pot

climb

Intestines

The 90

Intestines Last p

Last p

sump

Lower Stream Passage

a rift which slopes up for 21m but becomes too tight, passing a 4.5m long boulder-choked bedding on the way.

In the Upper Main Chamber a waterfall enters to cascade down into the Lower Main Chamber. An easier route is to turn right and climb down into the NW Rift and crawl left under boulders. The passage gains height and doubles back under an aven to a short tube and boulder slope into the Lower Main Chamber where the water sinks into a choked pot 6m deep.

Ahead a large dry passage has a floor slot which affords a slippery climb down into a chamber. Below is a hidden choked pitch of 15m which often contains standing water and above is a large window into Great Aven, scaled for 12m to a ledge and a further 18m to the top, where 21m of small phreatic tubes end in mud and boulder chokes.

The obvious exit from the chamber above the hidden pitch is a long, irregular fissure – the 240 foot Rift. Easy going continues past a traverse over the blind Pillar Hole to Stink Pot. Across the pot is a roof passage 37m long becoming too low, while below it a gash in the floor is the start of the Intestines Route. Across the gash a short passage opens onto 'The 90' – a fine ladder climb. Up to the left is a connection with the Intestines and down on the right is the last pitch into a muddy complex of greasy 6m climbs. These are avoided by a sloping crawl emerging in the Lower Stream Passage. Downstream are fissure sumps linked by a traverse and upstream is a crawl to the base of the last pitch of the Intestines. An excavated fissure continues to where it is choked by cobbles. Downstream sump descends an 18m pot to a low passage explored for a further 160m.

Tackle

Pitch	Ladder	Belay	Lifeline
Gully	37m	4.5m	46m
Stink Pot	8m	3m	15m
'The 90'	29m	2.4m	37m
Last Pitch	11m	1m	15m

The Intestines

Explored 1948, CPC; extended 1969, North Manchester Caving Club.

Below Stink Pot climb down a fissure (rope useful) into small crawl to short pitch. A further low crawl ends suddenly in a roomy pitch with a series of steps below. A traverse to the N is the link to 'The 90' on the classic route. Down the steps to the S is a high chamber with an inlet waterfall which may be scaled up falls of 11m, 6m, 4.5m and 3.7m before becoming too tight. Downstream a walking passage ends in the last pitch into the Lower Stream Passage.

Tackle

Pitch	Ladder	Belay	Lifeline
Climb	8m rope useful		
1st	4.5m	3m	
2nd	11m	0.6m	21m
Last	15m	6m	21m

Wet Route

At stream sink carefully bridge down boulders to a small wet pitch into pool. Fine passage to another wet rift, which is climbable. Above it is a step across and up into a short passage to a large window over The Gully. Below, the stream cascades down into an easy passage to the pitch into the Main Chamber.

Tackle

Pitch	Ladder	Belay	Lifeline
1st	6m	2m	15m
Main Chamber	18m	1.2m	24m

Lost Inlet Series

Explored 1969, HWCPC and 1970, ULSA.

From Upper Main Chamber climb down into NW Rift and follow high narrow passage to the Branch Aven with a choked sink on the left. Climb waterfall to spacious ledge and traverse back into high, dry hading rift. Fine long climb up into roof passage. Inlet crawl to left is the route into a high fault rift but way forward is along a decorated fissure into a spacious sandy aven. Climb up a narrow gully into tortuous passage opening out into high canyon. Awkward 4.3m climb is succeeded by a crawl and pleasant scramble up into a chamber. Narrow rift intersects fossil streamway which is good going upstream until it lowers to a crawl, after a narrow sink in the floor.

Downstream is a shingle choke but a body-sized tube is the way to the Trunk Route. A small drop terminates the tube and meets a parallel crawl. Winding rift, whose floor falls away to a 4m climb, joins a small stream. Upstream splits impassably but downstream is a further climb and a large choked tube enters on the left. Cascades end at top of Branch Aven which has waterfalls of 8.5m, 8m and 4.5m. From first ledge it is possible to traverse forward and up into decorated fissure at top of initial climb.

Poly Passage

Explored 1972, BSC.

At end of 240ft Rift climb up into rift and through very tight squeeze to 4.5m pitch into wider section. Outlet fissure soon chokes with fill. Be sure of return before passing squeeze.

BOLT BELAYS – see Warning, page 13.

Permission – Masongill Hall, Westhouse, via Carnforth.

THE MOHOLE   **NGR SD 686769**   **Grade III**
Alt. 404m   Length 40m   Depth 82m

Explored 1969, ULSA.

Shakehole by Blea Dubs wall. Scramble down rift to boulder floor with holes off in both directions. One opening is a blind chamber but the other opens out above the first pitch. Best laddered down narrow rift, but one traverses across to climb down sharp chimney until shaft widens and ladder can be gained. Next pitch follows at once as a slot under the wall which pops out into a small chamber. Short passage to the third pitch opening out into a fine climb. Steep boulder slope offers no shelter so descend final pitch into chamber. Possible to get down another 6m between boulders and the wall.

Tackle

Pitch	Ladder	Belay	Lifeline
1st	17m	1m	21m
2nd	8m	–	12m
3rd	29m	2m	37m
4th	6m	3m	12m

Permission – Thornton Hall, Westhouse, via Carnforth.

MOTHERING SUNDAY POT   NGR SD 683767   Grade II
Alt. 399m   **Depth 8m**
Explored 1982, NPC.

In SW corner of field just over wall at start of Turbary Road is obvious shakehole. Climb down 8m into chamber with small rift leading off.

NORTH END POT   NGR SD 683765   Grade III
Alt. 395m   **Length 110m**   **Depth 48m**
Explored 1987, EPC.

Entrance is large open shaft 7m deep, 330m SSE of Large Pot. Dig in centre of hole under hanging wall unearthed human bones. Excavated entrance shaft at S end drops 9m onto a loose boulder slope down a rift to a pitch down jammed boulders (care!). From foot of pitch is way forward into St. George's Hall with steep calcited boulder slope up on right to choked aven. To left is tight passage opening out into a larger inlet emerging from a drainpipe. This has been bailed and forced through tight squeeze to a boulder choke.

Tackle

Pitch	Ladder	Belay	Lifeline
Entrance	10m	1m	15m
2nd	15m	3m	30m

Permission – Mr. R. Shuttleworth, Thornton Hall Farm, Thornton in Lonsdale.

NORTH END QUARRY CAVE   NGR SD 681766   Grade I
Alt. 372m   **Length 8m**

In small quarry on right where Turbary Road emerges from walls is bedding plane which becomes too low.

PILGRIM POT   NGR SD 687769   Grade I
Alt. 402m   **Depth 6m**
Explored 1969, ULSA.

Deep shakehole E of the Mohole. Wet fissure descends in a series of steps to a choked crack in a small chamber.
Permission – Thornton Hall, Westhouse, via Carnforth.

RAPUNZEL POTS   NGR SD 689767
Alt. 373m

1.   **Depth 4.5m**   **Grade I**
 Hole opening into chamber (rope advisable) where debris is stacked behind
a tail board. Ends in narrow fissure.

2. Length 20m   **Depth 38m**   **Grade II**
Extended 1988, NCC.

 8m rift to descending crawl. 5m forward is 3m drop into sizeable chamber
which slopes down to the head of a shaft. This shaft is very unstable, but can
be descended with care via two free-climbs of 7m and 10m and a pitch of 9m
to where it becomes too tight.

Tackle – 10m ladder; 2m belay; 12m lifeline.

RIFT POT   NGR SD 679769   **Grade IV**
Alt. 365m   **Length 2720m**   **Depth 101m**
Total length with Large Pot is 4.17km
Explored 1984, DCC and NCC. Extended 1985, KCC and 1988, KCC and
NCC.

 Massive shakehole S of Marble Steps Pot.
 Scramble down entrance to 10m shored pitch and bedding plane to 'T'
junction. Left is tight and to right is floor slot with climbs of 2m and 3m
into small chamber. Across 3m drop is Telephone Chamber with roof inlet
becoming too tight after 15m. Blasted passage continues to two more 2m
climbs and head of large pitch (Route 66).
 Pitch is awkward at first, with ledges, but after 10m becomes airy and
breaks out into roof of Coates Cavern (60m by 20m).
 From the cavern three passages radiate. To the NW is the huge fossil All
Fools Passage which finishes after 50m in a boulder choke which draughts
strongly. A small inlet passage enters here and can be followed for 20m to
a choke and climb up to the Pleasure Dome extensions.
 To east of Coates Cavern is Crosspatch Inlet and main way forward is
Acacia Avenue running SE as a bedding plane in the roof. The crawl quickly
enlarges to a large well decorated tube with calcite slope into decorated aven
to the left. Continuation leads to large stalagmites behind which is Crystal
Inlet with another decorated passage on left. **This must not be entered** since it
is only an oxbow. Crystal Inlet itself is 40m to a choke which is near the
Chisholm Trail and branch to left which becomes too low.
 Main passage down steep mud bank emerges in high fault chamber with bolt
routes in roof to aven and two oxbows. Way on is part way up boulder slope on
left where route through boulders leads to hands and knees crawl in bedding
with strong draught. After 50m the Mousehole is a small muddy crawl and a 3m
drop to a muddy wallow which can be almost dry or sumped and impassable
depending on the weather. Beyond is the Eldon Extension and Large Pot.

Tackle

Pitch	Ladder	Belay	Lifeline
First	10m	1m	15m
Route 66	60m	1m	75m

Chisholm Trail
  Several bolt routes have been pursued in Coates Cavern leading to high level oxbows or short offshoots. A tube is gained from the main Route 66 pitch which heads due south to a hole into the chamber taking a small stream. A traverse leads to the Chisholm Trail which is crawling until after 40m the Gee Cross junction is reached. Right is a small inlet for 40m which becomes too low 2m from the Pleasure Dome. Straight on past a boulder run in is a 3m climb to a choke.

Pleasure Dome and Temple of Doom
  Original entry from choke at All Fools Passage was up through very loose choke at end of 20m rift. Safer way is up through tight squeeze before this choke to emerge in roof tube. Drop down into larger passage and follow stream up until branch on left can be followed to choke near Chisholm Trail.
  Continue upstream to squeeze and sand filled passage and further squeeze into way forward to two cobble chokes – The Temple of Doom.
  Into choke and to right are two small chambers and way under blocks (extreme care!) into alternate crawling and walking to the more stable Pussy Cat choke and more sandy crawling to a chamber with blind side passages. Ahead is a 'T' junction with a much larger passage, generally 3 by 4m. To the left is upstream and water emerges from roof where a series of climbs leads to a tight rift and aven with continuing small passage. Continuing main crawl has a crystal floor to a flowstone chamber with a further crawl to the final choke.
  The right branch at the 'T' junction passes a false floor to another choke. The stream sinking near the 'T' junction has been tested to East Inlet in Ireby Fell Cavern.
BOLT BELAYS – see Warning, page 13.

ROBINSON CRUSOE POT   NGR SD 688766   Grade II
Alt. 393m   **Depth 18m**

  In clints 90m out on bench from Turbary Road, in same field as Kail Pot and 4.5m from wall. Entrance in clints is not obvious; replace boulder cover. Climb down 4.5m to short passage into chamber. Inlet soon chokes. Crawl through blasted hole under boulders leads to climb down into excavated rift passage which becomes blocked by calcite after 8m.

ROLAND RATS HOLE   NGR SD 689754   Grade III
Alt. 300m   **Length 80m**
Explored 1984, NCC.
WARNING – Floods completely in wet weather.
  Flood resurgence for Hunts Cross area. Entrance in field before old quarry 30m W of Kingsdale road at side of farmers track (use gate), Behind boulder is crawl in deepening water. Awkward duck under flake after 49m is followed by further crawling in water in wider silt floored passage. Ends in sump.

SAFARI CAVE   NGR SD 691754   Grade I
Alt. 275m   **Length 14m**

Entrance on edge of limestone outcrop. 14m crawl to where daylight can be seen. Too tight to exit.

STEPS POT   NGR SD 680771   Grade III
Alt. 375m   **Length 40m**   **Depth 23m**

Explored 1966, ULSA and 1968, MUSS.

WARNING – Pitch is tight and difficult to reverse.

First opening on right of slope down to gully of Marble Steps Pot. Descend through chamber into crawl to a high rift and pitch. This is very restricted and finally becomes too tight at a depth of 18m. Across the pitch the crawl divides and then is choked by calcite.

Tackle – 18m ladder; 1m belay; 21m lifeline.
Permission – Masongill Hall, Westhouse, via Carnforth.

THORNTON FORCE CAVES   NGR SD 695754   Grade II
Alt. 229m

1.   Explored 1979, NCC.   Length 4.5m   Grade II

Entrance on left of main waterfall where stream emerges from bedding cave 8m up vertical cliff face; best approached by abseiling from above and swinging in. The wide bedding passage ends quickly in big slipped blocks barring the way on.

Tackle – 30m rope for abseil.

2.   Explored 1982, NCC.   Length 12m   Grade III

Situated to right of waterfall on steep face just below 2.4m overhang. Difficult entry involves a pendulum and use of chocks, and a ladder is also useful. Cave is a hands and knees crawl to a small fallen block, then flat out to where daylight enters from narrow slot in stream bed. No exit possible.

Tackle – 30m rope; assorted tapes and chocks; 10m ladder.

TRACK CAVE   NGR SD 689770   Grade I
Alt. 390m   **Length 18m**

Explored 1971, KCC.

Low entrance to W of Turbary Road. Muddy bedding plane runs back under track and enlarges somewhat before choking. It trends towards Sheepfold Pot.

Permission – Thornton Hall, Westhouse, via Carnforth.

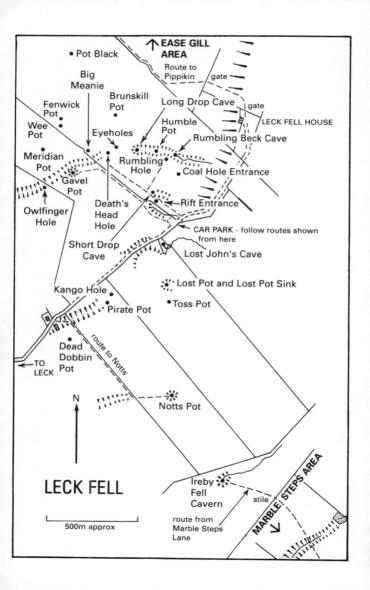

LECK FELL

BIG MEANIE   NGR SD 667791   Grade IV
(Hawthorn Pot) (Nostril Pot)
Alt. 335m   **Length 315m**   Depth 73m

Big Meanie/Death's Head/Long Drop is 1km long and 92m deep.
Explored 1971, MUSS and HWCPC.

WARNING – Beware of loose rock on entrance pitch.

     Entrance in small deep shakehole by wall. Rift narrows quickly to top of deep pitch and first 3m are tight and awkward. Fine climb into tall fissure passage which may be followed westwards to chamber with short high level series, and mud choke. East passage proceeds through another large chamber to a series of avens and a division of ways. Left ascends and descends as a rift which becomes restricted, while right through boulders drops to a crawl with pools before opening out to the head of a broken pitch into Death's Head Main Chamber. An impressive spot.

Tackle

Pitch	Ladder	Belay	Lifeline
Entrance	49m	6m	61m
Main Chamber	21m	3m	30m

BOLT BELAYS – see Warning, page 13.

Permission – CNCC.

BRUNSKILL POT   NGR SD 667794   Grade III
Alt. 344m   **Length 76m**   Depth 45m

Explored NPC.

     Entrance in line of shakeholes 183m N of Eyeholes. Stream sinks in middle of three shakeholes and entrance climb of 5m is through small hole in the side of that shakehole. At bottom of climb two short constrictions lead to head of 1st pitch, which can be free-climbed. Short crawl leads to 2nd pitch, descending into chamber where stream sinks in impenetrable slot in floor. Way on is low crawl for 12m to head of 3rd pitch, belayed to bar. Pleasant free-hanging climb with crawl at foot, which quickly divides. Left is flat-out crawl for 4.5m, breaking out over streamway; upstream becomes too small and water from chamber below 2nd pitch enters at two points, while downstream drops down a narrow pitch to small chamber and sump. Right where crawl divides is sideways crawl, interrupted by an aven, to a pitch with bar belay. The passage below becomes too tight.

Tackle

Pitch	Ladder	Belay	Lifeline
1st	4.5m	1.5m	–
2nd	8m	0.6m	9m
3rd	11m	0.6m	12m
Sump chamber	4.5m	4.5m	–
Crawl	3m	0.6m	–

BOLT BELAYS – see Warning, page 13.

Permission – CNCC.

COAL HOLE ENTRANCE   NGR SD 671790   Grade III
Alt. 361m   **Length – see Short Drop Cave**

First through exploration to Short Drop Cave 1977, CPG.

A very sporting alternative entrance to Short Drop Cave. Obvious entrance in small shakehole SE of Rumbling Hole. Downward squeeze into slightly larger passage which leads past small inlet on left. Continues as crawl with pools for 40m. Short climb over partial flowstone blockage leads to more low passage. 15m forward passage narrows at floor level and traverse cum crawl leads to drop back into wider section. Low crawl leads into bedding chamber with coal seams exposed in walls. Excavated squeeze through coal seam meets Canals Inlet of Short Drop Cave, with Canals Inlet water emerging from large passage on right which rapidly becomes too tight. Canals Inlet can be followed downstream by traversing or crawling in water to emerge at Short Drop Main Entrance.

Permission – CNCC.

DEAD DOBBIN POT   NGR SD 665781   Grade IV
Alt. 294m   **Length 122m**   **Depth 56m**

Explored 1972/73 BUSS and CPG; Extended 1974, Sheffield Univ. Speleo. Soc.

WARNING – Parts of the cave are very unstable and the lower part of the Entrance Shaft in particular should be treated with respect.

In prominent shakehole 137m SE of the shooters' hut. Obvious entrance below prominent bedrock lip. Climb down of 3m into small circular chamber. Descending squeeze to left into rift chamber followed by short crawl into bigger chamber with floor of huge boulders. At far end unstable route down through boulders leads to small stream but no way on.

Entrance shaft continues, best laddered from bolt on far wall to avoid dubious shuttering. Very tight muddy crawl into easier going down short climb to top of second pitch. Fine shaft into chamber. Short crawl behind foot of ladder leads to short free climb into Jane and Ethel, twisting tortuous passage for 37m to Lofthouse Aven. Across bottom of aven short squeeze through pool into hands and knees crawl, past short inlet on left, for 12m. Crawl degenerates, passes through a canal section and continues for 15m to a gravel choke. The canal section is very difficult to enter on return due to limited air-space and awkward crawl.

Tackle

Pitch	Ladder	Belay	Lifeline
Entrance	8m	Karabiner	15m
2nd	18m	2m	24m

Permission – CNCC.

DEATH'S HEAD HOLE   NGR SD 668791   Grade IV
Alt. 341m   Length 351m   Depth 82m

Big Meanie/Death's Head/Long Drop is 1km long and 92m deep.
Explored 1889, YRC; extended 1949, 1968 & 1981, GC.

Impressive fenced shaft 0.4km down the fell from Short Drop Cave, in shallow valley. Belay main shaft ladder back to stake at W end or hang from ledge in gully at E end. Landing is on an unstable boulder slope descending to pitch over massive jammed boulder, into Main Chamber, 12m x 18m and 46m high.

Waterfall descends from East Passage, 23m above floor, reached by a steep gully climb (two pitches). Second pitch is rising traverse to outside of bridged boulders. Roomy passage leads below a series of avens before dwindling to a silted crawl after 152m. A chimney aven just beyond Candle Chamber has been climbed for 43m to a choked inlet. Where main stream enters from under left wall is Dolphin Passage, starting low and wide to where tight left branch enters. Winding streamway leads to fault-controlled canal where baling improves air-space in two ducks followed by a sumped tube with soft mud floor into the 'final' chamber of Long Drop Cave.

Tackle

Pitch	Ladder	Belay	Lifeline
Main Shaft	64m	12m	91m
Main Chamber	6m	–	–
East Passage	–	–	27m

BOLT BELAYS – see Warning, page 13.
Permission – CNCC.

EYEHOLES   NGR SD 668792   Grade II
Alt. 341m   Depth 15m

Three prominent entrances N of Death's Head Hole. Two westerly are divided by a rock bridge. Walk down and very short crawl at W end. Smallest entrance is rift pitch to choked fissure.

Tackle

Pitch	Ladder	Belay	Lifeline
East Eyehole	9m	3m	18m

Permission – CNCC.

FENWICK POT NGR SD 665793 Grade III

Alt. 332m **Length 30m** **Depth 35m**

Explored 1977, CPG.

Prominent double shakehole N of Wee Pot. Entrances in both shakeholes, that to N giving the safer descent.

Mud and boulder slope leads past digging spoil to entrance which is a window into a large chamber. The ladder for the first two pitches is best belayed from a good thread high on the left. Descend to chamber with floor of mud and boulders. Enormous boulder wedged in rift holds up chamber floor. Thread remainder of ladder through hole at south end and descend Bechstein Pitch in impressive rift to debris floor. Hole at north end gives access to further shaft, under false floor, which is the site of a dig. This latter shaft can be free-climbed, but if laddered the safest belay is at the level of the false floor above.

Tackle

Pitch	Ladder	Belay	Lifeline
Entrance ⎫ Bechstein ⎬	23m	1m	46m
3rd	12m	1m	24m

Permission – CNCC.

GAVEL POT NGR SD 666791 Grade III-IV

Alt. 323m **Length 1971m** **Depth 110m – dived to 174m**

Gavel/Short Drop/Lost John's/Rumbling is 10.6kms long and 147m deep – dived to 211m.

Extended 1970, NPC & CPC; 1971-1989 CDG.

WARNING – Final pitches are liable to flooding.

Entrance is huge shakehole surrounded by fence. Path descends from stile to natural bridge and short chockstone pitch. Through canyon beneath bridge is window into final pitches of Short Drop Cave. Floor of daylight pot is steep boulder slope to second pitch which may be climbed (rope advisable) into chamber which was original limit of exploration.

Climb down walled shaft into rift passage with stream rising from low bedding plane to the right. Downstream is a wide passage of variable height to a chamber with a crawl on the right into October Series. Mudbath leads through this crawl into easy going for 61m to traverse beyond aven and climb down. Main rift continues beneath aven and becomes too tight 91m forward but low crawl on right enters the main stream in a wide crawl. Upstream becomes low, then tight fissure leads to blockage and constriction at upper level. Downstream emerges below the wall climb near the entrance.

Beyond October Series the Gavel streamway cuts down a narrow canyon and drops quickly to the two final pitches and terminal sump. This is a flooded window. Upstream is a 120m dive past an airbell to a complex area where a shaft descends to a gravel choke at 64m depth. Downstream leads to a junction with the downstream sump in Lost John's after 198m. The gradually deepening sump continues to a further junction at 25m depth and 787m from base. The passage on the right is the second sump in the Lower Streamway of

Pippikin Pot. On the left is the downstream continuation towards Leck Beck Head dived for 100m in a large tunnel.

Above the final wet pitches and cascades is a roof passage leading to Southbound Passage; a rift with two branches, one choked and the other becoming tight.

Before the streamway begins to cut down into the canyon there is a dry oxbow on the right with a narrow passage leading off into Glasfurd's Chamber. Inlets enter from an aven and a tight duck, beyond which is 9m of larger passage, ending in a liquid mud choke. Outlet passage ends in a very constricted sump. Glasfurd's Passage runs E through a series of well decorated chambers (care!) and crawls to a choke of mud and boulders.

Tackle

Pitch	Ladder	Belay	Lifeline
Chockstone	8m	Karabiner	12m
2nd	–	–	12m
3rd	26m	Karabiner	30m
4th	17m	Karabiner	21m

BOLT BELAYS – see Warning, page 13.

Permission – CNCC.

HUMBLE POT   NGR SD 670791   Grade I
(3½ Hole)
Alt. 347m

Depth 4.5m

A small choked pothole 61m NW of Rumbling Hole in a shallow, dry gully. No tackle required.

Permission – CNCC.

IREBY FELL CAVERN   NGR SD 673773   Grade III
Alt. 396m   **Length 4.9km**   **Depth 128m**

Ireby/Notts is 10.1km long and 183m deep.

First explored 1949, BSA. Extended 1964, CDG; 1966, RRCPC and North West Pothole Club; 1968, 1975, 1988 NCC; 1991, YSS; 1993, BSC.

A favourite system for training, with short pitches and long but easy passages. A magnificent cave, linked to Notts Pot by diving.

Entrance is approached from Marble Steps Lane via stile over fell wall. Stream sinks into steep sided shakehole and there is a complex cave behind boulders on left. True entrance is concrete pipe. Climb down and forward into chamber and steeply descending passage to Ding Pitch. Landing is a spacious ledge above Dong Pitch and passage spirals down to Bell Pitch. Climb above Dong Pitch, or inlet passage below it, leads to a shaft with window into alternative aven to Bell Pitch.

Streamway continues down climbable cascade (Pussy Pitch) to cross rift chamber where water sinks into shingle. Window in wall opens into twisting trench which soon rejoins stream in high passage which lowers to shingle chokes upstream. Inlet almost immediately downstream indicates complex

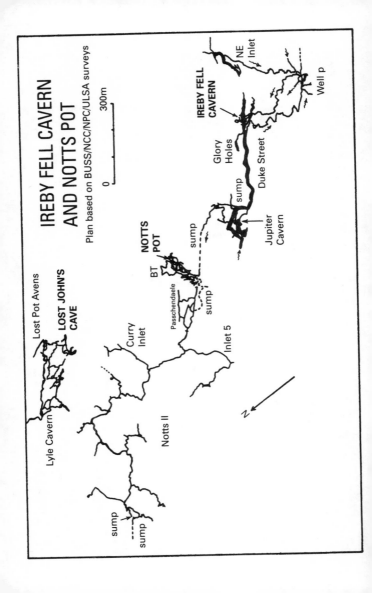

IREBY FELL CAVERN AND NOTTS POT

Plan based on BUSS/NCC/NPC/ULSA surveys

0   300m

Lost Pot Avens

LOST JOHN'S CAVE

Lyle Cavern

Curry Inlet

NOTTS POT

BT

Passchendaele

sump

sump

Inlet 5

Notts II

sump

sump

IREBY FELL CAVERN

Glory Holes

sump

Duke Street

Jupiter Cavern

NE Inlet

Well p

N

area of roof passages between a large aven and the abandoned trunk route of the Glory Holes. Stream sinks into cobbles and crawl continues past oxbows into twisting walking size passage through pools. Massive formations create two short wet crawls but otherwise the going is very easy until passage cuts down via cascades to the head of the Well Pitch. Traverse across pit while lifelined and fix ladder to bolt on rock bridge. Below is chamber with pool and high canyon leads on to boulders at base of large chamber. Roof passage from this chamber is link with North East Inlet and high level traverse may be followed upstream. Beneath boulders stream drops to short pitch where a rope or ladder is useful. Now massive avens are encountered before roof drops into small tunnel with shingle floor and stream runs away under left wall of Main Stream Passage. A flat out crawl over cobbles with the water leads to the Bolton Extensions which quickly enlarge to walking size. 50m forward is an inlet on the left trending towards the cavern below the Rope Pitch, and the stream drops down a 5m climb to a handsome passage and a sump.

Back in Main Passage, East Inlet to right is crawl to silted sump. Right branch of inlet is low crawl to dam and 12m of minimal air-space passage (negotiated on one's back). Slightly better going for 9m reaches a junction. Left chokes almost immediately and right is too low just beyond another dam; a waterfall can be heard ahead. Left hand passage carries water from stream beyond Temple of Doom in Rift Pot.

The Main Stream Passage rapidly enlarges to a spacious walk through pools for 0.4km until water turns left into crawl. Deserted canyon rises to 'T' junction with wide cavern. To the right the cavern is choked and sandy crawls become impassable 91m distant. To the left the cavern enlarges, before lowering and descending to the stream, which may be followed back via a duck to the sink. Downstream Duke Street is an impressive march through Whirlpool Chamber until sadly the roof shelves into Sump 1.

Tackle

Pitch	Ladder	Belay	Lifeline
Ding	9m	Tether	15m
Dong	11m	Tether	18m
Bell	11m	0.6m	18m
Well	8m	Tether	24m
Rope	–		12m

Shadow Route and Overshadow Series

Traverse over top of Ding pitch and drop 4m to window and 5m descent to head of Shadow Route pitch, which drops 24m directly to streamway below Bell pitch. Traverse over Shadow pitch to short climb and muddy crawl to step into small chamber. Up to left is massive collapse and two other passages quickly close down. Way on is down through Plughole to the right (loose boulders!) and steep descent to pitch dropping onto boulder slope. Way forward is up 4m to window into another chamber and scramble down through small hole in boulders (care!) to 7m pitch and 4m climb down flowstone to sandy floored high passage and down hole to Chamber of Dark Sound. Wet crawl down in floor, or well splashed climb up and over, unite in Ireby Streamway.

Tackle

Pitch	Ladder	Belay	Lifeline
Traverse	–	–	30m
Shadow	25m	Bolt	40m
Plughole	12m	Bolt	20m
Second	8m	Bolt	15m

Well Pitch Series

Traverse over Well pitch for 10m to large block. Passage on right is 30m of easy crawl to the Aberfan choke. Traversing on for 10m to further large blocks and Cornflake Inlet, again on the right. After a few metres is a small climb and easy going for 30m to a junction. Right is a mud choke and left up a 4.5m climb is a squeeze into small chamber with two impassable inlets.

Rope Pitch Series

Below Well pitch is boulder slope and large chamber with 8m ascent (requires ladder) to boulder littered platform. On right is scramble over blocks and squeeze into chamber with inlet at roof level which is too tight.

From platform two small climbs enter the high level route to North East Inlet but on the right is the tortuous start to Adulterer Passage with a very awkward 4m drop. 70m of mixed going leads to a small inlet where calcite almost blocks the passage. The way then becomes smaller and too low at the closest point yet reached to Rift Pot.

Just before climb down into North East Inlet is another passage on the right where 30m of flat out crawl ends in a draughting constriction with a stream audible ahead.

North East Inlet   **Grade IV**

Ascend slope on left of first aven downstream of Rope Pitch and climb up into trench passage. A further climb out of a chamber meets the stream which flows down a small passage and showers into the next aven down the main streamway. Up the inlet is 183m of twisting passage to a wet squeeze. In this series are two roof passages – one connecting with the top of the chamber above the Rope Pitch – the other a small passage to an isolated chamber. Beyond the wet squeeze are fine formations (care!) and a final crawl over blocks into a roomy tunnel. The stream emerges from a low inlet which splits into three and the tunnel chokes beneath a sandy aven. NW along the tunnel is a choke of liquid mud and an inlet leads to a fine chamber.

Ireby II   **Grade IV**

Sump I is 18m long with an airbell, and should not be free dived as it is prone to silting up. Beyond it the roof rises dramatically into the massive tunnel of Duke Street II. Small inlet on left emerges from a deep sump and joins the Ireby water which enters a canal 152m long to the start of the 226m long sump which connects with the inlet sump above the last pitch in Notts Pot. The remainder of Duke Street II is an inlet of magnificent proportions terminated by a choked sump. A side passage on the left divides into E and W branches. The W inlet soon becomes silted but the E inlet is the key to Jupiter Series.

Jupiter Series
Follow up the high inlet of Escalator Rift and climb up choke to route through boulders back to stream. Ascend waterfalls to 'Y' junction. The left passage soon chokes and the right is well decorated to a series of ducks. After a long period of very settled weather, and after digging away two silt obstructions, the ducks were passed. A 9m long, low wet crawl enters a chamber 3m wide and high, and 6m long. The way on is a wriggle up into a rift passage 2m high and 0.5m wide with many sharp projections. After 76m is a small inlet which has been followed for 9m before becoming too tight. The main way continues for a further 61m to an 8m high aven chamber with water cascading down the far side from a passage 4.5m above; this has not been entered. At the entry to the chamber is an 8m aven with what appear to be two large passages going off at the top – also unentered.

Traversing back over the boulders before the 'Y' junction enters Jupiter Cavern – a huge chamber 30m long, 15m wide, and 46m high. Up on the left a tight chimney ascends into a round chamber with a further awkward 4.5m climb into Milk and Honey Passage. A crawl past an aven leads to 61m of well decorated tunnel (care!) to a calcite choke.

At the bottom left hand side of Jupiter Cavern a short climb and tight passage lead to a pit in the floor 8m deep. This is crossed by laddering the pit and scaling out of it into 30m of passage trending towards the Glory Holes but choked by calcite.

At the far end of Jupiter Cavern is a crawl to a chamber with high and low routes forward. The low route terminates in pitches of 6m, 15m and 12m back into Escalator Rift. The high route requires an 8m scaling pole to gain a low passage and 4m pitch into Frink Chamber and an adjacent large boulder chamber. A decorated passage ends in avens and a 9m climb down at this point to a mud choke.

BOLT BELAYS – see Warning, page 13.

KANGO HOLE	**NGR SD 667783**	**Grade I**
Alt. 320m	Length 18m	Depth 12m

Explored 1972, HWCPC and MUSS.

At edge of valley to side of the dry valley below Lost John's. Narrow passage descends quickly to a very tight fissure.
Permission – CNCC.

LONG DROP CAVE	**NGR SD 669792**	**Grade III**
Alt. 351m	Length 283m	Depth 61m

Big Meanie/Death's Head/Long Drop is 1km long and 92m deep.
Extended 1965, GC; 1981, BCC.

Below cliff at end of dry valley beyond Rumbling Hole. Short passage to first pitch onto loose boulders. Crawl to second pitch. Low passage to top of Fault Chamber where three rift pitches are best tackled using a continuous length of ladder.

Stream rises from impassable fissure and flows into wet crawl. Easier going follows under avens to chamber and sumped tube, which may have small air-space, into Dolphin Passage of Death's Head Hole. Tube has soft mud floor and can be partially baled from the Death's Head end.

Crossing floor of 4th pitch there is a climb up of 11m to a window and squeeze through Double Joints. Bedding plane slopes down to Crutch Pot and High Stream Passage. Upstream is traverse to aven and Pool Chamber, from which a narrow trench ends at an aven.

Downstream is traverse to pitch into High Stream Chamber, where water sinks. Waterfall descends from Humble Inlet, starting with 11m VS climb into ascending passage which emerges in aven – Patterson Pot. A 22m bolt route enters a well-decorated upstream passage ending at a choke on a fault. The deserted downstream passage on the other side of the aven ends at an 18m pitch – Dungeon Pit – below a 2m drop. Way on at foot of pitch is too tight.

Tackle

Pitch	Ladder	Belay	Lifeline
1st	9m	2m	15m
2nd	4.5m	4.5m	9m
3rd ⎫ 4th ⎬ 5th ⎭	32m	9m	46m
Climb	4.5m	0.6m	15m
Crutch Pot	9m	2m	15m
High Stream ⎫ Chamber ⎭	8m	1.5m	12m

BOLT BELAYS – see Warning, page 13.

Permission – CNCC.

LOST JOHN'S CAVE   NGR SD 670786
Alt. 354m   **Length 6km**   **Depth 141m**

Lost John's/Gavel/Short Drop/Rumbling is 10.6kms long and 147m deep – dived to 211m.

An intriguing, classic system offering routes of all standards. From moor gate on Leck Fell Road follow stream on right to twin entrances on either side of wall. Stream sink is 1.5m high passage to junction with another streamway which can be followed up to dry entrance and 91m beyond to a choked passage. Downstream a fine canyon is easy going with scramble over chockstone just before Quicksand Junction. Here there is a grotto in roof of main cave and the inlet (Quicksand Passage) eventually splits and ends in boulder choke. Main Cave continues to Traverses.

Old Roof Traverse   **Grade IV**

Explored 1928, YRC. Fully descended 1935, NCFC.

Main cave cuts down to a small climbable waterfall and obvious traverse line into Hampstead Heath Passage and Pitch. After rejoining stream second obvious traverse leads to head of Monastery Pitch. Traverse out or swing into oxbow 3m down to give drier hang in wet conditions. Attractive streamway of Cloister Passage drops to Piscina Pitch and outlet continues beyond Portcullis Pool to Six Feet Straddle over deep pool. A further obvious traverse and

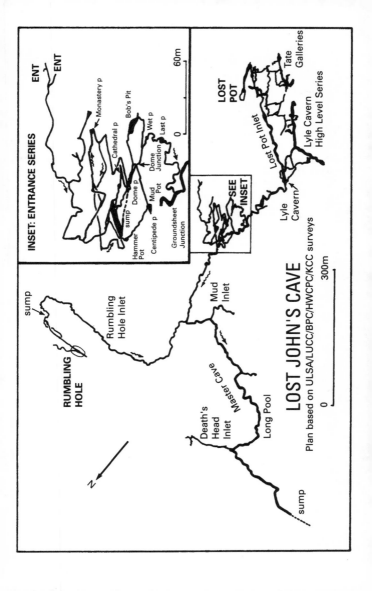

INSET: ENTRANCE SERIES

ENT
ENT

Monastery p
Cathedral p
Bob's Pit
Wet p
Last p
Dome p
Hammer Pot
Mud Pot
Centipede p
Dome Junction
sump
Groundsheet Junction

60m
0

SEE INSET

LOST POT

Tate Galleries

Lost Pot Inlet

Lyle Cavern High Level Series

Lyle Cavern

sump

RUMBLING HOLE

Rumbling Hole Inlet

Mud Inlet

LOST JOHN'S CAVE

Plan based on ULSA/LUCC/BPC/HWCPC/KCC surveys

300m
0

Death's Head Inlet

Master Cave

Long Pool

sump

N

climb down to top of Pinnacle Pot, broken into 12m and 8m sections and landing in Sink Chamber. This is below Shale Cavern and water enters a sump which has dives of 3.4m, 9m and 2.7m through to the Battle Axe streamway. No line in place and free-diving not advised.

Tackle

Pitch	Ladder	Belay	Lifeline
Hampstead Heath	4.5m	3m	9m
Monastery	34m	Bolt	43m
Piscina	4.5m	3m	9m
Pinnacle Pot	20m	1.5m	24m

New Roof Traverse   **Grade III**
Explored 1928, YRC.

Take obvious traverse line above first waterfall downstream of Quicksand Junction. Roof passage has three holes in floor which lead to Dome route, while upper passage continues to Hammer Pot and the Centipede Route. Hammer Pot lands in small chamber and twisting exit gives easy going to Mud Pot followed immediately by the Centipede pitch. The latter is broken by a ledge 8m above the floor and succeeded by a series of small climbs down to Dome Junction, where the New Roof Traverse routes unite.

Tackle

Pitch	Ladder	Belay	Lifeline
Hammer Pot	4.5m	0.6m	8m
Mud Pot	11m	2m	15m
Centipede	30m	Bolt	37m

The holes before Hammer Pot unite. No.1 Hole providing the easiest alternative into passage to the Vestry which is a short climb to head of Pulpit and Cathedral pitches. Crypt Passage shortly ends at Dome pitch, a fine climb into chamber with trenched floor. Traverse above Crypt Passage to Dome alternative involving two pitches into the same chamber.

Three passages radiate from Dome chamber. In SE direction rift may be followed up two interesting 6m climbs to emerge above streamway just below Monastery pitch. To NW a twisting passage leads to short pitch into Shale Cavern, 8m wide and 18m long. At far end is further pitch into Sink Chamber of Old Roof Traverse.

Way on towards Centipede Route is low passage on ledge which enlarges rapidly, dropping down two 3.7m climbs to Dome Junction. Muddier walking ends at Bob's Pit which is 9m deep and ends in narrow fissure close to Battleaxe streamway. Across pit, Candle and Shistol Pots descend into a short gothic section passage to Battleaxe pitch in roof of streamway.

Traditional route is pitch into Thunderstorm Depot, where stream is encountered on last 4.5m. Succeeding Wet Pitch avoids worst of water if belayed to bolt up on left. Better all-weather routes are along traverse above Battleaxe. The first is a short pitch to a ledge and then dry alternative hang down Wet pitch shaft. The second is fine free-hang at end of traverse. Passage passes under large aven to Last Pitch which is usually laddered dry by stepping up above water chute. Outlet is twisting rift with deepening water to Groundsheet Junction and the Leck Fell Master Cave.

Tackle
Dome Route

Pitch	Ladder	Belay	Lifeline
No.1 Hole	–	–	9m
Pulpit	9m	3m	12m
Cathedral	14m	2m	18m
Dome	21m	Bolt	27m
Dome Junction	–	–	15m
Candle	4.5m	1.5m	8m
Shistol	3.7m	3m	6m
Battleaxe	14m	Bolt	18m
Wet Pitch	18m	Bolt	24m
Battleaxe Alternatives			
1	9m	Bolt	15m
	20m	Bolt	27m
2	36m	Bolt	42m and 25m for traverse
Last Pitch	8m	1.2m	12m
Shale Cavern			
Short Pitch	4.5m	18m	6m
Sink Chamber	11m	2m	12m

The Master Cave
Explored 1928, YRC. Extended, BSA.

WARNING – Floods seriously after heavy rain. Long Pool sumps in moderate flood.

From Groundsheet Junction a fine, gently meandering, passage gives easy going for 305m to where Rumbling Hole Inlet is seen as a 2.4m waterfall into large pool. 91m forward a 3.7m climb on left gives access to Mud Inlet which is 91m of well-named passage to a sump. Main drain continues in splendid style through pools to the Long Pool just beyond inlet on left which is 46m crawl to a sump. Long Pool is a canal up to 4.5m wide and 183m long, which involves a short swim in damp weather. Roof rises as pool ends and stream cuts down into canyon. Waterfall on right is Death's Head Inlet.

Master cave eventually lowers to a sump, which joins the Gavel Pot sump after 15m. The continuing downstream sump meets the second sump in the Lower Streamway of Pippikin Pot at a junction 604m from base.

Rumbling Hole Inlet
Explored 1957, NSG and 1963, BPC/HWCPC; connected to Rumbling Hole 1985, LUSS.

From pool in Master Cave 3.7m climb overcomes waterfall into walking passage lowering to a wet crawl. Roof rises into high but narrow rift for 305m until tortuous progress degenerates into further wet crawl and series of ducks under formations until rift becomes tight and waterlogged. Fifteen constricted corners lead to a 0.5m duck into the canal at the bottom of Rumbling Hole.

Death's Head Inlet
Extended 1980, Wessex Caving Club.

Climb up 3.7m waterfall gives access to 107m of easy going to a junction. The water comes from the left and a boulder choke can be penetrated upwards for 15m or so. Right at the junction leads via an excavated boulder choke to a climb into a sloping chamber and choked aven close to the boulder choke in the left hand branch.

Lyle Cavern
Extended NPC.

Upstream of Groundsheet Junction is large cave with little water which passes under a high aven. Climb up boulders (**very loose – care!**) and over-hanging stal into Lyle Cavern, a 24m high rift chamber. Down in streamway 4.5m climb up stal chute into bedding plane rejoins main water behind Lyle Cavern. Inlet straight ahead is easy crawl to aven at base of Five Pitches route into Lyle Cavern Upper Series. Main cave is the Lost Pot Inlet, 213m of roomy passage to point where three tributaries unite. Two are impassable and third is a wet crawl to climbs of 4.5m and 9m into a rift and two massive avens. The 2nd pitch of Lost Pot drops down NPC Aven, at the end of the Inlet.

Lyle Cavern Upper Series   Grade IV
Explored 1969, HWCPC; Extended 1980, MUSS.

At top of Lyle Cavern use wire to hoist ladder into roof passage, which is extremely well decorated (care!). Short climb over flowstone and passing crystal pools and gours leads to junction of two large passages and pit in floor. Pit is Pete's Climb (best laddered) succeeded by two short pitches and small passage to pitch into aven at N end of Lyle Cavern. At junction West Passage is 91m long and well decorated to a choke. Slit in floor is top of Five Pitches (one climbable) into inlet upstream of Lyle Cavern.

SE Passage is equally large and passes under avens. It terminates after 137m in a massive aven scaled to 24m by LUCC in 1971. Halfway along passage a flat crawl under E wall opens onto top of 4m pitch. Outlet has vicious bends and small drops to 4.5m pitch. Difficult to return.

The prominent aven half-way along SE Passage, Slum Aven, has accessible passage at the top of a 16m climb. A route through boulders leads to a junction, the way to the SE is a narrow rift terminating after 5m at a mud choke, whilst the route continues through 50m of tight fissure passage to where it becomes too narrow for further progress.

Tackle

Pitch	Ladder	Belay	Lifeline
Lyle Cavern	21m	Spreader	49m
Pete's Climb {	12m	2.4m	18m
	4.5m	1.2m	9m
	4.5m	1.8m	9m
Lyle Aven	11m	1.2m	15m
	8m	3m	30m
Five Pitches {	12m	–	30m
	4.3m	–	30m
	9m	3m	15m

Tate Galleries   **Grade IV**
Explored 1985, KCC.

Confusing maze of streamways which is intriguingly close to inlets in Notts 2.
In Lyle Cavern Upper Series, 30m before LUCC Aven, is hole under boulder which leads to a 12m pitch. Crawl below leads to junction with larger passage which chokes with fill in downstream direction. In other direction crawl passes two small avens to another streamway where Straw Chamber lies upstream. To left in Straw Chamber is Handshake Crawl and continuation upstream becomes too low.

Downstream is a walk until water sinks in floor and way on is through small chamber into boulder area and upstream route which passes slope up to right into far end of Handshake Crawl. The continuing upstream passage is half filled with water and passes through a breakdown area to a final pool after 100m.

From the breakdown area a 9m climb up a rift enters a classic keyhole passage 60m long. A 20m deep hole in the floor (The Bear Pit) is climbable but becomes too tight, and just beyond is a 'T' junction. To the left is a stooping height passage over two more blind pots, one of which connects to the Bear Pit, and a continuing crawl which emerges 12m above the floor of the Lost Pot Avens. This pitch is climbable with care and a rope.

Right near the Bear Pit leads to Crowbar Pitch which drops into a sandy rift and another streamway. Downstream is a chamber with calcite veins and a 20m aven inlet. The streamway becomes too low very close to Straw Chamber inlet.

At the top of the 20m aven is 7m of tight rift to a 'T' junction with a roomy well decorated passage. Upstream is a stal choke and Wednesday Night Avens – 15m high and impenetrable. A traverse back over the 20m aven enters Epiglottis Grotto and a gradually descending tunnel links back above Crowbar Pitch.

Upstream below Crowbar Pitch is crawl to two avens. One is blind but Tantrum Aven has been climbed for 40m before it too closes in.

Tackle

Pitch	Ladder	Belay	Lifeline
First	15m	2m	20m
Crowbar	10m	1m	15m

Lost Pot Avens
Explored 1988, KCC.

From ledge between the Lost Pot Avens where passage enters from Tate Galleries a bolt route rises 23m into large block filled passage. Small hole on left drops into Lost Pot above last pitch. More upward climbing leads to edge of massive shaft and passage opposite chokes after 17m. Pitches of 10m, 20m, 12m, and 10m have been ascended to 20m of passage with a tight branch on the right. Final choke is immediately below surface sink which is only 6m above. This has now collapsed to give a highly unstable entrance.

Maypole Passage
Explored 1972, LUCC.

At bottom of Wet Pitch traverse upwards on obvious ledge and cross to

right of stream canyon. Two 6m pitches are scaled into short section of
walking passage, Two pitches drop into mud floored chambers and low crawl
ends at pitch with awkward take off. Choked by mud.

Tackle

Pitch	Ladder	Belay	Lifeline
1st	3.7m	2m	15m
2nd	3.7m	–	15m
3rd	11m	3m	18m

Rough Pot Inlet
Explored 1972, NCC.

   Aven immediately below Last Pitch in Lost John's is 14m climb overcome
using bolts. Small upstream passage to two avens and crawl which becomes too
low. Roof passage in first of two avens emerges on ledge 6m above Maypole
Passage Traverse from bottom of Wet Pitch. Best reached by laddering 8m
pitch out of Maypole Passage.

BOLT BELAYS – see Warning, page 13.

Permission – CNCC.

LOST POT   NGR SD 671784   Grade III
Alt. 360m   **Length** – see Lost John's Cave.
Explored 1982, RRCPC/NPC.

WARNING – Unstable boulders are a considerable hazard. Entrance sealed.

   Isolated impressive shakehole 12m deep with steep descent to choke. At SW
end of shakehole – opposite stream sink – is 9m climb down excavated shaft
(presently blocked) into large chamber. Letterbox squeeze under entrance
opens into top of 8m deep shored rift. Climb down with care onto unstable
cobble slope at bottom, descending to top of 1st pitch, belayed in crack in
roof. Pitch is a continuation of main rift and at present is extremely unstable.
Fine descent onto large ledge from which a 6m climb down reaches the floor
of a large rift passage where water from Lost Pot Sink emerges. The rift
continues straight for 61m to chamber beneath large aven. Way on is small
passage on right, immediately opening out at head of 2nd pitch, dropping
down NPC Aven at the far end of Lost Pot Inlet in Lyle Cavern of Lost
John's. Beneath wet aven halfway along rift is floor trench leading directly
to 2nd pitch.

Tackle

Pitch	Ladder	Belay	Lifeline
1st	30m	2m	37m
2nd	23m	6m	30m

Permission – CNCC.

Footnote: sinkhole to south has collapsed to give a very unstable entry at the
top of Lost Pot Avens.

LOST POT SINK   NGR SD 671784   Grade III
(Lost Pot)
Alt. 359m   Length 40m   Depth 12m
Excavated 1968, NPC; extended 1969, ULSA.

In same impressive shakehole as Lost Pot, with steep descent to choke. Near water sink on slope is 4.5m excavated shaft (climbable) to dry crawl which joins water in small passage. Downstream is small but technical drop and fissure becomes very tortuous with cobbles in floor. Water tested to Lost Pot.
Permission – CNCC.

MERIDIAN POT   NGR SD 664792   Grade II
Alt. 315m   Length 45m   Depth 25m
Explored 1985, EPC.

Oil drum entrance in square hollow 250m NW of Gavel Pot is top of 7m pitch into sloping boulder floored chamber. Way on is roof tube crawl up far wall which leads after 6m to a 2m drop into a second chamber. Again, the way on is a tube crawl at the top of a mud bank which ends at a 1.5m drop into a third, and final chamber, with only a hole in the floor leading into a small enlargement at the foot of a 3m climb.
Permission – CNCC.

NOTTS POT   NGR SD 671778   Grade III-IV
Alt. 370m   Length 1097m   Depth 127m
                  Length including Notts II to IV 5.2km.   Depth 157m
First explored 1946, BSA.

The most concentrated vertical maze in Britain, offering a bewildering choice of combinations, much of the fascination being missed by those who stick to the trade routes.

Follow wall up eastwards from shooting hut on Leck Fell Lane. Strike half left up marked dry valley crossing wall to reach deep and complex shakehole near sink.

Tackle requirements

The description is divided into the following sections: 1, the entrance passages; 2, the upper series; 3, the main descent routes; 4, the variations to the main descent routes; 5, the lower main stream passage; 6, Notts II; 7, the other passages.

Sections 1 and 2 describe the pot from the entrance down to Three Ways Chamber, where routes begin to diverge. Section 5 describes the pot from the point where all routes have rejoined, down to the sump.

For a complete descent of any route, tackle for sections 1 and 5 (entrance passages and lower main stream passage) is necessary, together with the appropriate tackle for the chosen route as listed in sections 3 and 4. Thus, for any of the main descent routes the complete tackle requirement from entrance to sump comprises that listed in sections 1, 3 (for whichever route is selected) and 5. It is important to note that for any of the variations to the main routes, listed in section 4, partial tackle lists only are given and must be read in conjunction with the descriptions and lists in section 3 so that tackle requirements may be worked out accordingly.

In section 7 only the tackle required for the passages described in that section is listed.

1. ENTRANCE PASSAGES

Shaft may be laddered from metal stake above main hole. Alternative shaft blocked at present due to run in. Ladder may be simply avoided by bridging down rift at NE end of hole and following ledge round northern side. Walk down to hole under south wall protected by dry walling. Narrow rift breaks into small chamber then continues to short drop at oxbow where stream is met. Follow stream to 1st pitch with eyehole belay high on left. Easy traverse from head of pitch leads immediately to oxbow on left leading right to dry alternative pitch. 1st pitch lands in Three Ways Chamber, where water normally sinks at foot of ladder.

Tackle

Pitch	Ladder	Belay	Lifeline
Entrance (optional)	9m	12m	30m
1st	6m	2m	12m
Oxbow bypass	6m	0.6m	12m

2. UPPER SERIES

Left and up in oxbow enters gallery above stream passage with impressive rift and phreatic upper level leading off. This leads back towards entrance before ending in stal choke. Awkward climb up before choke leads to large chamber with impressive main inlet cascading in. Follow water through deep pools and climb up to emerge just inside entrance. Chamber can also be entered by taking passage from ledge in NE rift of entrance shaft to pitch down into chamber.

Tackle – 8m ladder; 1.2m belay; 12m lifeline.

3. MAIN DESCENT ROUTES

3a Left Hand Route

Immediately to left at bottom of Three Ways Chamber pitch large trench passage leads to Double Bucket Pitch. In dry conditions ladder direct from thread belay high on right, leading to spacious ledges. Oxbow on left gives dry alternative in wet conditions. Second half of pitch may be laddered direct in dry conditions. If wet traverse round left wall to spacious muddy ledge at level of thick shale bed on far side of shaft. From foot of pitch clamber down into high chamber where Adamson's Route joins via avens. Last pitch drops into main streamway at junction of Centre and BT Routes.

Tackle

Pitch		Ladder	Belay	Lifeline
Double Bucket	{	15m	3m	24m
		24m	4.5m	37m
Dry alternatives	{	15m	2m	24m
		24m	2m	37m
Last pitch		9m	1.5m	15m

3b Centre Route

Cross Three Ways Chamber to two obvious holes under left wall. First pitch can be laddered free down first hole or against rock (with ledges) at right end of second hole. Remaining pitches follow in quick succession. 2nd pitch belay to secure chockstone. 3rd pitch good thread on left. Hole in floor at foot leads to Lower BT Passage (ladder required). 4th pitch in two parts separated by further hole down into BT – care required crossing to sharp arete between. Below 4th pitch scramble down to junction with streamway, passing high inlet of Dubious Tactics Route and connection to Adamson's Route on right.

Tackle

Pitch	Ladder	Belay	Lifeline
1st	23m	1.5m	30m
2nd	9m	2m	15m
3rd	8m	2m	12m
4th	15m	2m	21m

3c BT Route

The most demanding and varied of the trade routes. On right in Three Ways Chamber scramble up into low crawl which crosses blind pit in floor. Passage continues low and awkward, enlarging towards 1st pitch. Across 1st pitch is Latham's Aven Inlet which can be reached by intricate maypole manoeuvres into impressive aven with tight passage leading off 9m up (maypole required). Pitch is in superb circular shaft and stream sinks in floor below. Continue in narrow rift requiring traversing to head of 2nd pitch. Main stream is met at foot of pitch emerging from BT Inlet and flowing immediately down steep chute into Fossil Pot of BUSS Route. BT continues as dry passage down short 3rd pitch to 4th pitch with eyehole belay high on left. Pitch leads to very high rift passage passing beneath high avens of Fossil Pot and Centre Route connections. Stream runs into waterlogged passage and short duck leads to junction of Left Hand and Centre Routes.

Tackle

Pitch	Ladder	Belay	Lifeline
1st	15m	3m	24m
2nd	6m	2m	12m
3rd	4.5m	1.2m	9m
4th	15m	0.6m	24m

3d   Adamson's Route
Explored 1967, ULSA.

WARNING – Beware of loose boulders.

From Three Ways Chamber proceed NW up large dry inlet pasage until it swings sharply E. Climb up to short length of fixed metal ladder and past remains of unstable boulder bridge into mud-floored rift. Forward is 5.5m climb down into chamber. Hole at far end is Birthday Pot, best tackled in three sections. At foot of 2nd section three holes lead off. Two to right join at once and drop into Left Hand Route above last pitch. Left hole leads to 6m drop into Centre Route below 4th pitch and just downstream of entry of Dubious Tactics Route. Slope up from ledge at 15m leads to Deprofundis Series (see below).

Tackle

Pitch		Ladder	Belay	Lifeline
	⎧	15m	3m	24m
Birthday Pot	⎨	34m	1m	46m
	⎩	9m	–	15m

4.   VARIATION DESCENT ROUTES

4a   BUSS Route
Explored 1970, BUSS; 1976, CPG.

Belay ladder to thread on right at top of Double Bucket Pitch (Left Hand Route) and using bollard on ledge hang ladder as far out as possible. Descend about 4.5m where it is possible to work leftwards along wall and pull into circular passage. Thin fixed rope in position, but good holds present if approach correct. Last person across must secure end of ladder for pendulum return and whole manoeuvre requires careful thought and planning.

Passage leads at once to junction. Right too tight. Left leads over hole in floor (extremely tight connection to Centre Route) through tubular passage to Mud Pot, belayed to rock bollard back up passage. Climb down one of several connected holes into chamber with major shale bed. Several alternative descents now possible.

(i)   Ladder through left hand passage out of chamber and descend Fossil Pot direct to floor of Lower BT Passage.

(ii) 8m down Fossil Pot step onto arete and thread ladder down parallel shaft. Scramble down to bouldery floor and ladder down Thread Pot to Lower BT Passage.

(iii) Traverse right (while lifelined) from head of Thread Pot to re-emerge at top of 4th pitch of BT Route.

(v)   Descend Fossil Pot for 2.4m and step onto obvious ledge on right. Through window into tiny chamber. Ladder belayed back through window must be threaded over fixed scaffold pole for awkward take off of Thrutch Pot, landing between 2nd and 3rd pitches of BT Route.

Tackle

Pitch	Ladder	Belay	Lifeline
Pendulum	8m	1.2m	15m
Mud Pot	6m	6m	12m

Tackle

Pitch	Ladder	Belay	Lifeline
Fossil Pot Direct	30m	3m	40m
Parallel shaft	15m	–	21m
Thread Pot	18m	1.2m	24m
Traverse	–	–	15m
Thrutch Pot	6m	2m	12m

4b   Handshake Route

Explored 1970, LUSS; 1971, BUSS; connected 1977, CPG.

A rather contrived, though interesting route, for thin masochists only.

Enter Left Hand Route and where passage swings sharply right climb up to wider roof level. Traverse forward past formations to enter low passage above dry bypass to Double Bucket Pitch. Sandy crawl leads past hole in floor (very deep – watch tackle!) to emerge in chamber with unstable boulder chokes and small inlet. Climb up on right and enter tight rift. Pass feet first through short enlarged section and climb down rift aven into South Inlet. Down slope to junction. Right leads to unstable descending slope (care!) onto 15m ledge of Birthday Pot (Adamson's Route). Ahead leads to impressive shaft of Deprofundis Pot. Hole in floor of chamber below Deprofundis leads back to Birthday Pot at 30m level.

Tackle

Pitch	Ladder	Belay	Lifeline
Deprofundis Pot	24m	2m	30m
Lower Birthday ⎰	18m	3m	24m
Pot ⎱	9m	–	15m

4c   Dubious Tactics Route

Lower part explored 1967, ULSA; complete exploration 1977, CPG.

Proceed via BT Route or Thrutch Pot of BUSS Route to point between 2nd and 3rd pitches of BT. Instead of descending 3rd pitch traverse forward in rift to enter passage above BT 4th pitch (care!). Passage leads at once to Dubious Pot which has no convenient belay point, requiring very long belay or rope back along traverse. Pitch leads to chamber which was limit of exploration. Tactics Pitch follows, free-climbable but rope advisable. From chamber below crawl leads forward to break out into wall of Centre Route below 4th Pitch. Pitons at both sides of exit assist 4.5m free climb to floor or can be used to belay handline.

Tackle

Pitch	Ladder	Belay	Lifeline
Dubious Pot	6m	15m or rope	9m
Tactics Pitch	–	–	8m

5.   LOWER MAINSTREAM PASSAGE. (Pitches numbered as continuation of Centre Route.)

From junction of Left Hand, Centre and BT routes follow stream down high rift to wet pitch (5th). Large chockstone in roof allows dry ladder hang.

6th pitch follows quickly and is always wet, into chamber with large inlet chute. Final wet pitch lands in large sump pool, choked with rubble at a depth of 5m, whilst short dry passage on left ends in a static sump – the route to Notts II.

Above 6th pitch traverse upwards and forwards leads to roof oxbow and high aven. Alternative dry pitch from oxbow leads to ledge above inlet to mainstream chamber. Inlet passage is fissure leading to deep sump discharging Ireby Fell Cavern water, and has been dived by CDG for 226m to emerge in Ireby II.

Tackle

Pitch	Ladder	Belay	Lifeline
5th	11m	3m	15m
6th	18m	4.5m	24m
7th	6m	2m	12m

6. NOTTS II

The static sump reaches a depth of 9m and is 210m long to where it surfaces, the main stream entering near the deepest point, Taffy Turnip's Turnaround. Beyond the sump the main stream passage can be followed for 1.3km to sump 2, the first 700m being a fine phreatic tube to a nick point, which is followed by a narrow canyon for the remaining distance.

Many inlets are encountered, and the Near Inlet Series can be entered at three places. Inlet 1 is a tube rising to the right immediately beyond the sump and quickly meets a junction. To the left ends in a boulder-floored aven chamber, climbed for 8m to a choke, whilst to the right a tubular crawl enters Inlet 0. A muddy ramp to the right descends to the sump, but a walking sized passage ascends on the left until it reaches Prospector Pot which drops into an impenetrable sump. A bold leap across the pot enters the 4m long Moribund Inlet.

Before Prospector Pot is reached a muddy crawl off to the left can be followed to Passchendaele; a small streamway. Upstream soon lowers to a tight sump, whilst downstream encounters a choke. Just before this a crawl off to the left reaches a junction, to the left continuing as a crawl through dug boulders to end at a small choked chamber, whilst going right regains the main stream passage at Inlet 2.

Swimming is necessary in places to follow the main passage through a canal, and where this finishes the boulder dam marks the entry of the wet and loose Daylight Aven off to the left. On downstream leads past Inlet 3 and Inlet 4, both of which quickly choke, whilst Inlet 5 is situated at 180m from the sump, in the left wall. Stooping height passage ends at a sump after 190m, but a crawl to the right gains a chamber followed by a 3m climb into a well decorated passage. Wet crawling then follows to a chamber with four ways on, three of which quickly choke leaving only the downslope route which continues as an unpleasant muddy crawl for 125m to where digging is required. A stream is audible beyond the mud blockage.

The fine tubular main passage beyond Inlet 5 requires wading in places and after 150m Curry Inlet enters from the right. This can be followed easily for

80m to where main route is choked, but water enters from low crawl on left and can be followed a further 60m to a sump.

Beyond Curry Junction the main passage starts downcutting near the large solitary stalactite; Vlad the Impaler. A roof dome 115m on is the entry of the short Inlet 6.5 whilst 90m beyond a second larger roof dome Inlet 7 enters from the right. This is a low muddy passage for 50m to a junction. To the right a low cobble-floored crawl ends after 50m at a muddy aven and small mud sump, but the left route quickly enters the impressive Oliver Lloyd Aven with two waterfalls. This has been bolted for 27m to a slope up boulders and a choke, with no way through to the active inlet above.

Inlet 8 enters the main streamway only a few metres beyond Inlet 7 and is only an alcove above a cracked mud slope on the left. Past this point the passage widens and becomes block-strewn, but the impressive dimensions terminate after 50m where the stream cuts down into a narrow canyon at the nick point. By traversing in the roof tube for 60m Dome Inlet is reached on the right. Entered by a short climb, 40m of passage can be followed to a short wet crawl to the foot of a 12m aven.

On downstream the canyon can be followed to where Sir Digby Spode's Inlet enters on the right. A short climb leads to 30m of large passage, and Count Lazlo Stroganoff's Aven which has been climbed for 37m to a rift leading to a further 6m aven. Above this a short crawl ends at another 10m aven with two small choked passages at its head. This point is believed to be only 20-30m below the surface.

To the left before entering the main aven the continuing crawl can be followed to the impenetrable Bruno Kranski's Rising sump.

Back in the canyon a climb on a right hand bend enters the short Echo Inlet which gets too tight, whilst 45m further on a showerbath beyond some jammed boulders marks the entry of Showerbath Inlet (Inlet 12). Chimneying up through the boulders and stepping across the canyon gains a crawl which emerges in a high fault-aligned passage with the water descending from an aven. Ahead, the passage rises steeply over calcited boulders to end at a cobble choke 60m from the main passage.

130m downstream from Showerbath Inlet a high narrow passage (Inlet 13) enters on the left at stream level. After 50m a 'T' junction is reached, the route to the left quickly choking. To the right can be followed upstream to Mincemeat Aven, and beyond to a series of narrow climbs ending too tight. A further passage to the left beneath the aven ends after 60m at an inlet sump.

The next inlet (Inlet 14), indicated by an active flowstone cascade has yet to be entered, but Inlet 15, 65m further on, can be entered by climbing a flowstone cascade below some calcited blocks bridging the passage. A stooping height passage continues for 170m to a sudden drop into a small chamber, and a further passage ends after 22m in a sump.

Where the main streamway narrows again the unobvious Green Tape Inlet (Inlet 16) enters via a slippery climb on the right, and can be followed through 140m of low, wet crawling to a 'hanging death' boulder choke. Just before this is reached three low interconnecting crawls lead to an inaccessible streamway.

Below this last inlet the main passage cuts down steeply, with small cascades followed by a 2m drop, into the boulder-floored chamber; Kleine Scheidegg. The low outlet passage soon reaches a roof dome, and not far beyond sump 2 is met. In normal conditions this is 30m long, and only 20m beyond lies sump 3. Inlet 17 enters between the sumps as a significant stream and can be followed for 80m to a sump.

Sump 3 is 295m long, with a large airbell after 210m. An inlet entering this can be followed up a chute and through varied going for 50m to a junction. Left ends in a small sump, whilst right encounters a further junction. To the right here is an impenetrable cobble-filled bedding, whilst a 1.5m diameter tube to the left ends at a sump beyond a 2m climb and low crawl.

Downstream from sump 3 is a block-strewn streamway which gives way to a silt-floored passage over which the stream meanders for 70m to reach sump 4, with a short boulder choked inlet on the right just before the start of the sump.

Sump 4 begins with a diminishing air-space for the first 25m, beyond which the roof dips to water level. No underwater route onward has yet been found, although a short cross-rift air-space has been entered.

7.   OTHER PASSAGES

7a   Acrobat Series
Explored 1967, ULSA; extended 1970, LUSS.

Traverse over Birthday Pot (CARE!) to boulder-floored passage and 4.5m climb down at Rubble Pot. Cross crumbling slope over top of blind Plant Pot and enter roomy tunnel to Acrobat Pot. There are short passages above this shaft which is well-named but safe if rigged with thought. There is no safe natural belay point. Below is awkward climb into inlet ending under choked floor of Plant Pot. At foot of Acrobat Pot, in alcove to right of way on, excavated route under enormous boulder drops into phreatic rift passage which is part of the system leading off from Far Chamber. Way forward is narrow rift leading to Far Chamber with very steep boulder slope. Tricky climb on right leads to steep Circus Inlet. At base of slope is way into series of tubes and rifts and squeeze into larger passage with small stream. This enlarges into a series of interconnected tunnels ending in solid chokes.

Tackle

Pitch	Ladder	Belay	Lifeline
Acrobat Pot	20m	6m	27m

7b   Deprofundis Series
Explored 1970, LUSS.

From foot of Deprofundis Pot (reached from Adamson's or Handshake routes) crawl to 'T' junction. Right leads into larger mud-filled passage which chokes to the left and becomes tight to the right. Left at junction leads steeply upwards to reach choked chamber of Yellow Clay Terminus.

7c   BT Inlet
At foot of BT 2nd pitch or Thrutch Pot of BUSS main route stream falls from obvious passage. Entry requires 4.5m maypole and ladder or combined tactics. Small but pleasant streamway leads to fault-controlled chamber almost below blind pot at start of BT Route.

7d   North Inlet

Follow trench from N end of Three Ways Chamber, rising steadily to eventual choke. Close to end roof intersects small tubular passage which can be followed until it breaks out into top of rift opposite start of Adamson's Route.

Numerous other short passages exist, notably in the entrance and Upper Dry Series area and leading off from Three Ways Chamber.

BOLT BELAYS – see Warning, page 13.

Permission – CNCC.

OWLFINGER HOLE   NGR SD 664789   Grade II
Alt. 305m   **Length 8m**   **Depth 6m**
Explored 1977, CPG.

Immediately after wall across dry valley below Gavel Pot, hole in left side of valley above obvious spoil heap.

Awkward climb down of 2.4m into circular phreatic chamber. Hole in west wall drops into rift passage which is solidly choked. In opposite wall of chamber very tight passage, best tackled feet first, leads left into short tight rift. A passage can be seen continuing but has yet to be entered. Access is partially blocked by a large collapsed slab.

PIRATE POT   NGR SD 667783   Grade II
(Committee Pot)
Alt. 320m   **Depth 15m**

In dry valley below Lost John's. Climb down muddy rift beneath boards covering the hole. Ends in choke of mud and boulders. Rope useful for return. Permission – CNCC.

POT BLACK   NGR SD 664797   Grade III
Alt. 305m   **Depth 21m**
Explored 1980, RRCPC.

Excavated hole in shallow shakehole 275m SW of Pippikin wall. Climb down with care past Acrow stemple and slide through boulders to squeeze between blocks and further climb down onto rubble slope into small chamber. 8m pitch led to short rift and another undescended drop. Top of pitch now collapsed.

RIFT ENTRANCE   NGR SD 670789   Grade II
Alt. 354m   **Length – see Short Drop Cave**

Shakehole just over wall from main sink. Entrance blocked at present. Climb down into end of high rift chamber. Crawl forward until twisting passage heightens into traverse to First Oxbow in Short Drop Cave.

RUMBLING BECK CAVE   NGR SD 671791   Grade II
Alt. 357m   **Length 61m**

Entrances at the sink of Rumbling Beck. The stream enters a wet crawl to the dry entrance and an even wetter crawl under a boulder and skylight to a

fine deepening trench discharging into the pit of Rumbling Hole, 8m below
the surface.
Permission – CNCC.

RUMBLING HOLE   NGR SD 671791   Grade IV
(Fairies Workshop)
Alt. 351m   **Length 213m**   **Depth 119m**
Rumbling/Gavel/Short Drop/Lost John's is 10.6km long and 147m deep –
dived to 211m.
Explored fully 1932, YRC; connected to Lost John's 1985, LUSS.

Impressive open shaft with isolated tree. Use stile to cross fence and belay
ladder to stake or tree. A rope is handy for the climb down the gully and
under the waterfall into a long fault passage with a series of cascades. Second
pitch may be hung dry via a passage to the right and a window communicates
with the waterfall. Above the third pitch is a short dry passage and the fourth
pitch is brief but wet. Last ladder hangs down a waterfall and the succeeding
canal soon sumps. A 1m awkward duck under calcite leads to a waterlogged
chamber and an outlet with diminishing fissure air-space which has been
forced into Rumbling Hole Inlet in Lost John's.

An inlet below the last pitch has a wet crawl bypassed by a higher level
before the trench rises to a bedding plane sump.

Tackle

Pitch	Ladder	Belay	Lifeline
Entrance	30m	2m	43m
Gully	–	–	21m
2nd	18m	2m	24m
3rd	12m	1m	18m
4th	4.5m	1m	9m
Last	17m	3m	24m

BOLT BELAYS – see Warning, page 13.

Permission – CNCC.

SHORT DROP CAVE   NGR SD 670789   Grade II-III
Alt. 354m   **Length 2.5km**   **Depth 55m**
Short Drop/Gavel/Lost John's/Rumbling is 10.6km long and 147m deep –
dived to 211m.
Explored 1898, YRC; extended 1966, ULSA & BSA.

An impressive system suitable for novices.

Through Cave
Top entrance is small hole at termination of shallow dry valley. Short drop
into stream passage. Upstream is Canals Inlet, starting as a canal, followed by
a traverse and further canal until rift becomes tight. Squeeze on right before
end is junction with Coal Hole Entrance.
Main downstream passage is easy going to First Oxbow where stream takes
crawling route, and dry rift passage (with high level complex) rejoins water at

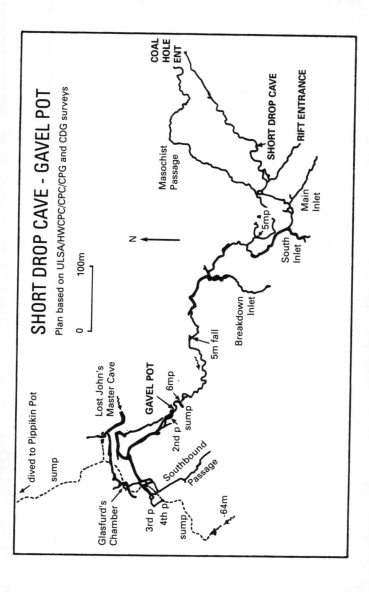

junction with Rift Entrance Passage. On return journey crawl to Short Drop Entrance is easily missed.

Walking passage continues to split level meander complex at Masochist Junction and higher canyon leads on to shower at junction with Main Inlet. Stream continues its steady descent past short oxbow until gradient slackens and canyon enlarges to impressive dimensions beyond entry of South Inlet. Main Drain swings N past Avens Inlet on right before resuming the NW trend of the cave to Breakdown Inlet. Beyond is the remarkable boulder bridge just before the massive passage terminates in a choked roof chamber and the stream cuts down into a narrow meandering canyon. Short cascades end at 1st pitch, down 5m fall, which is a serious climb without aid, into chamber. High canyon meanders on to head of 2nd waterfall pitch and 6m climb into sump pool which chokes at a depth of 9m. Just upstream of pitch is high level complex of rifts and series of climbs out to daylight at SE end of Gavel Pot, also reached by ascending traverse from upstream.

Below 1st pitch is climb into roof and traverse on ledges for 15m to passage veering off on right. This passes a large boulder slope to choked 9m aven (care needed). A window drops into a continuation of the passage, emerging on large ledges over the main streamway. Step over canyon to large ledge, at back of which is an awkward 6m rift climb (rope needed) into 4.5m square breakdown passage. This continues for 61m to breakdown and sand choke.

Tackle

Pitch	Ladder	Belay	Lifeline
1st	6m	12m	9m
2nd	8m	3m	18m

Masochist Passage

Obvious inlet at Masochist Junction. Starts in a promising way as a high rift but develops into tortuous going with traverses and crawls through mud. After a long struggle the passage becomes too narrow and tortuous only a short distance from a small sink near Rumbling Hole.

Ancient Highway and Avens Inlet

At Masochist Junction the highest level is an abandoned outlet in the form of a twisting meander. This drops into a circular chamber with a crawl onwards into a pool. Wriggle over calcite flow (Tollgate Squeeze) to passage with soft 'moon-milk' ledges. Gours descend to loose chockstones above formation chamber and outlet ends above pitch into Avens Inlet. Roomy chamber below leads to 'T' junction. To right is another aven and low crawl. To left is climb down into Main Drain.

Tackle – 6m ladder; 2.4m belay; 9m lifeline.

Main Inlet

Above cascades water rises from low bedding plane but traverse back over falls gains a pleasant rift passage. Crawl over cobbles soon opens up and rejoins stream which sinks in the floor. Upstream over boulders is choke, which is beneath Main Sink.

South Inlet

'T'-section passage divides after 30m. Right is crawl into narrow rift choked by stal and sludge after 30m; left is a small passage which sub-divides and becomes impassable.

Breakdown Inlet

Large passage on two levels which unite at a 4.5m cascade. Calcite infilling reduces passage size and water rises under right wall. Ahead is boulder-strewn passage to narrow slot and flat roofed cavern. From breakdown chamber a suicidal crawl in water beneath boulders terminates in choked sump.

Splashdown Inlet

On S side of main streamway, 18m upstream of 1st pitch, and 4m up from floor is hands and knees crawl to calcite blockage. Tight squeeze beneath is succeeded by further crawling to loose blocks and stal-choked fissure.

BOLT BELAYS – see Warning, page 13.

Permission – CNCC.

TOSS POT	**NGR SD 671783**	**Grade III**
Alt. 370m	Length 53m	Depth 56m

Explored 1988, NCC.

Entrance in shakehole just to the S of Lost Pot.

A series of climbs leads to a pitch onto jammed boulders. Further climbs descend to a solid floor and short walk to a crawl in the roof tube for 30m and short final pitch to complete choke below a shaft.

Tackle

Pitch	Ladder	Belay	Lifeline
First	6m	1m	12m
Second	3m	3m	12m

WEE POT	**NGR SD 665793**	**Grade II**
Alt. 328m		Depth 12m

Small hole just N of gateway in the wall. Rift descends as a series of steps to a mud floor where trickle of water sinks into a fissure.

Permission – CNCC.

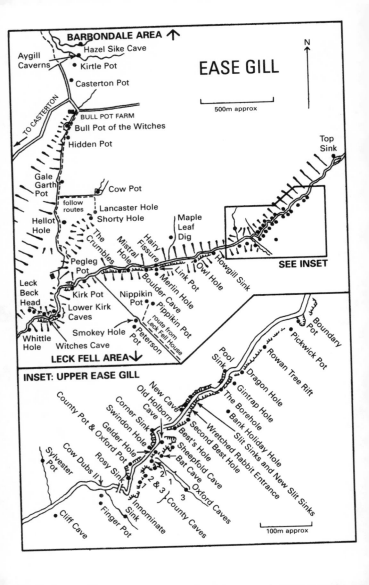

EASE GILL

Due to certain problems which have arisen the CNCC no longer deals with access arrangements on behalf of the landowner. It is suggested that intending visitors to any of the holes in this area contact the agent for the landowner, Davis & Bowring, 6-8 Main Street, Kirkby Lonsdale, Carnforth, Lancashire, LA6 2AF.

Alternatively, the CNCC can be contacted for up to date information on the situation.

AYGILL CAVERNS   NGR SD 663818   Grade III
(Aygill Hole)
Alt. 295m   **Length 2438m**   **Depth 55m**
Explored 1965, NSG; extended 1966, HWCPC; 1965, RRCPC; and 1971, ULSA.

A fascinating system developed at several levels in the Dent Thrust. Hole under cliff on right bank of Aygill is surrounded by a rampart of stones. Climb down into a crawl which enlarges and then chokes. Way on is climb up further back into another crawl and squeeze to a short drop and traverse into the First Chamber. Beneath large boulders are a series of crawls to a 4.5m pitch into the Inlet Series but the normal route out of the First Chamber is the obvious exit down to the Traverse Pitch. The pitch may be laddered or avoided by an exposed traverse (rope advisable). Large passage below rises to a boulder choke and slot under pitch is the way forward. Clean crawl leads to small chamber and chute to head of Second Pitch, belayed through a thread above small ledge at base of the chute. Landing is in a high chamber where the main inlet enters and falls over a series of fine cascades. A chimney up the cavern above the cascades brings one onto a massive block and ledges on each wall. Two side passages at this level are narrow and soon choke.

Tackle

Pitch	Ladder	Belay	Lifeline
Traverse	9m	9m	15m
2nd	11m	2m	18m

Junction Complex and the Sump

From the chamber below the cascades several passages radiate at different levels. To the left 1.5m above the stream is a high rift with a traverse and oxbow to a muddy passage and 2m drop into a wet crawl which connects back with a floor passage. At the beginning of the rift a roof passage communicates with three more high level routes originating in the roof of Cascades Chamber. Up to the right at stream level a ramp ascends to Bridge Chamber where one of the high level routes is encountered. A climb up steep boulders has a visual connection with Middle Series and leads to a muddy passage choked by boulders. The stream can be followed out of Cascade Chamber into a wet crawl or a dry crawl taken to the right which pops out in a small chamber with two exits. At roof height a passage splits to communicate with Bridge Chamber and Cascades Chamber, at high level. The way on is down a ramp into a wide low passage and from here the stream may be rejoined or a dry crawl followed left to Sand Junction. As a finishing touch two routes at stream level and two high level crawls from Sand Junction unite in Shatter Chamber which has an unstable choke high in the roof.

Downstream a simple crawl emerges in Middle Chamber with steep choke to left and roof quickly lowering to the Wet Crawl which has low air-space (liable to flooding) for 18m. Fine tunnel continues to the impressive terminal sump. Stream reappears in Bull Pot of the Witches. Low passage in left wall of sump has been dived for 30m, where it needed digging.

Inlet Series

Proceed upstream from bottom of second pitch to junction of streams. Ahead (right) are a series of chutes and pools rising into a maze of shingle crawls. Left is a climb into the roof above a waterfall into a stream passage. Waterlogged section may be avoided by a dry crawl up into a chamber where oxbow rejoins the passage. There are a series of crawls partway round the oxbow and an exit into a strike passage where small streams enter and sink into the floor. Slot from oxbow chamber leads to stream again but also rises into higher level strike passage where stream is encountered once more and 4.5m climb at N end leads to a short sandy passage. 4.5m pitch at end of crawl from First Chamber in Entrance Series lands in this strike passage.

New Year Series

From Sand Junction continue N along a roomy tunnel past a sump on the left to a stal chamber. Step up into a crawl to rift with a blind aven. The crawl continues to a grotto where a manhole drops to a sump and tight upstream passage. Easier high level crawl from grotto joins stream below boulder pile rising into Curtain Chamber where a fine aven climb ends in choked roof passages. From the chamber a wet crawl enlarges and passes under three avens. In the third aven a crawl to the right ends in a boulder choke and a staircase to the left leads to a tube crossing a deep pool but the passage splits into two levels which both choke.

At boulder pile below Curtain Chamber crawl upstream into good going to a cross joint where water rises from an impassable bedding plane. Climb up into roof passage with boulder ramp across pit and crawl forward towards New Year Cavern. Small inlet at N end soon closes down but main inlet is flat crawl at back of cavern. The crawl rises dramatically into a fine passage which eventually chokes with mud and boulders just beyond a 10m aven, leading to an 15m long draughting inlet.

Middle Series

Climb up into passage in right wall of Middle Chamber and crawl past formations (care) to complex junction. Up to the right is a maze of passages at three levels and low level route soon chokes but straight ahead is a crawl to a 'T' junction. Right is easy going to a steep sand slope and crawl to a calcite choke where the waterfall in Waterfall Series can be heard. Back over sand slope is a high level passage with odd traverses over the 'T' junction until it enters the maze area. Up to the right is a mud slope and tunnel to yet another junction. Left leads back into the maze and right soon splits again. To the right the active branch is a squeeze into two choked chambers while straight ahead a mud floored crawl leads to a boulder choke and a visual connection with Bridge Chamber in the Junction Complex.

Waterfall, Lefthand and Red Rose Series

Just before terminal sump climb up into a large window to two passages. The Lefthand Series crosses an eyehole over the sump and rises to a 'T' junction. Right leads to a squeeze and choke while left becomes tortuous and splits into two blocked passages. Right above the climb quickly reaches a crossroads and a stream channel in the floor emerges at the sump. Upstream a handsome passage ends in an aven and noisy waterfall with an accessible inlet rising tortuously to a sump and dry passage to a choke.

Opposite the stream channel at the crossroads is a narrow high fissure which continues beyond a choked branch and small chamber to a crawl above a small stream. The streamway becomes very low but to the left a crawl breaks out into Red Rose Chamber – a fusion of avens. Ascend flakes into a much higher passage which becomes narrow but up through sharp rock is a section of larger passage choked by mud at each end.

Precambrian Series   Grade IV

Two passages may be entered by swimming across the terminal sump pool. Straight ahead is a crawl 15m long which becomes tight. Precambrian Series is gained by a similar passage to the left. The crawl passes through a duck and a squeeze to a junction with a streamway. Downstream after 30m is a pool with diminishing air-space. Upstream a 1.5m high meandering passage (Carotid Passage) leads to an inlet bedding plane, which has been forced to a chamber and zig-zag passage above a small fall. Carotid Passage continues to a waterfall and alternative climb up into a chamber whose exit is a long inclined bedding plane. Beyond a small inlet a low crawl at water level enters an aven with a narrow fissure near the roof. The point is very close to the end of Casterton Pot.

BOLT BELAYS – see Warning, page 13.

Permission – Estate Office, Cowan Bridge.

BANK HOLIDAY HOLE   NGR SD 677806   Grade II
Alt. 349m   **Length 111m**   **Depth 10m**
Explored 1983, RRCPC.

A small cave located on the limestone bench on the east side of Ease Gill Beck. The entrance is in a prominent shakehole, where a small stream sinks, about 150m across Leck Fell from the entrance to Slit Sinks and due south of the Borehole.

A 2m entrance climb into a chamber leads to a hands and knees crawl for 25m to a flat out squeeze over cobbles. This breaks out into a 2m high rift

passage developing into a winding stream canyon averaging 3-4m high and 1m wide for 100m with some formations including a fine 2m long curtain. A small muddy inlet enters on the right and can be followed for 10m. The cave ends in a boulder collapse which is near to the surface and the resurgence, located on the limestone bench above and on the opposite bank from Slit Sinks.
Permission – CNCC.

BAT CAVE   NGR SD 675805   Grade II
Alt. 332m   **Length 107m**

High entrance in obvious rift opposite Swindon Hole where a stream emerges. Twisting canyon to a junction. Right soon splits into two impassable branches while left continues some distance to small chambers and tight inlets.
Permission – CNCC.

BEST'S HOLE   NGR SD 676806   Grade II
Alt. 328m   **Length 24m**

Slit entrance at stream level in left bank of Ease Gill. Twisting, sideways going for 12m to impassable inlet on the left. Short crawl into small chamber and window to wide aven. Roof inlet is too tight and outlet is a muddy crawl.
Permission – CNCC.

THE BOREHOLE   NGR SD 677807   Grade III
Alt. 322m   **Length 0.4km**

Explored 1964, North Lonsdale Speleological Club & RRCPC.
WARNING – The entrance section and further parts lower down the system flood completely and rapidly in times of wet weather.

Large open entrance in SE bank of Ease Gill some 252m upstream from County Pot. A short length of descending passage leads to a 3m pitch, followed by a long meandering streamway with a deep canal in places. This gives way to a well decorated bedding section leading to a further length of winding stream canyon which enlarges to the head of a 15m pitch. Top of pitch is loose boulders and is best laddered by climbing into roof back from edge, and belaying ladder to large block near head of pitch. Two small passages can be followed by traversing on beyond top of pitch.

From foot, in a clean washed chamber, an inlet can be followed up to a choke, whilst downstream continues as a narrow snake passage descending quickly until it emerges in a larger passage, where an inlet enters on the right. The passage is followed downstream to a large flat roofed chamber, Motterhead's Chamber. To the left the chamber can be followed past an aven to a low dug crawl into a series of loose chambers heading towards Dry Dock Passage.

Down through the boulders to the right of Motterhead's Chamber is the main way on to the lower passages in Pool Sink. Several minor inlets are passed and a 3m climb down leads to a walking passage descending to the stream. Several passages branch off in this area and a low bedding on the right enters T-piece Passage just upstream of its junction with Green and Smelly

Passage. A low wet crawl on the left, the Eccles By-pass, emerges a few
metres downstream of the choke at the head of Green and Smelly Passage.

Tackle

Pitch	Ladder	Belay	Lifeline
1st	–	–	6m handline
2nd	15m	6m	23m

Permission – CNCC.

BOULDER CAVE   NGR SD 667683   Grade I
Alt. 274m   **Length 9m**

91m upstream of Mistral Hole behind a boulder against scar. Short crawl
into chamber with floor of boulders separated by deep fissures. Bedding
plane at rear of chamber soon closes down.
Permission – CNCC.

BOUNDARY POT   NGR SD 679808   Grade III
Alt. 331m   **Length 671m**   **Depth 44m**
Explored 1950, NPC and RRCPC.

**WARNING – Entrance passages liable to total flooding after a little rain.
Watch out for loose boulders in Hiroshima Chamber.**

The furthest upstream entrance in the left bank of the gill, in a long open
depression. A short low crawl and climb down lead to a chamber where
daylight enters from a fenced shaft 6m above on the bank. Way out drops to
a wide crawl followed by climb down to a second chamber. Passage straight
ahead ends in a mud choke after 37m but crawl to right leads to clean-washed
passage which originates in an inlet chamber with a roof connection to the
daylight chamber. Way forward is flat crawl under left wall to short drop into
a dark aven. Tortuous passages enlarge to a shingle crawl which chokes where
a small downhill tube (Bar Stewards' Passage) meets a high inlet dropping to
a fine pitch. Belay to blade of rock directly over pot. Before Bar Stewards'
Passage a tight shingle-floored crawl goes off to the right. This leads to a
series of exposed climbs dropping 12m into the main inlet passage at the
upstream end of Fusion Cavern.

Below is the massive Fusion Cavern with a complex of inlets. Up to the
right is a high chamber with further climbs up into a complex of oxbows and
deserted streamways. At the end of Fusion Cavern a tight crawl bypasses a
boulder choke into a wide arched passage with fine formations and false
floors (care) leading to Hiroshima Chamber. Just before the chamber is a
short passage up on the left and a 6m climbable pitch past jammed flakes to a
small stream trench amongst boulders. Hiroshima has choked roof passages
and an extensive bedding plane to the NE where a tight 'L' shaped slot leads
to an old inlet and the inevitable choked boulder chamber.

Tackle

Pitch	Ladder	Belay	Lifeline
Fusion Cavern	15m	4.5m	21m

Permission – CNCC.

BRONTE CAVE NGR SD 621798 Grade II
Alt. 62m **Length 80m**
Explored 1992, LUSS.

Small stream emerges from rift entrance on true right bank of Casterton Beck. Crawling to awkward small chamber and guarded by a duck. Branch on right is 10m to a blockage where waterfall can be heard. This water probably comes from Casterton Beck. The main cave continues as a hading rift for 15m until a low section is bypassed to the left. Stream emerges from blockage and sink in quarry is only 30m distant.
Permission – The Gamekeeper, Underley Hall.

On opposite side of Casterton Beck is 4m long narrow rift passage to a pool.

BULL POT OF THE WITCHES NGR SD 662813
Alt. 293m **Length 2.5km** Grade III
Explored YRC; extended 1966 and 1968, BSA and 1969, RRCPC.

A cave with fossil phreatic development at several levels in a thrust plane. Large open shaft where stream sinks, a short distance along track behind Bull Pot Farm. The entrance pitch can be laddered but the more usual route is via a short passage leading off from the slope at the S side. The passage leads to an easy chimney descent into the wide South Chamber a few metres from the open hole. South Chamber is just one of several routes leading from the entrance and it can be followed to where the mud floor gives way to a climb down into the extensive, boulder-filled Cavern 32. At the far end of this chamber an awkward climb up leads to a further length of passage and a dangerous choke whilst under the left wall was the original route through to Hidden Pot, now blocked.

At the opposite end of the open hole lies North Chamber and a short section of rift passage leading to further small chambers and a mud choke. At the start of North Chamber a route down through boulders, The Cathole, leads to an 8m pitch to join the route taken by the stream, and a further short climb drops down to join Burnett's Passage. Excavated U-tube squeeze at end of North Chamber leads to a further 4.5m of passage and choke.

Burnett's Passage Area
The last passage out of the open hole turns sharply back alongside South Chamber and a series of drops, best laddered, reaches a large passage. A climb up over boulders enters a chamber, and a climb up on the left leads via a dangerous route into Cavern 32 whilst to the right comes to a 'T' junction after only a few metres. The large passage to the left leads via either of two levels to a climb down into the large Burnett's Great Cavern. The main route on quickly leads to a choke which can be penetrated a short distance via a climb to an upper level whilst high in the left wall, reached via a 12m scale is the short BSA Passage. A further passage can be entered from shelf on the right and an awkward climb leads up to where the way on is too tight.

To the right from the 'T' junction is Burnett's Passage, a hands and knees crawl which enlarges where the main stream enters on the right. A few metres further on in a recess to the right is a large aven which can be scaled to a short length of rift passage and a further aven. This is free-climbable, and 9m up enters Robert's Inlet, an awkward crawl which terminates very close to the surface streambed where the way on is choked.

Upstream Passage

From the foot of the first aven a large passage slopes away to the left and ends at a muddy climb up into a hading rift. A traverse along this followed by a climb up leads into the beautiful Gour Chambers, whilst continuing along the rift by-passes a sump in the upper section of the bottom stream passage to emerge in a large sloping chamber. A traverse across a mud slope and a careful descent reach the start of the Upstream Passage. The first few metres consist of a low air-space crawl in the stream, but soon the roof lifts and the way continues as an easy walk. An obvious climb up leads into the high level '49 Cavern, or a low passage following the stream meets a slope down from the far end of the chamber. Only a few metres on is the upstream sump where water from Aygill Caverns enters. Sump is 46m to an airbell. The next sump has been dived for 175m to a point which would require digging, beyond, but to one side of the downstream limit of Aygill.

Cascade Aven

Climb into passage in right wall upstream of ducks in Upstream Passage. Crawl forward to chamber then via tight squeeze to sudden emergence in Cascade Aven, 18m high, scaled to impenetrable bedding inlet. Outlet in floor of aven is drop to narrow stream passage and acute bend.

Long Gallery to Downstream Sump

If, instead of leaving the large passage below the series of drops, the continuing passage is followed, a climb down leads to an enlargement in a roof bedding, and an extremely tight crawl runs off to the left to emerge at the head of a small aven at the choke at the downstream end of the Long Gallery. A short distance on downstream is Hidden Pot Pitch of 5m which is an awkward climb, possibly best laddered. At the bottom a short length of passage and a short climb down reaches the bottom stream passage which can only be followed a few metres in either direction before sumps are reached. However, just to one side is a short climb up into The Long Gallery which by-passes both sumps.

Upstream is a hands and knees crawl in a slanting passage to where the way slopes down to the right to the stream and the bottom end of the sump by-passed via Robert's Passage and the hading rift. In the opposite direction The Long Gallery reaches the aven and choke already mentioned, and just before this twin holes against the right wall lead down an easy climb to The Canal. Upstream here sumps immediately but downstream leads into a wide but low passage running to a complex junction.

To the right is a large complicated oxbow whilst to the left is Junction Chamber and a way through a choke up into the Far Gallery, and also The Dry Way. This is a large abandoned passage which finally re-unites with The Wet Way, a low crawl, in a roomy chamber containing a large sump. This has been dived downstream, past a large airbell, for approximately 122m to emerge in Wilf Taylor's Passage in Lancaster Hole. Off the airbell a muddy rift is reached via climbs of 2m and 4m. This splits after 60m, one way becoming too narrow, the other choking.

Tackle

Pitch	Ladder	Belay	Lifeline
Entrance	15m	3m	23m
Cathole Pitch	8m	3m	12m
Main Route			
1st	9m	Sling	15m
2nd	6m	Long sling	9m

At least 12m of scaling pole is needed to reach BSA Passage, and 8m to reach Robert's inlet.

BOLT BELAYS – see Warning, page 13.

Permission – CNCC.

CASTERTON POT   NGR SD 663816   Grade II
(Tip Pot)
Alt. 300m   **Length 37m**   **Depth 30m**
Explored 1959, EPC.

Midway between Bull Pot Farm and Aygill are twin shakeholes. One contains a mass of scrap iron; the other is Casterton Pot. Climb down into first chamber via original entrance has now collapsed. Entry is now on S side of shakehole by direct pitch into first chamber. Way continues via second chamber to Guillotine Pot, where the small stream sinks. A rift leads to an aven and wet crawl which becomes too tight only a few metres short of Precambrian Series in Aygill Cavern.

Tackle

Pitch	Ladder	Belay	Lifeline
Entrance	8m	6m	12m
Guillotine Pot	9m	6m	15m

Permission – Estate Office, Cowan Bridge.

CLIFF CAVE   NGR SD 674805   Grade II
Alt. 305m   **Length 12m**
On ledge in cliff on S bank of Ease Gill and opposite Houe Gill. Low crawl meets a small stream and enlarges but beyond an impassable side passage the way is blocked by a boulder.
Permission – CNCC.

CORNER SINK   NGR SD 675805   Grade I
Alt. 317m   **Length 37m**
WARNING – Liable to rapid flooding if gill starts to flood.
Entrance is in right bank on corner where gill turns sharply to the left. A squeeze down over large boulders enters a rift passage which quickly becomes a crawl. Beyond a small oxbow to the right the floor starts cutting

down and walking is possible to a climb down into a pool. On far side of this the fissure narrows and the only way on is in a wide bedding crawl to connection with Swindon Hole.
Permission – CNCC.

COUNTY CAVES   NGR SD 675805   Grade I-II
Alt. 328m

1.   Length 8m

Obvious bedding plane entrance across Ease Gill from County Pot. Quickly lowers to a crawl and choked passages. Two other caves to left and right of No.1 are short and choked by boulders.

2.   Length 33m.   Depth 8m

Upstream of No.1 and higher in the scar. Stooping passage to sudden entry into a fine chamber. Climb down overhanging blocks to floor with blind holes and short passage. Climb up onto shelf with two inlets – one a narrow fissure, the other easy going to a small aven.

3.   Length 21m
Explored 1951, NPC.

Immediately left of No.2 is a sideways slide into a high canyon and easy traverse past a short side passage on the right, to a boulder choke.
Permission – CNCC.

COUNTY POT   NGR SD 675805   Grade III
Alt. 314m
Length – included in Ease Gill Caverns total.
Excavated 1952, NPC and RRCPC; extended 1972, MUSS.

The most popular route into the ramifications of Ease Gill Caverns. Excavated entrance shaft with steel lid, on right bank of gill 73m up-valley from Cow Dub. An easy climb down into a low passage quickly enlarges to become a winding canyon with several short climbs down to the head of a 4.5m pitch. Below is a chamber with an inlet entering on the right, and a short passage on the left to a 2.4m climb down into a spacious passage, The Broadway. Upstream to the left is an easy walk to a crawl and aven, with a short climb into upper passage which emerges in a large chamber with a waterfall inlet.

Oxford Circus downstream to Molluscan Hall and beyond.

Almost opposite the point of entry into The Broadway is Oxford Circus. The downstream passage continues from here as a twisting streamway to a high level junction on the left with Green Passage, a low crawl which soon becomes too tight. On downstream reaches Toadstool Junction, where a large inlet, Butterfield's Passage, enters on the left. This can be followed up a 4.5m waterfall into a long crawl to a further canal and low exit at Cow Dubs II. The main way continues with several cascades to Razor Passage where small climbs down over breakdown finally lead to Platypus Junction.

About 30m up Razor Passage from Platypus Junction a wide low bedding on a shelf on the right above the stream leads to a hole up through boulders. A slope up over boulders leads into a large passage heading upstream above Razor Passage back towards Broadway to a choked area. From the hole up through the boulders an awkward crawl containing a squeeze continues for about 40m. To the right is a way on through several small phreatic tubes and an unstable boulder choke which break out into the Gallery above N.W. Stream Passage downstream of Poetic Justice. To the left the bedding plane crawl continues. After 60m there is a junction and the crawl continues straight on. A climb up over slabs on the right leads into the Gallery Extension, a short section of large well decorated passage. To the left Dismal Bypass continues through boulders to Funnel Chamber with a hole in the floor to a wide bedding plane. This can be followed through two separate passages both breaking out in the roof of Upper Molluscan Hall. An awkward climb down and traverse leads to the lower part of the chamber and hence provides a bypass to the flood prone route via Dismal Junction. Continuing along the crawl below Gallery Extension more flat out crawling leads to a complex junction where up to the left a small chamber Hall Hall is entered. This is the start of Luft's Passage which continues as a high meandering streamway to Delicate Sound of Thunder Boulder Choke. A way through to Sylvester Pot has been forced up the right hand side of the choke but is very unstable. It leads through a large flat roofed chamber and a rift to Rocky Horror Show. A loose climb down from here leads into the Main Chamber of Sylvester Pot whilst back in Hall Hall Northern Passage leads to a point very close to Molluscan Hall.

Below Hall Hall the crawl, Iraq-naphobia, continues as a sandy grovel for over 50m until it breaks out in the roof of Clough's Passage close to the point where it gets low as it pops out at Dismal Junction.

Continuing downstream from Platypus Junction the well decorated North West Passage soon degenerates to a wet crawl past Dismal Junction where Clough's Passage leads off left to an aven and 9m climb enters Mancunian Way Extension.

Downstream crawl ends at squeeze past massive block where stream quickly backs up in flood. Holes between fallen blocks lead up to slippery climbs into the high-level cavern of Molluscan Hall. At the lower level holes between boulders rejoin the stream before it runs into a low bedding cave which can be bypassed by climbing chimney into a wide, muddy passage above. Branch on left is another oxbow back to Molluscan Hall while a series of climbs and traverses over blockfall regain the stream, where dry branches enter from the left. Large passage continues downstream for some distance until the main Ease Gill water is met at Surprise Junction, where both ways quickly terminate in hazardous crawls beneath masses of collapsed blocks.

Molluscan Hall to Cornes' Cavern

One of the branch passages beyond the oxbows downstream of Molluscan Hall enters an 11m aven. Scaling this leads to a series of large passages running back to the left to The Surprise, a large chamber, and a considerable length of passage beyond. To one side of the chamber is a 3m climb up into the Sideline, a low crawl which eventually emerges 6m up the wall of Snail Cavern in

Lancaster Hole. The other route from the top of the aven, The Mancunian Way, leads via a series of low chambers to a larger passage which enters Cornes' Cavern in Lancaster Hole, behind a tremendous dropped block.

Mancunian Way Extension

Beyond the Surprise is the well decorated passage, Nice Way. Near the end of the left hand branch of Nice Way a hole on a shelf on the right hand wall leads down a 5m pitch to a dug and blasted section. After a short flat-out crawl there is a second 7m pitch with a scaffold bar in place. This is in a rift and is tight and awkward on the return. At the bottom of this pitch is a larger passage. Up dip it quickly chokes, close to passages in Sylvester Pot. Down-stream progress is through a shattered chamber to a stream passage which can be followed down to a 9m pitch which is the top of Clough's Aven in Clough's Passage.

This route provides yet another Ease Gill round trip as it provides a quick route out of the far end of Mancunian Way using a 20m rope to abseil the three pitches described above. This should only be attempted in dry weather to avoid being cut off by flooding at Dismal Junction.

Oxford Circus to Poetic Justice

Back at Oxford Circus a further passage leads off up and over a rock slope and down into Showerbath Passage. Easy walking in a twisting streamway brings one to Confusion Corner and the junction with the original route from Oxford Pot. Also at Confusion Corner is a large abandoned upper passage which enters a highly shattered area with a connection through to The Upper Trident Series in Battle of Britain Chamber. On down the main streamway leads to a climb down into Spout Hall which can be by-passed via an old route on a shelf to the left. Spout Hall slopes steeply down to two outlet passages which quickly unite, and only a few metres further on, tucked away under the right wall, is the chimney up to Poetic Justice and the connection with the further reaches of the system. The stream passage continues to Platypus Junction, already described, with a further high level connection to the Far Series via Ignorance is Bliss.

The Manchester By-pass enters the active streamway just upstream of the climb down into Spout Hall. This by-pass is important as it provides what is probably the least complicated flood escape route from the Stop Pot area of Lancaster Hole, and consequently from large lengths of Ease Gill Caverns. It is decribed on p.144.

Poetic Justice to Eureka Junction

A short crawl at the head of the chimney – Poetic Justice – leads to a drop down into a separate stream passage, and only a few metres downstream is a 5.4m pitch into Pierce's Passage. Upstream above the pitch leads via a complex route to a link, with Carrot Chamber in Lancaster Hole, or alternatively into the Upper Trident Series and Spout Hall. Below the pitch Pierce's Passage is easy walking to a large junction on the right where Trident Passage enters. This can be followed up to where the way splits into three. Scaling any of the waterfalls at the ends of these passages enters the complex Upper Trident Series which virtually defies description. Back in the main passage a climb up a muddy boulder slope leads to a drop back down to the stream, and a twisting canyon passage which descends numerous cascades. Gradually the gradient flattens out and a drop in the roof is followed by a climb up into a mud floored section, lowering to a crawl which emerges down a slope into the spacious main drain of Ease Gill at Eureka Junction.

Tackle

Pitch	Ladder	Belay	Lifeline
1st	8m	3m	9m
2nd	8m	Sling	12m

Wretched Rabbit Passage

Just before this point is reached a gap in the right wall leads into Wretched Rabbit Passage, a long meandering streamway that can be followed to the surface at Wretched Rabbit Entrance.

Eureka Junction to Stop Pot

At Eureka Junction the stream can be followed down in a gradually lowering passage until a flat crawl in the stream takes one to a climb up through a tremendous collapse area into the complex below Snail Cavern. Upstream from the junction is a large passage which enters an enlargement on a corner. Here there are two routes on, that to the left following the stream through a bouldery section, whilst up the slope straight ahead a low bedding crawl can be followed, to where both ways emerge into the vastness of Stop Pot. A climb up the huge boulder slope leads to an iron ladder and climb up to the usual connection with the high level route through from Lancaster Hole.

Depot Passages

From the foot of the Stop Pot boulder slope two passages can be entered from a rock shelf on the right. The first one, Depot Passage 2, can be followed as a crawl to a choke whilst the other, and more obvious passage, Depot Passage 1 is more complex. Commencing as a wide crawl it gradually narrows and passes three sharp bends to a long straight section. At the end of this two chambers can be entered, and the far one has an awkward 3.7m climb to an upper level. Further small passages continue to more small chambers and a further climb to a junction, both ways soon becoming too tight. Right hand fork above 3.7m climb in Depot 1 is Depot 1.5, starting with the flat-out Flashbang Crawl for 46m to blasted squeeze, then narrow rift to sudden climb up into Ahaa Chamber. First exit on right is low triangular crawl for 30m to choke. Second exit is small passage and squeeze to calcite choke. Straight ahead from point of entry is step into walking size passage to shattered rift chamber on right. 6m climb at far end and narrow rift crawl emerge in lofty chamber. Climb into old stream trench on left leads to Pretty Passage which eventually splits and chokes. Below rift chamber, short crawl and chimney up, then via squeeze onto boulder slope down into Wretched Rabbit Passage above the waterfalls.

Stop Pot to Holbeck Junction

On the opposite side of Stop Pot to Depot Passages a climb up a loose slope reaches the start of Double Decker Passage which after a short climb up enters the large high level Straw Chamber at roof level. At far end of Straw Chamber a steep slope up boulders leads to the well decorated start of Dry Dock Passage, a walking size passage which terminates in an extensive choke. To the left of the entrance to this passage is the climb up into the link passage to Green and Smelly Passage, whilst under the left wall a hair-raising descent down loose boulders brings one back into the main stream passage just upstream from Stop Pot. From here an involved route over huge fallen blocks leads to a narrow section, and a climb down to the stream at Holbeck Junction.

BOLT BELAYS – see Warning, page 13.

Permission – CNCC.

COW POT   **NGR SD 664808**   **Grade IV**
Alt. 305m   **Length 244m**   **Depth 76m**
Explored 1899, YRC; extended 1948, NPC and 1969, BSA.

An interesting route into Lancaster Hole, with a classic final pitch. Open shaft at end of stream course, in walled enclosure at corner of field. The entrance pitch can be laddered in several positions, the easiest being down the gully on the east side. Leading off from the sides of the open shaft are several short inlet passages, and FX5 Inlet. This is up the rock slope to the right of the pitch, and is a series of short climbs up into avens and a balcony overlooking the open pot. From here a bedding leads to a stream inlet which can be followed for 40m, over a blind 6m pitch, to end at two avens.

Almost opposite the bottom of the ladder a large, meandering passage descends several short cascades to where the roof lowers, and a short crawl over large cobbles leads to a wide but low chamber formed in a washed out shale bed. A number of passages radiate from here, the first one being on the left of the point of entry. This is a short crawl running back in the direction of the entrance and soon chokes. Only a few metres on round the wall from the start of this passage is a further short crawl in a phreatic tube several metres above floor level. Moving on round the chamber a hole in the floor down through large boulders is met, and this can only be followed a few metres before choking completely.

The next passage is up a shelf in the washed out shale bed, and a crawl leads to a step up of 1m into an old phreatic tunnel. Continuing past a hole in the floor leads to a junction, the way to the left spiralling back round into the chamber, or continuing on to the top of a short pitch. The other direction continues as a stooping walk to a further junction. To the left leads up an inlet to a choke very close to the foot of the entrance waterfall, whilst to the right is a squeeze and 2m climb down into a small chamber, the only outlet being an impassable slot taking the stream.

The final exit from the chamber is the one that connects with this last passage, but to one side is an opening giving straight onto a 4m pitch. From the foot a short crawl leads to an acute corner and a short drop into a small chamber. The way on is an awkward squeeze in the right wall and this ends abruptly at the lip of a further pitch of 4m. A small chamber at the foot leads to a very narrow rift passage which becomes too tight within a few metres.

Fall Pot route
   The only other passage leading off from the entrance shaft is up the rock slope to the right of the ladder, and is the route which connects with Lancaster Hole. This starts as a narrow rift which quickly swings to the right and after a short climb down reaches a junction. To the right ends at a choke after a few metres, whilst to the left is the main way on in a low crawl. After passing several acute bends a stream inlet enters on the left and the crawl is through a long pool. Gradually the passage enlarges to a short climb down into a wide chamber, with thick shale bed in walls, where stream sinks in floor. Continuing on upper ledges leads to direct pitch down into the vastness of Fall Pot. Alternative route is short traverse in gully to boulder platform and pitch down to rejoin stream before it drops into Fall Pot. Across stream passage and through window is dry pitch down N wall of Fall Pot. 15m down, it is possible to step off onto ledge, level with top of huge boulder, reached (lifelined) by an exposed traverse or up slippery mud slope to passage from Lancaster Hole.

Tackle

Pitch	Ladder	Belay	Lifeline
Entrance	23m	Sling	30m
Old Series			
1st	6m	3m	8m
2nd	6m	Sling	9m
Lancaster Hole Route – Direct Pitch			
Fall Pot	46m	6m	55m
Lancaster Hole Route – Gully			
Gully Pitch	9m	1.2m	12m
2nd pitch (to ledge)	17m	4.5m	30m
2nd pitch (to floor)	30m	4.5m	37m

BOLT BELAYS – see Warning, page 13.

Permission – CNCC.

COW DUBS II   NGR SD 674805   Grade III
(Blind Pot)
Alt. 300m   Length included in Ease Gill Caverns total
Explored 1990, NCC.

   Entrance in rock walled hole, just downstream of Cow Dub, leads to flat out crawl to head of a 3m drop. Below, a body sized tube is followed by more crawling to where way enlarges to permit walking to head of 5m drop into head of Butterfield's Passage.

Tackle – 8m handline.

Permission – CNCC.

THE CRUMBLES   NGR SD 666803   Grade II
Alt. 267m   **Length 61m**   **Depth 18m**
Explored 1972, HWCPC.

WARNING – Much shattered rock; take care.

   Entrance in cliff 30m down Ease Gill from Mistral Hole. Drop into loose chamber with precipitous slope and cross to short roof passage. In alcove on right is Black Rabbit Chimney which descends to Square Cavern with twin chimneys on each side. W chimney leads to a series of crawls and avens, while E chimney drops into Mint Crawl leading to a climbable pot and very unstable boulder choke.

Hole at bottom of entrance chamber opens into South Chamber which has a muddy crawl straight ahead blocked by boulders. A hole in the left connects with Mint Crawl and a slot between blocks drops into a lower chamber.
Permission – CNCC.

DRAGON HOLE
Alt. 335m

NGR SD 678807
Length 12m

Grade II
Depth 6m

Hole under boulder up on S bank of Ease Gill drops 3.7m into roomy passage. One end chokes at once but the other continues through a deep pool to a very tight twisting fissure.
Permission – CNCC.

EASE GILL CAVERNS
Length 52km, vertical range 137m including Bull Pot of the Witches, Lancaster Hole, Link Pot and Pippikin Pot.

Ease Gill Caverns, strictly speaking, are the many inlets from Ease Gill Beck between Oxford Pot and Top Sink inclusive. However, it is also a convenient heading under which to consider the great complex of interconnected cave passages extending on both sides of Ease Gill, and together forming the longest known cave system in the British Isles. The present total length of the Ease Gill–Lost John's complex is 62.6km.

The several parts of this complex are described in the following manner: Bull Pot of the Witches is divided from Lancaster Hole at the sump linking with Wilf Taylor's Passage in Lancaster; Link Pot comprises the passages between the top of Echo Aven in the Stake Pot Series of Lancaster Hole; and the sump and crawl where the links to Pippikin Pot were made; Pippikin Pot is described as far as the connections to Link Pot; Lancaster Hole description extends to Stop Pot; County Pot includes the various passages to Lancaster Hole between Stop Pot and Cornes' Cavern (except the important flood escape route of Manchester By-pass, described under Lancaster Hole), and extends upstream to Holbeck Junction; Pool Sink and Wretched Rabbit Entrance deal with these entrances and associated inlets down to Holbeck Junction, and finally Top Sink includes the upstream passages down to Holbeck Junction.

Such an extensive and highly complex system defies adequate description in a book of this nature. There is no comprehensive account of the whole network, although the Cave Research Group Transactions Vol.9 No.2 (1967) 'Lancaster Hole and the Ease Gill Caverns' is still the most detailed description of much of the cave, despite being outdated by subsequent explorations.

All newcomers to the system are advised to make their first exploration in the company of someone who knows the system well. Great care should be

CAVERNS OF THE EASE GILL AREA

Plan based on RRCPC / NPC / HWCPC / ULSA / MUSS / CUCC / CDG surveys

0   600m

ABBREVIATIONS

BTP	Bill Taylor's Passage
CC	Colonnade Chamber
DJ	Dusty Junction
EH	Equinox Hall
LG	Long Gallery
MH	Molluscan Hall
MMS	Misty Mountain Series
MP	Mortuary Passage
MR	Magic Roundabout
MWP	Montagu West Passage
PJ	Poetic Justice
PR	Pooh's Revenge
RI	Ratbag Inlet
RRS	Red Rose Series
RWC	Red Wall Chamber
SJ	Sausage Junction
WP	Waterfall Passage
WRP	Wretched Rabbit Passage
WTP	Wilf Taylor's Passage

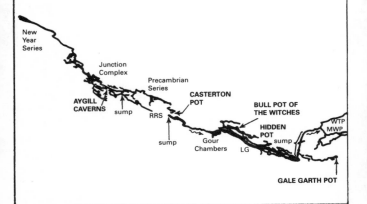

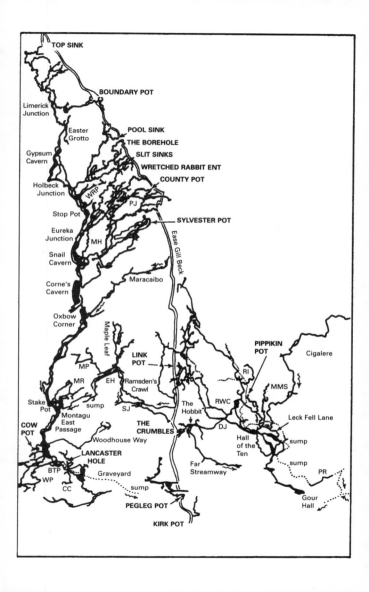

taken to avoid damage to the marvellous formations, which have already suffered severely at the hands of earlier visitors, and taped routes should be followed.

FINGER POT   NGR SD 674805   Grade II
Alt. 314m   Depth 9m
Explored 1954, RRCPC.

Top of shaft is covered by boulders in thick patch of bracken about 18m down-valley from the wall joining Ease Gill at Cow Dub, and well up on left bank near large pointed boulder. A straight descent in a rift lands on a sloping floor which funnels down to a short drop and a squeeze into a section of larger passage. This quickly chokes in both directions.

Tackle – 8m ladder; stake & sling belay; 12m lifeline.

Permission – CNCC.

GALE GARTH POT   NGR SD 662809   Grade III
Alt. 301m   **Length 229m**   Depth 27m
Explored 1971, RRCPC.

Entrance is excavated shaft in shakehole by track between Bull Pot and Lancaster Hole. Below the short shaft is a squeeze and way through a boulder choke into Octopus Chamber. Ahead is a breakdown cavern with roof inlets and a high level route back over Octopus Chamber to a choke under the entrance shakehole. Wide crawl at N end of breakdown cavern soon leads to a rift and pitch on the right down into a large abandoned passage and mud choke. The crawl continues via the China Shop and Dracula's Altar to Equality Crawl and a large choked fault chamber.

Tackle – 6m ladder; 3m belay; 12m lifeline.

Permission – CNCC.

GELDER HOLE   NGR SD 675805   Grade III
Alt. 314m   **Length 10m**
Directly below Bat Cave. Water falls into a nasty wet bedding plane.
Permission – CNCC.

GINTRAP HOLE   NGR SD 676806   Grade I
Alt. 335m   **Length 9m**
Notable shakehole on bench above Ease Gill. Short bouldery cave strewn with straw and earth.
Permission – CNCC.

HAIRY FISSURE   NGR SD 668803   Grade II
Alt. 274m   Depth 6m
Explored 1970, HWCPC.

Rift in rock outcrop in the bed of Ease Gill. Tight section partway down is

easy to traverse for small people – almost impossible for fatties. Ends in a series of constricted shingle-choked crawls. Blocked at present.
Permission – CNCC.

HAZEL SIKE CAVE   NGR SD 663819   Grade I
Alt. 305m   **Length 12m**

Hazel Sike is next stream N of Aygill. Entrance is on the true right side of small gorge under dry waterfall. Pleasant hands and knees crawl to small chamber with dig in floor.

HELLOT HOLE   NGR SD 662806   Grade II
Alt. 296m   **Length 20m**   **Depth 21m**
Explored 1946, BSA.

Shaft by track to Hellot Scales Barn is straight descent into a passage. Inlet to the NW ascends rapidly to become tight and choked. Small stream runs down tunnel which chokes where water sinks into a narrow fissure.
Tackle – 18m ladder; 3m belay; 24m lifeline.
Permission – CNCC.

HIDDEN POT   NGR SD 662813   Grade II
Alt. 296m   **Depth 9m**
Explored 1927, YRC.

On opposite side of track, and only a few metres from Bull Pot of the Witches in a steep sided, fenced shakehole with drainage gully entering. A straight climb down leads to small chamber and loose boulder choke. At one time a passage through this led into Cavern 32 in Bull Pot of the Witches.
Tackle – 8m ladder; 3m belay; 12m lifeline.
Permission – CNCC.

HOWGILL SINK   NGR SD 672804   Grade III
Alt. 297m   **Length 137m**   **Depth 12m**
Explored 1970, RRCPC.
WARNING – Entrance is underwater when Ease Gill flows beyond Cow Dub.

Beneath bedstead on left bank of Ease Gill below the confluence with Houe Gill. Small climbs drop to first squeeze into a wider passage and Hanging Death Squeeze past loose blocks in a choke at entrance to Consortium Cavern. At base of steep upward boulder slope are two short drops into a wide, low streamway. Upstream is a wet crawl to a breakdown chamber, and downstream is a wide silted bedding plane to 46m of easier going to a junction. Straight ahead soon ends in a boulder blockage and choked avens while the crawl continues for 61m to a low chamber and sump. The far reaches of this cave, now blocked, is the Silver Streamway in the Lone Ranger Series in Link Pot.
Permission – CNCC.

INNOMINATE SINK   NGR SD 675805   Grade II
Alt. 328m
Explored 1951, NPC.

Up side valley immediately above Cow Dub. Climb down into short passage and further drop into choked bedding cave. Blocked at present.
Permission – CNCC.

KIRK POT   NGR SD 662802   Grade II
(Upper Gunbarrel) (Sputnik)
Alt. 252m   **Length 183m**   **Depth 38m**
Explored YRC and extended RRCPC, 1958.
WARNING – Total flooding within minutes when Ease Gill floods.

At base of dry waterfall in Upper Ease Gill Kirk. Twin entrances behind large flakes on the S bank unite in a series of rifts and bedding planes. Fissure crawl into descending bedding plane and small passage to a 3m chockstone climb and the spiralling pitch and final climb down into a large passage. Upwards over boulders soon chokes but other branch descends through pools to crawl over boulders into wider section. Continuing wide passage lowers into choked sump.
Tackle – 14m ladder; 2.4m belay; 18m lifeline.
Permission – CNCC.

KIRTLE POT   NGR SD 663817   Grade II
Alt. 305m   **Length 12m**   **Depth 9m**
Explored 1975, GC.

In large shakehole between Casterton Pot and Aygill.
Fissure descends to squeeze under right wall and loose debris slope into low chamber from which a short passage descends to a hole in the floor with choked crawl below.

LANCASTER HOLE   NGR SD 664807   Grade III
Alt. 294m   **Depth 112m**
Length 52km including Bull Pot of the Witches, Ease Gill Caverns, Link Pot and Pippikin Pot.
Explored 1946, BSA; extended by many other clubs since, particularly the RRCPC, NPC and EPC.
WARNING – In extremely wet weather the Master Cave backs up to a height of at least 15m above the downstream sump and drowns many low level passages. Such flooding of Wormway (below Echo Aven) and Woodhouse Way, for example, could cause parties to be trapped.

Lancaster Hole is one entrance to the superb, vast series of caves connecting with Bull Pot of the Witches and Ease Gill Caverns to form the longest and most intricate cave system in Britain. A more detailed description than there is room for here is given in the Cave Research Group's Transactions, Vol.9,

No.2, 'Lancaster Hole and the Ease Gill Caverns' by J. Eyre and P. Ashmead (1967).

For convenience the description here is divided into three main sections: West of Fall Pot, East of Fall Pot, and Stake Pot Series and Inlets. These are further divided into many sub-sections. The division between Lancaster Hole and the Ease Gill Caverns is taken as Stop Pot.

Great care should be taken of the superb formations, which have already been severely damaged by careless visitors.

WEST OF FALL POT

The lidded entrance shaft of 33m lies in the shallow valley to the S of Cow Pot, by an isolated group of boulders. Narrow at the top, the shaft soon opens out to large dimensions, passing two ledges to reach a boulder floor. A short climb up leads into a large rift passage with a slot in the floor and a short walk emerges at the top of a steep boulder slope down into Bridge Hall. Immediately on the left are two routes into the Sand Cavern Series which ultimately chokes whilst slightly further down the slope, and also on the left, is a concealed crawl which leads to a 6m pitch and The Graveyard Series.

The Graveyard Series

From the foot of the ladder the passage enlarges quickly, and a branch to the left ends in two fine avens; the left hand one has been bolted for 24m past several alcoves to a ledge, from which a route up through boulders enters the Chapel of Rest – a large chamber with very fine formations and all ways out choked. Ahead below the avens a large chamber with a further aven is entered, and beyond stretches The Graveyard itself. The mud floor, abundantly decorated with stalagmites, is split by a gully containing a small stream. Climb down gully and past large blocks to streamway. Upstream in gully leads to choke beneath Bridge Hall, or downstream to a junction. The right passage joins the Stump Cavern Extension, whilst the left passage descends a 6m pitch with no obvious belay to reach a short duck into a small airbell, and a sump that was found by divers to be badly silted up and impassable.

Continuing beyond the gully a slope up and a crawl leads into Stump Cavern, from the far end of which a further crawl over breakdown eventually enlarges at a junction with a far larger passage. To the left here leads to the Skittle Alley and a deep sump which has been dived unsuccessfully with an exposed traverse in the roof leading over sump to a choke, and a climb up right wall to series of avens in loose rock (care), whilst to the right leads to a muddy sump, Aqua-Mud Sump, which can be bailed to enter Montagu South Passage. This commences as a low passage, but enlarges into a rift, seemingly to terminate at a blank wall. However, an 8m scale followed by a similar pitch down enters a large chamber, Newton Hall. From the far end of this a large passage gradually degenerates into a wide, low crawl which can be followed for about 61m to where it gets too low.

Bridge Hall and Colonnade Chamber

By continuing down the slope into the chamber proper, and passing a hole down through boulders at the lowest point, Kath's Way, a mud slope can be ascended on the right to a blind 6m pitch, Barker's Pot. To the left at the bottom of the slope an easy climb up and a traverse round to the right enters a large passage. This closes to a short crawl which enters the Colonnade Chamber with its beautiful columns. At the far end of the chamber the way swings to the right and narrows to a rift which quickly chokes, as also does a high level route reached by an 8m climb.

Bill Taylor's Passage

At the foot of Kath's Way a low crawl is reached, with a branch off to the right into a complex low series connecting with Sand Caverns and the slot in the floor of the passage from the entrance pitch. The main route enlarges to an alcove on the left where a showerbath descends, and just beyond, a couple of holes to the right lead to The Craters. A descent of the largest enters a squeeze to a sump which can be bailed. Beyond, a small passage leads to a climb into a larger section and an 18m pitch into the Master Cave canal just upstream of the final sump. A low crawl continues beyond the pitch for 91m to a small sump.

Back in Bill Taylor's Passage the way on enlarges considerably and then splits into two, both ways uniting in the vastness of Montagu East Passage where it encounters Fall Pot. If the left hand route is taken, a descent of several small steps leads to a cleft in the floor which is a 24m pitch into the Master Cave. A careful traverse round to the left here, on a sloping mud-floored shelf, leads to the start of Montagu West Passage. This in turn joins in its further reaches with Waterfall Passage and Wilf Taylor's Passage – two separate routes back down to the downstream section of the Master Cave.

Montagu West Passage

A climb up the mud slope leads to a narrow passage and a strategically placed fixed ladder. A short descent enters a larger section, and a short crawl emerges in a chamber with several holes in the floor leading direct to the Master Cave nearly 30m below. Alternating stretches of walking and stooping leads to a junction with the far larger Portcullis Passage. To the left here narrows in to a rift with two holes in the floor which connect with Waterfall Passage 9m below, whilst beyond them another junction is quickly reached. Both ways, which have been excavated, soon end, and it is possible that this area is connected to Montagu South Passage.

To the right at the junction with Portcullis Passage continues as a hands and knees crawl, past The Portcullis itself, to where the mud floor slopes down to a rock floor. Just beyond the roof lifts and two rifts cross the floor, the first of which connects on the left with Waterfall Passage. The continuing passage now has banks of sand and shingle along the sides, and eventually a 'T' junction is reached at Cross Passage. To the left here leads in a few metres to a drop down into the active streamway of Waterfall Passage, whilst to the right enlarges considerably as it enters Wilf Taylor's Passage.

Waterfall Passage

A short climb down from Cross Passage enters a narrow canyon passage which can be followed upstream for a short way to where the roof lowers and the stream splits in two, both routes sumping almost immediately. The right hand sump is too tight after 38m; the left hand sump has been dived for 15m and is very low. Downstream from the point of entry continues as a high, narrow canyon passage with dark mud-covered walls. Easy walking leads steadily on to where the gradient increases to descend several small chutes, and finally, an easily descended 3.7m sloping waterfall. At the foot is a large cross rift, and the stream flows into the right hand extension and sumps. The chamber itself, Waterfall Chamber is fairly spacious and very tall, and from the far side a narrow rift leads down a steep mud slope to enter the Master Cave at a sharp corner.

Wilf Taylor's Passage

At the junction with Cross Passage a step down leads into the large Wilf Taylor's Passage, and to the left (upstream), can be followed in a gradually lowering route to a pool which finally sumps. It is here that the underwater connection to Bull Pot of the Witches commences. Downstream from the junction the passage narrows and becomes a high rift with clean washed rock floor and walls – obviously a flood route in wet weather. Easy walking leads to a series of chutes and Double Decker Pot with a fairly easy climb down to the floor of the chamber, although rather frightening when viewed from above. From the far end of the lower chamber twin rift passages quickly unite, and a zig-zag route with several small chutes emerges finally from an un-inspiring entrance into the Master Cave only a few metres upstream from the junction with Waterfall Passage.

From halfway ledge on Double Decker climb, slot in left wall pops out in parallel rift. South from here leads through a sand dig for about 30m to a narrow pitch down. The base of this can be reached from the Main Drain just upstream of where Wilf Taylor's enters, where a short passage leads to an aven and a vocal connection to the narrow pitch above. To the north, upstream way continues in stooping passage for 60m to sump. Very constricted sump should not be free dived, but leads to canal and further rift to climb up and short bedding plane crawl back into Wilf Taylor's at top end.

Fall Pot and downstream section of the Master Cave

By following one of several routes from the end of Bill Taylor's Passage, taking care of the deep holes in the floor, the lip of Fall Pot itself is reached, with the stream entering from Cow Pot far above. To the right is a pitch descending past a tremendous fallen block to a boulder floor. To the right at the foot of a short slope is a 12m pitch taking the water, or to the left a descent down between the boulders, both uniting in the Master Cave, here some 3.7m wide and 5m tall.

On downstream the passage skirts the boulder pile of Fall Pot, enlarging suddenly into a tall rift, and after only a few metres a small, keyhole passage enters on the right at floor level. This is Burgess' Passage, and scaling two climbs here leads into Aardvark Country, a series of crawls one of which chokes, the other entering an inlet region with pitches down to water level and a large aven.

Only a few paces on downstream lies the entrance to Wilf Taylor's Passage – already described – and a similar distance brings one to the large slope up into Waterfall Passage at a sharp bend to the left. Ahead is a long straight passage with a steadily lowering roof; and deepening canal to the final downstream sump 81m below Lancaster Hole entrance. Underwater the Master Cave can be followed down to wide bedding plane at an average depth of 10m. At 140m from base The Ramp descends into a huge submerged chamber, and the continuing tunnel at over 30m depth has been followed to a point 585m from base.

Tackle

Pitch	Ladder	Belay	Lifeline
Entrance	34m	Short spreader	38m

Graveyard Gully Passage

1st	8m	4.5m	12m

Montagu South Passage
8m of scaling ladder or pole and electron ladder.

1st	8m	2m	12m

Bill Taylor's Extension (Crater Passage)

1st	18m	3m	23m

Fall Pot

1st	13m	Short spreader	30m

Burgess' Passage and Aardvark Country
At least 9m of scaling gear is needed to enter, with sufficient ladders and lines to match.

1st	9m	2m	12m
2nd	15m	3m	23m
Graveyard	8m	Spreader	18m

EAST OF FALL POT

Upstream section of the Master Cave

Continuing upstream from the foot of Fall Pot a small inlet immediately on the right is the start of Woodhouse Way. The Master Cave continues as a high rift with several boulder obstacles to where the way narrows and a series of deep pools and small chutes are encountered. Eventually more breakdown is reached and the passage swings left beneath the large collapse area of Stake Pot. A narrow passage entering on the right here is one way into the Stake Pot Inlets and the Stake Pot Series (EPC '71 Series) – whilst another route can be followed from the high level route of Montagu East Passage. The inlet passage can be followed to a squeeze and a crawl which emerges in a large chamber containing four avens. To the left another crawl enters a further chamber with a high level route through dangerous boulders to near Bob's Boss on the upper route.

On up the Master Cave from Stake Pot the roof lifts and there are some fine formations, until after about 275m a large passage enters from the right up in the wall. An easy climb enters Breakdown Passage which although large initially, gradually closes down with piles of collapsed blocks littering the floor, to where the way on is completely choked. This passage should be treated with caution as the roof appears in danger of imminent collapse. Beyond the entrance to this passage the main way on can be followed through boulders to Oxbow Corner, a perfect example on the left, to end not far beyond in a complete choke where the passage decreases in size.

Maracaibo
Explored 1973, RRCPC.

Various entrances downstream of the oxbow at Oxbow Corner lead to a fairly narrow inlet passage. Lengthy walking and crawling along a well decorated streamway degenerates into a more restricted section where the widest level must be sought. Any passing body wreaks havoc amongst delicate formations and regular visiting can only result in their destruction. Passage ends in chokes under Ease Gill. Crystal pool in side passage is particularly liable to damage and **must not be crossed** since passage ends just beyond.

Montagu East Passage and the high level route to Stop Pot

From the bottom of the pitch at Fall Pot a steep boulder slope leads up to the continuation of Montagu Passage, here a fine wide passage with a mud floor. Holes in the floor should be avoided, and soon the gaping hole of Stake Pot is reached. A pitch leads down onto a boulder bridge, from where a steep slope leads down into the Master Cave below, and a climb up the opposite side leads into the continuation of the upper route. Again the way on is large with many formations to where a fixed rope at Bob's Boss marks the way on. The floor gives way to boulders and the passage narrows in to the Painter's Palette, beyond which the twin holes of Scylla and Charybdis are soon reached. The traverse round these should be treated with care as they drop direct into the Master Cave far below.

Ahead, the boulder floor causes confusion until the top of a steep boulder slope on the left is encountered. This leads down to the Master Cave at Oxbow Corner, whilst the way on lies in a crawl over mudbanks along the right wall. A sharp turn to the left after a small chamber leads to a larger chamber, and off to the right here is Diamond Hall, a large passage which soon ends in a tight crawl and choke. The main way on enlarges dramatically at Oakes Cavern, and stops as abruptly at the start of the Minarets – a series of parallel fissures linked by short crawls. At the far end a climb round a tremendous fallen block reveals the huge Cornes Cavern stretching away into the distance. A central gully can be followed through this, with banks of mud and boulders sloping up to the walls. Tucked away behind a large block against the right wall is the start of the Mancunian Way leading into the Ease Gill Caverns at Molluscan Hall.

Cornes Cavern narrows in somewhat and then enlarges when Snail Cavern is entered. To the right here is the way down into Lower Snail Cavern, whilst a few metres further on lies Main Line Passage which provides an alternative route to Main Line Terminus, usually reached by following the large open passage to where it splits into four separate passages, one being the other end of Main Line Passage. Straight ahead leads through a crawl to enlarge again, and end in Carrot Chamber, whilst the other passage on the right is winding fissure terminating in a choke. The large passage on the left leads over fallen blocks for a short distance to the top of Stop Pot, where a fixed ladder drops to the steep boulder slope down into the Main Drain, and the vast ramifications of the Ease Gill Caverns.

The whole of the high level route should be treated with respect as parts of it are confusing, as well as the more obvious dangers of the holes to the Master Cave, slippery mud slopes and loose boulder piles.

Tackle

Pitch	Ladder	Belay	Lifeline
Stake Pot	8m	Spreader	20m

MANCHESTER BY-PASS   **Flood Escape Route**

Because of its importance in providing what is most likely the least complicated flood escape route from the Stop Pot area of Lancaster Hole, and thus large lengths of the Ease Gill Caverns, back to County Pot entrance, it has been decided to describe the route here rather than in the County Pot description.

On the high level route from Stop Pot to Lancaster Hole is Main Line Terminus, the point where a number of different passages merge to form the large upper level on towards Snail Cavern. By taking the eastern branch of Main Line Passage from Main Line Terminus, walking and scrambling leads to where the floor rises suddenly, with the way on being a shattered crawl-sized passage. This is followed up and to the right through a slot into Old English Chamber (while straight on emerges in the large Carrot Chamber). A small, muddy hole to the left of the point of entry into Old English Chamber is the low and narrow start of Spangle Passage. Various obstacles and short traverses at roof level lead on until finally a narrow descending rift is reached. Care is required here as the rift ends 3.7m above the boulder strewn floor of Brown and Smelly Chamber, and the walls are somewhat greasy. The climb down is awkward because of this, and a short line or couple of slings can be a great help. The way on is a crawl out of the chamber to the left of the bottom of the climb, followed quickly by a drop into a small shattered passage. This soon rises over muddy boulders and to the right here is the top of a 6m pitch with fixed ladder in place. For those slim enough it is possible to by-pass the pitch by continuing forward into Cono Crawl; a very narrow rift and corkscrew descent emerges over the top of two large unstable boulders at the end of the chamber encountered at the bottom of the pitch. From here a short crawl brings one to a short descent into a muddy fissure and a way on into a low cobbled crawl via a gap between two loose boulders. Ahead leads into a low bedding chamber with the route on being up and over some large fallen blocks on the left. A short scramble and a few metres of walking size passage emerge in the active streamway just upstream of the spout descent into Spout Hall. From here, walking upstream in Showerbath Passage enters Oxford Circus and the climb up on the left at the start of Broadway leading to County Pot.

Tackle

Climb into Brown and Smelly Chamber – 6m handline.

Pitch	Ladder	Belay	Lifeline
6m	8m	3m	12m

Woodhouse Way
Explored 1981, RRCPC.

WARNING – First 200m from the Master Cave is very flood prone and sumps completely by backing up from the Master Cave. The ducks sump in light rain unless cleared properly.

Immediately upstream of Fall Pot entry into the Master Cave is a small inlet up on the right. A short bedding crawl enters a fissure passage which continues for 61m with some traversing to a flowstone blockage.

A squeeze to the left of the flowstone drops into a flat-out wet crawl to the first duck, beyond which is a 1m high 'chamber' and the second duck – tight and awkward. The ducks usually need clearing of rubble. Continue along rift and through eyehole to junction after 30m. The right-hand inlet becomes too tight after 49m and the way onward is to the left through a 6m long bedding plane duck. Now the struggle eases and the passage develops into a 6m high. meandering streamway for 152m to a complex junction.

Here all ways close down or coalesce but to the right is a 6m climb up in the main inlet to a bedding plane and further chimney up to Haemorrhoid Hall. Across the 'grikes' flooring the hall is an inlet complex, the main way being via the first climb on the left, a 10m chimney up to an eyehole opening into Bat Chamber. The largest roof aven (Bat Aven) is an 8m climb which intersects another passage. Upstream is the blind Radio Aven with a choked tube at the base, and downstream the passage soon chokes.

Tackle – Bat Aven: 8m ladder; 15m lifeline.

STAKE POT SERIES AND INLETS   **Grade III-IV**
Stake Pot Series
(E.P.C. '71 Series)
Explored 1971, EPC.

WARNING – When the stream is running in Lower Ease Gill all the passages below the 88ft (27m) Pitch flood to the roof.

Follow the right wall of Stake Pot towards Ease Gill and take an irregular arched passage to a pit at Streamway Junction. Down the pit the passage is choked by stal upstream but straight ahead is a climb over a flake in a fissure and long joint passage to Thirsty Junction. Left is the streamway which soon terminates in Razor Aven but to the right is a roomy, sandy passage which splits into three branches. Only the right branch 'goes' as a short draughty crawl to Canuck Climb which requires combined tactics to scale. A fixed ladder is in position at present.

Equinox Hall
To NW the passage rises over calcited boulders and is too low 30m forward. In opposite direction crawl upwards into square chamber and wide sandy crawl. Down to the right a gothic crawl ends in a tight fissure and oral connection with Canuck Climb. Crawling left over sand into wide passage to Bridge Chamber. Decorated aven on right just before steep ravine in floor, which may be bypassed via a crawl. Continuation soon leads to a dribbly climb down into large passage. Further climb down boulders into chamber

and the Subway – 122m of small streamway to a choked sink. Below dribbly climb a large dry tunnel is Brew Chamber. Its continuation closes in to a crawl and final wriggle into Equinox Hall – a massive low chamber with a roof aven. Exit crawls soon choke.

Long Gallery and Mortuary Passage

In Brew Chamber a low bedding plane under the W wall leads into a small cavern and an oral connection with Equinox Hall. Near this bedding plane is a manhole and chute into The Long Gallery which has loose passages at two levels at its S end. Various holes in the floor communicate with a streamway which is best reached by sliding behind a boulder at the N end of Long Gallery. Upstream is easy to traverse to tributary straight ahead where cascades rise to base of Archway Aven. Main passage continues as interesting traverse followed by easy walk until mud wall blocks stream. Climb into high level with small pot back into water, which emerges from the Mucky Ducks. A low wet passage develops into a rift and ends after 152m in an aven. The high level at the Mucky Ducks continues as the gothic crawl of Mortuary Passage. Beyond a tortuous crawl is a climb up a boulder choked rift into another large aven.

Maple Leaf Junction and Ramsden's Crawl

Downstream below Long Gallery are shattered chambers and two routes unite in Rat Pit Chamber. Crawl past formations and traverse forward to head of 88ft (27m) Pitch. To the right at same level is an abandoned passage with stal masses until a short crawl expands at Maple Leaf Junction. The obvious way to the right is a crawl up into a wide passage and a high chamber with a roof inlet which chokes under Equinox Hall. The main crawl continues flat out as Ramsden's Crawl through pools of water for 183m to the junction with Far Pinnacle Streamway. Upstream the impressive passage quickly lowers to Border Sump, dived to an impenetrable bedding plane after 49m. Downstream are small drops into a high rift cavern. Pinnacle Pot drops to a static sump but a narrow slot and two 6m climbs emerge at Sausage Junction in Wormway.

Cape Kennedy and Maple Leaf Passages

At Maple Leaf Junction a muddy crawl to the left passes crystal pool (care!) to a roomy passage with choked deep pit to the right into Maple Leaf Aven. Narrow upward slit emerges in Cape Kennedy and Fire Hydrant Chamber with fine formations. Crawl beyond Fire Hydrant terminates in the 9m high Redhead Aven. To the left Maple Leaf Passage opens out above a deep stream trench with a 21m pitch down Maple leaf Aven into Cellar Passage. Inlet on right brings in trickle from Redhead Passage. Up main stream is a fine high level route above the trench for 150m until the large tube silts up. Smaller inlet passage may be followed past climb. At collapse aven climb up 6m into a large tunnel 46m long and choked at each end. The way upstream, or an alternative high level crawl from the tunnel, unite in an aven. Above a 9m waterfall is a narrow streamway to a series of cascades and a 12m aven, which has been climbed to enter a cross rift at the top. This is soon choked in both directions by gritstone boulders. Water enters from sink near Maple Leaf Dig.

The Lower Stream Passages

Belay ladder for 88ft Pitch to bolt in roof. Fine climb landing in pool. Under wall of high chamber low crawl meets Cellar Passage with 21m aven and tortuous inlet upstream. Downstream is easy going for 213m and Wormway enters straight ahead. Combined streams flow right into sump. Up Wormway is the inlet rift at Sausage Junction and beyond the passage first lowers then gains height. Dry oxbow bypasses sump and at the next junction The Grind is to the left. Wormway continues past short choked inlet to the left until it terminates in the towering Echo Aven with the connection to Link Pot at the top.

Up The Grind crawl under barriers on right into Zeppelin Aven. Muddy tube develops into tight meandering rift until Letterbox Junction is reached. Main passage ends in boulder choke 52m forward. Letterbox squeeze into clean tubular crawl past oxbow junction. Left passage soon becomes too low but larger crawl to right. After 61m pools appear and 152m forward exploration is terminated by a sump, dived for 15m in a small tube.

Tackle

Pitch	Ladder	Belay	Lifeline
88ft Pitch	27m	3m	30m
Pinnacle Pot	9m	9m	18m
Maple Leaf Rift	18m	4.5m	24m

THE MAGIC ROUNDABOUT   Grade III-IV
(Stake Pot Inlets)
Explored 1973, CPC.

Proceeding up the master cave from Stake Pot the first inlet on the right leads to Stake Pot Series and the second passes under Bob's Boss (chain in place) to an aven. Two 4.5m climbs separated by a squeeze, bypass the aven, which can be laddered for larger cavers. Ahead is Brass Monkey Passage with 91m of wet going and cascades to Aquarius Pot and a passage on a ledge which is a fossil series dropping back into Brass Monkey Passage. Bolt route of 23m up wet shaft to more walking passage and another aven. 11m above is a roof passage running towards Razor Aven (Stake Pot Series) as the beautiful Pristine Way (care!) which ends in a calcite choke. In the opposite direction the Old Kent Road terminates in abandoned inlets and a complex of climbs leading to a wall slot opening out dramatically over Arson Shaft. Passage at 26m level connects with the Lancaster High Level Route whilst at the bottom is a series of muddy tunnels linking Bob's Boss with the master cave at Stake Pot.

Tackle

Pitch	Ladder	Belay	Lifeline
First Aven	9m	2.4m	15m
Aquarius	24m	2m	30m
Third Aven	12m	3m	18m
Arson Shaft	43m	4.5m	46m

BOLT BELAYS – see Warning, page 13.
Permission – CNCC.

LECK BECK HEAD   NGR SD 660800   Grade I
Alt. 213m

Major resurgence for all the caves between Aygill and Ireby Fell, located in small tributary valley to N of Ease Gill. There are three main entrances:

1.   Main Rising   **Length 150m**   **Depth 24m**
Explored 1992/1993, CDG.

All weather resurgence accessible to divers only. Low bedding soon enlarges and passes several squeezes to reach a complex choked area 95m from the entrance. Unstable route through the choke enters large underwater continuation.

2.   West Flood Rising   **Length 10m**
Extended 1989, ULSA.

Entrance on left at head of dry valley. Short crawl beside silt bank to step up over boulders and complete choke. Dig in floor at entrance revealed rift sump which becomes too narrow.

2.   East Flood Rising   **Length 20m**
Extended 1970, CDG.

At head of dry valley on right. Low cobble strewn entrance chamber is sometimes floored by pool. The only way on is deep pool to left. 10m forward is choke, but narrow underwater rift in right wall can be followed to immature bedding plane at 2.5m depth.
Permission – CNCC.

LINK POT   NGR SD 668803   Grade III-IV
Alt. 276m   **Length 3.2km**
Explored 1978, NPC; extended 1980, CPC.

WARNING – Wallows on route to Pippikin Pot becomes impassable in very wet weather and Silver Streamway fills to the roof. The Serendipity pitches become very serious or impassable under high flow and are always wet. Several areas of the cave contain dangerous loose boulders.

A system of great variety and interest which joins the caves of Leck and Casterton Fells.

Obvious walled entrance on S bank of Ease Gill. Entrance pitch is narrow for first 6m but opens out thereafter. Short descent from foot of pitch enters the splendid 5m square Hylton Hall. Upstream is a low bedding to a complete choke. A rift in the N wall chokes under the gill and one in S wall is blind but with passage at high level through to Pybus Bypass. Downstream in Hylton Hall leads quickly to a large boulder choke which can be ascended for 20m to where all ways are blocked. At base of right wall just prior to choke is a low crawl to an aven. A once draughting tube at floor level is now sumped. A very difficult climb up the aven leads to a series of passages choked under the beck. In wet weather a large stream enters here, flows across Hylton Hall to sink under the south wall, and is next seen at the top of Echo Aven.

To Lancaster Hole

To the left of the choke at the downstream end of Hylton Hall is a descent to a chamber. Left here is flat-out crawl to Pybus Bypass. Right is further descent into solid 'T'-section passage. Either meandering trench or roof bedding lead to a bouldery area. Crawl down to right amongst potentially dangerous blocks (CARE) drops back into solid passage at a junction. Upstream is Echo Crawl – 30m of crawling heading under Ease Gill but becoming too small. Downstream is canyon to sharp left hand bend and the top of Echo Aven in the Stake Pot Series of Lancaster Hole. At the top of the pitch is an inlet and oxbow which rejoins the canyon.

To Pippikin Hole

From Link Pot entrance proceed down Hylton Hall for 6m to a slit in the left wall (Pybus Bypass) which is a wriggle up into a roomy passage. Right under the wall is a flat-out crawl which connects to the end of Hylton Hall and left is a climb into a short passage overlooking the Hylton Hall south wall rift. Straight ahead is the main passage with a fine false floor to reach Squid Junction. Here the right branch gives access to the rest of Link Pot whilst left goes to Pippikin. This is a single passage with various inlets and avens debouching into Pippikin at Dusty Junction.

Night Shift Series

Right at Squid Junction is an easy walk to Black Hole Chamber, and to right here leads up a loose slope which chokes. Ahead, across the chamber and above the obvious blind pit in the floor, is a crawl to a chamber with Snuff Rift in the floor, a stream enters this in wet weather. The main way on is down a rocky slope to the left, a short flat-out section enters a hands and knees crawl. Immediately to left a crawl leads through to Arrow Passage. Ahead leads to a left hand bend with the obscure and choked Missed Passage straight on. The main passage leads to a step across a floor slot (The Canyon) with a bridging rock. On the left just after this the small entrance to Arrow Passage is seen. This begins as a crawl but soon enters a large passage. Left chokes immediately but right leads to a large aven with very loose boulders and a good draught. The inlet which falls from above can be entered from the aven and leads via a beautiful passage to a narrow choked rift with high level boulder chamber. The main passage leads easily to the once finely decorated China Dog Chamber (sadly now very damaged). A traverse over the Canyon starts here and leads after 45m, to a ledge on the right next to an Inlet feeding the Canyon passage below. This is Tigers Inlet and the ledge marks the junction between the Canyon Chamber and the Serendipity Series.

The Canyon Streamway

This is most conveniently described and explored in two sections, an upstream bedding area and a downstream canyon area both of which are best approached from the ledge at Tigers Inlet. From the ledge a very exposed step to the left can be made to enter a boulder strewn area. A careful crossing of the boulders reveals a floor trench. A prominent stalagmite on the edge of the trench signals the easiest descent into the trench. Upstream in the trench is the very dangerous Panic Aven where one rock is holding back a large pile.

It is not advisable to cross under this aven and it is much safer to enter the upstream passage by an alternative route described below. Downstream the Canyon is high and narrow. After Tigers Inlet (falling in from the left) a descent is made and shortly after the stream enters a passage under the right wall which is a narrow struggle until a climb down is reached. The stream can be followed down The Ramp until it sinks under the right wall. This stream is next seen again at the end of Cobble Crawl. A series of dry oxbows, some muddy, also lead to The Ramp.

To enter the upstream passages the floor trench is not descended. The main passage is followed until it chokes after 16m. On the right, under the wall, is a low crawl. This leads under a climb, the passage at the top of which is too small after 15m, to a junction. Right is silted up, left is a descending tube to a 'T'-junction in a streamway. Downstream a flat-out wet crawl leads to the upstream side of Panic Aven. Upstream leads via several wet crawls to a too narrow choked rift just after a climb up.

Serendipity Series

From the ledge an exposed, but chain-assisted, step is made into Tigers Inlet which is a pleasant walk in a classic trench passage to a junction. Right soon lowers to a crawl to an ascending boulder pile. A passage on the right here is an outlet which can be followed for 30m until it becomes too low just after a pool. Up the boulders is Handpump Hall, a section of large passage choked at both ends. Both ends also have avens which are impassable although the one at the south end carries a draught. At the north end a low slot on the left leads back to Tigers Inlet near the junction and a wet crawl leads to Cairn Junction. Continuing left at the junction in main passage the way rises and becomes a 1m high bedding with an obvious passage off to the right. Straight ahead at this point leads through beddings to the large and dangerous Whisper Aven which contains some very large suspended blocks (care!). A descending tube in the right corner soon chokes. Just before the aven is reached a series of inlet passages on the right soon become too small.

Taking the passage to the right a crawl over fill and a scramble down leads to the impressive crossroads of Cairn Junction with four passages leading off. The left-most is a flat crawl which soon chokes while the right-most, hidden under the wall a little way back from the cairn, leads to Handpump Hall (see above). The second left passage is Molten Mars Bar Crawl, a generally flat-out struggle to an enlargement and the sound of falling water at Serendipity, a magnificent sight. Halfway through this passage is an aven which leads up to a higher bedding level which chokes in both directions. The easiest way to Serendipity is via the third left passage which passes Death Row, a fine group of stalagmites. The crawl ahead becomes too low (water tested from Expulsion Series) and the way on is through a squeeze on the left. More crawling leads to a larger continuation and a junction with Molten Mars Bar Crawl near Serendipity.

A traverse on the right of the floor slot gains the upstream passage, a fine walk for 100m until it lowers and divides in a region of wet crawls and boulder chokes. Two passages branch from this stream passage, both on the left. The most upstream, close to the lowering, is an ascending tube blocked by a large boulder. The other is Matchbox Aven, 30m upstream of Serendipity leading to the Lone Ranger Series.

The Lone Ranger Series

A 5m climb reaches a tight awkward crawl which pops out at a junction with a tubular passage. Right passes under two avens, both impassable at the top, until the passage becomes silted up. The small stream has been tested to Death Row (see above). Right at this point a dug out squeeze leads to an area of low crawls and a climb down into a very muddy and impassable bedding (Expulsion Passage). Left at the intial junction is a muddy crawl to Tontos Aven (impassable at top). Further crawling and two more avens (both impassable at top) leads to an area of flood deposited mud. Squeezes here pop out in the side of Silver Stream. Left is a dangerously loose aven. Right (upstream) is a bouldery bedding crawl to Consortium Cavern in Howgill Sink. Downstream leads to a sump (dived for 5m and too small) and Solitude Aven with a short crawl beyond it to a mud choke.

The Pitches and Easy Street

The floor trench at Serendipity can be descended as a 5m pitch from a thread at floor level or by a climb reached by going around the edge of the slot and across the stream to the left side. Both routes gain a trench and a bolt belay at the head of a wet 20m pitch. A third pitch of 8m drops into the beginning of Easy Street. This is a superb walking passage with some boulder falls and some fine decorations. Eventually the roof lowers and the stream sumps. This sump is 120m with several airbells to enter the final sump chamber of Pippikin Hole.

There are three inlets to Easy Street, all on the right. The first is just at the bottom of the pitches and is 10m to where it becomes too tight. The second (Sardine Inlet) is 90m down Easy Street. The third, and most extensive, is Cobble Crawl. Entered as a large tunnel it soon degenerates into a seemingly endless 210m flat-out crawl. Eventually a stream (tested from The Ramp) crosses at right angles from right to left. Both the stream outlet and the main crawl continuation become too low.

Tackle

Pitch	Ladder	Belay	Lifeline
Entrance	15m	0.6m	24m
Echo Aven	26m	3m	30m
Serendipity 1	6m	0.6m	9m
Serendipity 2	25m	Spreader	30m
Serendipity 3	8m	5m	12m

BOLT BELAYS – see Warning, page 13.

Permission – CNCC.

LOWER KIRK CAVES   NGR SD 660799   Grade I-II
Alt. 232m

Eleven small caves all situated by the Lower Ease Gill Kirk, with Nos.1-7 being in the left bank true and described going upstream whilst 8-11 are in opposite bank, and described going downstream.

1. Length 8m

30m before obvious cave in rocky banking below grass slope. Small passage giving awkward sideways crawling to where calcited false floor blocks the way.

2. Length 5m

In main rocky cove low down. A short, choked muddy crawl.

3. Length 8m

Larger entrance close to No.2 and above it. An ascending tube ends at a calcited choke.

4. Length 12m

5m beyond No.3 and low down. Muddy hands and knees crawl to step up and a 'T'-junction. Both ways quickly close down.

5. Length 12m

Reached by climb up, is a straight phreatic passage. The walls are covered in a powdery stalagmite deposit, and the way on is blocked by a calcited choke.

6. Length 5m

Directly above No.5, it requires a 5m ladder and 8m lifeline to descend from top of scar, belayed to a tree. A large phreatic rift passage soon ends at a choke of sand and mud fill.

7. Length 8m

Obvious opening in left bank at foot of waterfall leads into a chamber. To the right pinches out, but to the left an easy climb up a series of steps leads to another entrance above the fall.

8. Length 5m

Below falls, in right bank. Rift entrance quickly closes to where way on is choked with silt.

9. Length 12m

Large open rift can be followed to where it has been dug in a small tube.

10. Length 8m

Directly above No.9 and 10m above ground level. Can only be entered by a pendulum on ladder or rope into the awkward shaped entrance. A slippery phreatic tube ascends to a choke.

11. Length 18m

In opposite wall of cleft to No.1, and reached by awkward climb up dangerous peeling blocks. Stooping size passage leads to junction after 12m. Left leads to an over tight inclined bedding beyond an initial squeeze, whilst right and low down is a squeeze into a small chamber. Several small openings lead off, but all are impossibly tight.

Permission – CNCC.

MAPLE LEAF DIG   NGR SD 669806   Grade I
Alt. 312m   Depth 9m
Excavated 1973-75, EPC.

In large shakehole 40m S of stream sink close to wall. Timbered shaft entered small draughting chamber which has now collapsed.

Permission – CNCC.

MERLIN HOLE   NGR SD 668802   Grade II
Alt. 297m   Depth 11m

In large gully up on left bank of Ease Gill downstream of Hairy Fissure. Narrow rift on left to pitch into a small chamber and pool.

Tackle – 9m ladder; 2m belay; 15m lifeline.

Permission – CNCC.

MISTRAL HOLE   NGR SD 667803   Grade III
Alt. 267m   Length 18m   Depth 11m
Explored 1974, ULSA.

Prominent covered pit under cliff set back from Ease Gill. May be climbed with care to a hole into a cross passage. Right is choked, but left was a tortuous passage now much enlarged, and emerges above the 3.7m climb beyond the Hobbit in Pippikin Pot.

Permission – CNCC.

NEW CAVE   NGR SD 676806   Grade II
Alt. 319m   **Length** – included in Ease Gill Caverns total.
Explored 1972, RRCPC.

WARNING – Liable to severe flooding in wet weather.

Low bedding entrance in right bank immediately downstream of Slit Sinks, and some 61m down-valley from the obvious entrance to The Borehole in the left bank. A low crawl for 9m reaches the head of a short pitch, below which a tight squeeze leads to a short length of canal passage and connection via choke and squeeze to inlet in Wretched Rabbit Passage. From the head of the pitch a climb up leads into a dry, meandering canyon passage to top of another short pitch. At the foot is a small chamber with two small inlet passages entering, and the outlet passage can be followed in a twisting fissure passage until choked with sand. This possibly connects with the upper end of Wretched Rabbit Passage.

Tackle

Pitch	Ladder	Belay	Lifeline
Either Shaft	6m	3m	9m

Permission – CNCC.

NEW SLIT SINKS   NGR SD 676806   Grade III
Alt. 319m   **Length 30m**

Explored 1975, RRCPC.

WARNING – Entrance passage floods completely almost instantly!

Slab covered entrance in stream bed near top end of small scar, and only 1.5m upstream from Slit Sinks entrance. Tight, awkward slot, best entered feet first is followed by low passage to a 2.4m climb down to a small chamber. Beyond, passage narrows to awkward squeeze at head of a 4.5m pitch; dropping into a large canyon passage. Walking soon gives way to contorting in a narrow trench, which ends at a junction with the main passage in The Borehole not far upstream from the 15m pitch.

Tackle – 8m ladder; 3m belay; 9m lifeline.

Permission – CNCC.

NIPPIKIN POT   NGR SD 667801   Grade III
Alt. 323m   **Depth 55m**

Explored 1929, GC.

Large open shaft 137m N of boundary wall running down fell from Leck Fell House, and at end of shallow valley. The open shaft is 18m deep, and is completely choked. However, from a shelf situated 3m below the fence at the SE side of the pot a tight opening gives onto a 21m pitch which quickly bells out into a large shaft. At the foot a slope to the SW runs back up to the underside of the choke in the open pot, whilst to one side a climb up into a large washed out shale bed leads to a crawl to a junction with a small inlet passage entering on the right. By dropping down into the stream channel it can be followed down to a boulder bridge, and the top of the second pitch of 14m.

The foot of the pitch is a small chamber with a very restricted opening at the far side leading directly to the third pitch of 10m. Returning through this is awkward, and at times is very wet. The chamber at the foot is about 5m long and 2m wide, the outlet being a narrow fissure some 125mm wide. By traversing at the top of the third pitch ladder it is possible to enter a cross rift, and a 3m climb up and short crawl reaches the head of 11m rift pitch into the continuation of the narrow fissure. There is no passable way on from the foot.

Tackle

Pitch	Ladder	Belay	Lifeline
Open Pot	11m	3m	15m
1st	21m	3m	27m
2nd	15m	Long sling	21m
3rd	11m	2m	15m

Permission – CNCC.

OLD HOLBORN CAVE   NGR SD 667799   Grade I
Alt. 314m   **Length 10m**   **Depth 4m**

Explored 1993, RRCPC.

Located just upstream and on the opposite bank to Swindon Hole. A drop

down into a short section of rift leads to a calcite choke and a low wet bedding leading off at the base.
Permission – CNCC.

OWL HOLE NGR SD 671804 Grade II
Alt. 297m **Length 9m** **Depth 8m**

Entrance 137m downstream of Howgill Sink in boulders at foot of bank 14m from beck. Pitch in rift to short tight crawl into small chamber with boulder floor.

Tackle – 6m ladder; 1.5m belay; 9m lifeline.
Permission – CNCC.

OXFORD CAVES NGR SD 675805 Grade II
Alt. 335m

Series of caves associated with the tributary gill opposite Oxford Pot.

1. Length 12m

Resurgence cave where rapids rise to a low sharp crawl.

2. Length 46m

Below prominent scar in bedded limestone. Wriggle into wider passage where stream sinks in floor. Upstream is a pleasant crawl to a series of impassable or choked inlets beneath the surface stream bed.

3. Length 21m Depth 6m

Covered entrance manhole is up the gill on the right. Climb down and 'T' section passage lead to a chamber and further twisting passage which develops into a tortuous traverse.
Permission – CNCC.

OXFORD POT NGR SD 675805 Grade II
Alt. 314m **Length** included in Ease Gill Caverns total.
Explored 1947, BSA.

On right bank of Ease Gill only a few metres down-valley from the lidded entrance to County Pot, beneath large boulder. A short drop leads directly onto a 15m pitch, below which a low wet crawl leads into a large passage descending small cascades to a climbable 3m pitch. At the foot is a junction with a small inlet, and the continuing passage is the tortuous, twisting 'Snake'. Sideways shuffling and occasional crawling eventually leads to an enlargement and a junction with a large passage entering on the left. This point is Confusion Corner of the near series of the Ease Gill Caverns.

At present the top of the entrance pitch is blocked by collapse of the unstable boulders, although it is possible to enter the shaft part way down via a tight passage a few metres from the bottom of the entrance climb to County Pot.

Tackle – 18m ladder; 3m belay; 21m lifeline.
Permission – CNCC.

PEGLEG POT

NGR SD 663802   **Grade III**

(Lower Ease Gill Pot)
Alt. 259m   **Length 950m**   **Depth 43m**
Explored 1958, NPC; extended 1986, NCC.

WARNING – The entrance and lower passages are very flood liable.

The pot is located within a massive rampart of boulders and scaffolding 91m upstream of Upper Ease Gill Kirk. Drop through boulders into a clean passage and drainpipe crawl to a roomy tube choked at both ends. The outlet, through a pool, leads to a fine 4.5m climb into the second chamber and exit around an undercut block into a fine passage under two avens with short inlet crawls. Down through pools to 21m pitch into a high but narrow rift. Stream flows over shingle into a deep pool with diminishing fissure air-space. Upstream a succession of dry climbs rejoins the water which emerges from a canal.

A traverse at the top of the 21m pitch enters a roof passage to a 7m pitch. Above this on the right is a small trench to an alternative 24m pitch into the downstream rift and a high level passage which soon chokes. A climb down below the 7m pitch is difficult to reverse and lands in a blind muddy chamber. Above the climb a series of crawls unite and suddenly emerge in Surprise Hall, a flat-roofed cavern 24m by 18m and 9m high. At far side of the hall the floor shelves into a massive trench but a choked pool soon terminates the right branch. A muddy passage in the roof of Surprise Hall has floor slots communicating with the right branch and ends in two choked inlets.

The left branch of the trench continues above a great slab as the impressive Pennine Way to a side passage up on the left and a 4m pitch into a gravel-floored chamber. The Pennine Way lowers to a boulder choke and a low bedding plane to the right to a climb down a chimney with a chute into a tiny chamber.

A small exit at floor level is the Mud Tube Crawl towards the enticing sound of running water. Straight ahead a mud slope plunges into a static sump with a greasy, mud-choked inlet but the Reverse Streamway is gained by turning right. The water falls into a sump and upstream soon enlarges to walking size. Above the first cascades is a side passage on the left but it chokes with mud and ancient calcite after 9m. A wide pool marks the start of the second series of cascades up to a short crawl out into the large Mystery Passage, which lowers to a flat crawl just before a high chamber choked by calcite and boulders. The only way forward is a meandering canyon to a junction. To the left at roof level is a passage which eventually splits and becomes tight. Right is a boulder choke which has been forced into a walking passage to a junction. To the right the way finally degenerates to a choke of fill and left (downstream) leads to a high chamber, and upper route connecting back to right passage.

Tackle

Pitch	Ladder	Belay	Lifeline
Rift	21m	3m	30m
22ft	8m	1m	12m
13ft	4.5m	6m	12m

BOLT BELAYS – see Warning, page 13.

Permission – CNCC.

PETERSON POT

NGR SD 667799   **Grade IV**

Alt. 332m   **Length 116m**   **Depth 40m**

Explored 1929, GC; extended 1969, HWCPC.

WARNING – Very tortuous in parts. Think of the return journey.

Entrance is 30m S of Smokey Hole. Scramble down to the first pitch onto a scree slope and the second pitch with a choked crawl in the floor. On right is a small tube in a shale bed (Roly Poly Passage). This awkward crawl continues to a narrows and sharp bends below an aven to an inlet. Upstream is another aven but downstream at floor level becomes too tight. A roof crawl continues to a narrow rift and sudden exit above a 2m climb. The third, fourth and fifth pitches follow in rapid succession and the stream runs into an impenetrable crack.

Tackle

Pitch	Ladder	Belay	Lifeline
1st	4.5m	2m	12m
2nd	4.5m	1.2m	12m
3rd	9m	2m	18m
4th	4.5m	3m	18m
5th	6m	–	–

Permission – CNCC.

PICKWICK POT

NGR SD 678808   **Grade I**

Alt. 341m   **Length 11m**   **Depth 6m**

Explored 1956, PPSG.

About 30m SW of Boundary Pot eyehole. Bouldery rift covered by rusty wire. Climb down sharp rock into chamber and narrow passage to an inlet waterfall. Downstream a low passage chokes beneath the entrance chamber. Permission – CNCC.

PIPPIKIN POT

NGR SD 667800   **Grade IV-V**

Alt. 326m   **Length 7km**   **Depth 142m**

WARNING – Entrance series is narrow and strenuous. Keep the return journey in mind.

A superb complex system, linked with Lancaster Hole. Walk from Bull Pot Farm, or call at Leck Fell House, and follow wall down into allotment above Ease Gill. Pippikin is found by locating a shallow valley carrying the stream which enters the cave.

Entrance Series

Dry opening at sink drops quickly to first pitch into roomy chamber. Exit is low bedding plane crawl to the top of Cellar Pot, a broken ladder climb succeeded by a 2.1m drop into the stream of Cellar Passage. The water sinks into a joint and low bedding plane but upstream is the East Chamber 18m long, 2.4m wide and 12m high with a complex of active and abandoned inlets. Traverse across Cellar Pot (care!) to a shelf and short constricted tube to an awkward 2.1m drop. A window drops into a rift with two constrictions before a 4.5m pitch and below is a cross rift trending towards E Chamber. Beyond a further constriction is the shale bed above the 3rd pitch. A passage continues in the shale bed to a small blind rift and tight passage. Belay 3rd pitch to bolt and wriggle forward from base of ladder to an interesting 5.4m rift climb where a rope is useful. Immediately following is the 4th pitch and the junction with the streamway. The 5th pitch is short and damp leading to a stooping passage and an awkward 1.5m climb into a pool – great fun on the return! All but midgets are advised to traverse the next 46m until a high level passage enters a high chamber with formations. A scramble over and under calcited blocks emerges above the 6th pitch back into the stream through the roof of a chamber. A boulder strewn passage is an oxbow and a similar feature downstream intersects the Ratbag Inlet.

Now the streamway is an easy walk with occasional formations and odd interesting roof passages – one providing a link with Leck Fell Lane. Eventually the water runs into a boulder choke beneath the Hall of the Ten.

Tackle

Pitch	Ladder	Belay	Lifeline
1st	6m	3.7m	18m
2nd	5m	0.6m	9m
3rd	15m	Spreader	24m
Rope	–	–	9m
4th	8m	0.6m	12m
5th	3m	0.6m	6m
6th	4.5m	4.5m	12m
Cellar	12m	1.2m	21m

Ratbag Series

Ratbag Inlet provides easy going at first. Features of interest are an aven on the right, a short inlet to another aven on the left and fissures choked by cobbles again on the left. The main passage lowers slightly at the next junction, the most uninviting passage being straight ahead. This is Surveyors Dog Inlet which soon subdivides. The right branch quickly closes in but the left provides 152m of low crawl which has not been forced to any conclusion.

The Ratbag Inlet continues in easy style past fine formations (care!) to a squeeze over a huge stal blockage. Traversing and walking forward to a deep pool and 1.5m climb into the low crawl to Golden Wonder Aven. Scaling or prussiking tackle needed for 8m ascent into short passage emerging at base of Andromeda Aven – scaled to an impassable passage.

Hall of the Ten – Gour Hall

Crawl forward and upward in Pippikin streamway choke to enter the Hall of the Ten – a massive passage 18m high and wide. Ascend the S slope to silt balcony and junction of tunnels. The left route descends into the Hall of the Mountain King (floor connection with Leck Fell Lane) where Wellington Traverse gains the high level passages of Gothic Series and Hall of the Damned with its remnant fill and avens; one in the SE corner has been bolted for 27m to a very low passage, then around a buttress to an unstable boulder slope and an 18m aven which is choked with gritstone boulders less than 3m from the surface.

From the Hall of the Damned, to the right beneath an inlet the tunnel opens out into a wide chamber with fine stalagmites. At the far end is a silted link with Gothic Series and a crawl above a complex pot in the floor leads to a slot down to a small chamber 4m below; a sharp bend enters a narrow rift streamway with a constriction which has not been passed.

The main route continues wide and low to the vastness of Cross Hall where aven inlets sink into a mass of boulders. A bolting route only leads to a small roof chamber. A hole down in the bottom NE corner of the hall leads through a squeeze to a 7m pitch followed by a 3m climb, then an unstable boulder slope and 4m pitch into a small chamber. A waterfall can be heard and a dig through loose blocks descends for a further 8m. This whole section from the hall is extremely unstable.

The tunnel beyond Cross Hall soon breaks out into a rift which ascends into Gour Hall – a massive chamber floored by a dome of fine gour pools (care!). This floor descends rapidly into a small antechamber and a stal choke. A dig at the end of Gour Hall is 4.5m long and is still being excavated.

Lower Streamway

Crawl forward in the Pippikin streamway choke under the Hall of the Ten into the continuation of the stream passage. A fine tunnel eventually lowers to a wet section before the water sinks and a dry 7th pitch and 4.5m climb drop into Waterfall Chamber. The waterfall can be climbed via two pitches to an impassable bedding close to the sink.

In Waterfall Chamber a low, wet inlet on the left ends after 91m at the first of the sumps leading to Easy Street in Link Pot. Downstream quickly sumps on right, but ahead a continuation of the rift leads to a large aven. From ledge on left before aven is 29m aid climb, followed by further 4m ascent to passage crossing the head of the large aven by a precarious traverse. Beyond becomes too tight, but a branch to the right ends at a 9m aven with passage visible at the top.

The downstream sump is a shallow dive of 224m to Pooh's Revenge. This starts as a large passage, but after 80m the water disappears down a very aqueous rift and the way on is a short climb up into a stooping passage. Stepping over two holes in the floor a third drop returns to the stream via a couple of 3m climbs (handline useful). The continuing passage soon ends at a large pool and sump. This descends in a rift to 20m depth and 40m forward is the junction with the downstream sump of Gavel Pot.

Tackle

Pitch	Ladder	Belay	Lifeline
7th	12m	3m	30m

Dusty Junction – Red Wall Chamber

Take N slope out of Hall of the Ten and proceed along sandy tunnels to Dusty Junction where three ways diverge. Left is the way to the Hobbit, straight ahead is a wide bedding cave connecting with Link Pot. Right descends into a crater chamber.

Across the crater is a wide passage and climb over blocks to the top of Red Wall Chamber. From here a scramble up and 'U' section crawl leads into White Wall Chamber.

Back at the crater Dickeries Inlet is reached by descending a hole next to the obvious pit. Downstream the passage drops to a choke, bypassed by a hole in the roof. The water runs into a dismal canal with diminishing air-space. Upstream easy going lowers to a crawl and a junction where the arched passage straight ahead soon sumps. The inlet crawl continues past a high joint to Dropout Aven where a climb reveals 18m of passage to a choke. Below, the crawl has been forced another 61m to a tight sump.

Intercounty Passage starts in the roof of the Pippikin streamway just before the boulder choke. The crawl drops into a streamway which may be followed down to the choke under the Hall of the Ten. Good going upstream to tributary terminating in an aven and 61m beyond this is another aven through a window on the left. Now the way forward is a crawl to a high fissure and a further crawl to the bottom of Red Wall Chamber. Those wishing to complete the round must continue the crawl to an oxbow and aven rising into White Wall Chamber. A final waterlogged tube emerges between the first two inlets in Ratbag.

The Hobbit

The left passage at Dusty Junction drops into a muddy crawl finally relenting at an aven. 6m above at this point is Dinnertime Series, 152m of high level passages and chambers which are close to The Crumbles in Lower Ease Gill.

Ascending a slope in the next chamber N leads to the Hobbit – a flat roofed cavern. A crawl at the back breaks out into a shattered rift where the connection with Mistral Hole enters. A 3.7m drop is the way into 61m of passage and low crawls to a sump. To right is route up through unstable choke and down into 30m of large passage (The Frontier) to a choke. Back in the lowest tunnel a crawl over eroded calcite passes through a chamber to a three way junction. To the right a trickle emerges from an aven with a complex of passages in the roof. This trickle may be followed into a muddy crawl which becomes impassable beyond a chamber. The way forward is back to the left into Canyon Streamway which is 122m of walking to a sump. 15m before the sump is a crawl over blocks into an aven chamber succeeded by a larger passage to further avens until it intersects the Far Streamway rising from a wet bedding.

The Streamway is large and blockstrewn for 122m; the water sinks amongst boulders. Above the final choke is a climb into a roof chamber, whilst a passage to the left ends in a stal choke. From the latter passage a crawl ends in a series of rift climbs.

Leck Fell Lane and Cigalère

Climb into roof 30m before Pippikin streamway choke and crawl along muddy passage to emerge in roof of the canyon passage of Leck Fell Lane. Upstream is an abrupt choke but a climb on the right leads to a bedding plane crawl, aven and fine rift passage of Misty Mountain Series. 91m before the termination of the passage a series of fine climbs enters avens floored by flowstone.

At the old end of the Series a 3m climb on the right is followed by a tight squeeze into the Bastard Crawl. After several awkward bends the crawl breaks out at Birthday Aven which has been scaled for 5m to low wet progress in the Big Mean Porridge Machine. The passage enlarges into a rift and a climb up leads through boulders and another squeeze and a further crawl which emerges in Cigalère well above the Grand Cascade on a ledge half way up a waterfall.

Down Leck Fell Lane the Cigalère enters as a noisy cascade and flows into a choke beneath a way upwards into the impressive gloom of the Hall of the Mountain King. The Cigalère begins as a series of refreshing cascades and potholes to rapids and a rough crawl. Suddenly the floor drops into a deep canal, beyond which lies the atmospheric Grand Cascade. The 18m waterfall is best scaled as two sections (pole required). The succeeding passage is again well supplied with rushing water. To the left 152m of well decorated dry passage with a loose traverse ends in a flowstone blockage. Straight ahead is a superb little climb into a gothic streamway for 183m to a chamber and further waterfalls. At a fine rift chamber the stream splits; part falling from a low bedding plane high up and the rest spilling out from a shelf. The latter may be followed, through a decorated chamber and cascades, into a rocky crawl. After a long oxbow the streamway gradually diminishes in size as it splits into smaller passages.

BOLT BELAYS – see Warning, page 13.

Permission – CNCC.

POOL SINK   NGR SD 677807   Grade III
Alt. 323m   **Length** included in Ease Gill Caverns total.
Explored 1956, PPSG.

An entertaining direct route into the far reaches of Ease Gill Caverns. Entrance is a small opening in right bank of gill on rock shelf beside deep pool, 41m upstream from The Borehole entrance in opposite bank. A tight crawl leads round two acute bends to where the passage enlarges, and the head of the first pitch is reached. From foot a further short drop leads into a stream passage flowing from right to left. Upstream is an easy walk to a junction, the way to the right continuing as a high rift passage to terminate shortly in a choke, whilst the other way is a high meandering canyon passage which eventually emerges in Magpie Grotto. A short side passage here ends in a waterfall.

Downstream from the foot of the pitch continues in a large passage, Upper 'T' Piece Passage, to the 2nd pitch which can be by-passed by climbing into oxbow and a careful descent to the stream below pitch. The next pitch is only a short distance on downstream, and usually very wet. The 4th pitch follows almost immediately with a useful flake belay to keep ladder out of line of water. A high level traverse, very exposed in places leads to a climb down to the stream again thus by-passing the pitch, but this is best avoided. At the bottom a steeply descending streamway with numerous cascades leads to Jacob's Ladder, a spiral climb down which requires care, and after a further 2.4m cascade the passage levels out into Lower 'T' Piece Passage.

Easy walking, with occasional scrambling over boulders reaches a junction with a large passage, Green and Smelly Passage in a rather complex area. Turning left here soon brings one to a choke, with the crawl connection to the

Borehole dropping down and under the left wall, whilst just before this point is reached a passage leads off to the right into the start of Spiral Staircase Passage, a long narrow streamway which eventually ends in a choke. Downstream from the junction with Green and Smelly Passage continues in a most impressive passage with a large upper level, and a deep stream canyon. Finally, the passage enlarges and the stream leaves via a passage on the left to enter the Ease Gill main drain a short distance downstream from Holbeck Junction, whilst a dry abandoned level continues to a further junction. The narrow passage off to the left can be followed to emerge at the head of a climb down into the impressive high level Straw Chamber, and the main route continues to reach Holbeck Junction after a few metres.

Tackle

Pitch	Ladder	Belay	Lifeline
1st	17m	6m	23m
2nd	8m	3m	12m
3rd	6m	Sling	9m
4th	9m	Sling	15m

The by-pass routes to the 2nd and 4th pitches are both best tackled with a lifeline.

BOLT BELAYS – see Warning, page 13.

Permission – CNCC.

ROSY SINK   NGR SD 675805   Grade II
(Slaughterhouse Drain)
Alt. 314m   **Length 46m**
Explored 1951, NPC & RRCPC.

A low bedding entrance at foot of scar on right bank of gill a few metres downstream from County Pot. Crawl gradually enlarges where trench cuts down in floor, and meandering passage can be followed to a 6m pitch, or awkward climb down just upstream of short pitch in County Pot. The entrance is blocked at present by rocks and flood debris.

Tackle – 6m ladder; 3m belay; 12m lifeline.

Permission – CNCC.

ROWAN TREE RIFT   NGR SD 678807   Grade II
Alt. 333m   **Length 17m**
Explored 1956, PPSG.

Prominent rift in scar by Ease Gill Beck. Letterbox entry shaft to tight section and easy going to the Keyhole and wide passage. After a few metres debris reaches nearly to roof directly over boulder choke in Upper 'T' Piece Passage of Pool Sink. Blocked at present.

Permission – CNCC.

SECOND BEST HOLE   NGR SD 676806   Grade II
Alt. 332m   Length 9m

Small shallow cave above tributary waterfall just upstream of Best's Hole.
Enter from above into passage which quickly lowers to an impassable crawl.
Permission – CNCC.

SHEEPFOLD CAVE   NGR SD 675806   Grade II
(Ice Palace)
Alt. 328m   Length 40m

At back of prominent sheepfold upstream of Swindon Hole. Dry crawl to
stream in a 1.2m high passage and a junction. Right is sideways going for 18m
to a shingle choke. To the left the main inlet is an awkward struggle to a small
waterfall where it is possible to emerge beneath a huge boulder at the sink.
Permission – CNCC.

SHORTY HOLE   NGR SD 663807   Grade II
Alt. 291m   Length 20m   Depth 15m
Explored 1993, RRCPC.

Entrance is in enlarged gryke in the valley 50m S of Lancaster Hole. A tight
crawl leads to an awkward downward squeeze, immediately followed by a 6m
climb. A section of narrow rift follows to a squeeze in the floor which opens
out onto a 6m climb leading to a terminal rift.
Permission – CNCC.

SLIT SINKS   NGR SD 676806   Grade III
Alt. 319m   Length 183m
Explored 1951, NPC and RRCPC.

**WARNING – Extremely dangerous in wet weather as the beck totally floods
the entrance.**

Entrances are in right bank 46m downstream of The Borehole. Low crawl
to small drop into the start of a narrow canyon. Tight sideways shuffle to a
climbable 3.7m pitch and two ways forward. At foot of climb the trench leads
to another climb and a 9m pitch into the same chamber as the Borehole pitch.
Below the 3.7m climb a crawl to the right meets a separate streamway
which can be followed up to a tight section near the Borehole sink. Downstream is another pitch onto a large ledge overlooking the Borehole chamber
once more.

Tackle

Pitch	Ladder	Belay	Lifeline
1st	12m	15m	15m
Right Hand Route			
1st	17m	8m	21m
2nd	6m	4m	9m

Permission – CNCC.

SMOKEY HOLE   NGR SD 667799   Grade III
Alt. 332m   **Length 35m**   Depth 20m

Explored 1950, RRCPC; extended 1983, EPC.

Entrance is deep shakehole in wall kink near Peterson Pot. Small pitch leads to way into first chamber, with crawl leading on to second chamber. An upper level route (6m scale, and 6m pitch) also enters second chamber. Way on is 3m climb down rift in floor to head of 2nd pitch. This is very tight at top, but enlarges lower down, to land on boulder floor where stream sinks.

A step up and short rift passage leads to a 2m drop into a small aven chamber with an impassable floor rift as the only outlet. Just before the 2m drop a tight descent down a rift in the right wall is followed by a very tight crawl round a left bend to meet the same impassable rift.

Tackle

Pitch	Ladder	Belay	Lifeline
Entrance	5m	4m	8m
2nd	4m	4m	8m

Permission – CNCC.

SWINDON HOLE   NGR SD 675805   Grade I
Alt. 320m   **Length 107m**

Approximately midway between Corner Sink and County Pot is fissure entrance in right bank. A few metres of passage leads to step down into a bedding passage, and crawl through a pool. At far end of this a far larger passage is entered with a short inlet running off to the right. On downstream gradually enlarges, with a small chamber on the left, until eventually a complete choke is met. This point is very close to Upper Trident Series of Ease Gill Caverns. An inlet on the right near the end leads through a tight, flat-out crawl to connect with Corner Sink.

Permission – CNCC.

SYLVESTER POT   NGR SD 673806   Grade III
Alt. 330m   **Length** included in Ease Gill Caverns total.

Explored 1989, RRCPC.

WARNING – Entrance is flood prone. Loose boulders are a major hazard in several parts of the cave.

The entrance to Sylvester Pot is located in the bed of Houe Gill about 100m above its confluence with Ease Gill Beck and just below the first waterfall. An obvious dam has been built around the entrance but this should be checked before entering.

The entrance crawl soon becomes low at a squeeze which can be blocked by shingle. Beyond the squeeze the passage opens up to a small chamber. Right leads back to the entrance but straight on through boulders leads to a crawl to a 7m blind pot with a vocal connection to the First Pitch. To the right above the pot is a sandy tunnel which breaks out over the First Pitch (20m). The streamway above the pitch can be followed upstream for a few metres to a boulder choke which is immediately below the entrance. Downstream two short cascades are descended to the head of the pitch. Bolts are in place and the shaft is broken 15m down by a large ledge. At the bottom of the pitch is a boulder strewn chamber with several ways on.

Scrambling over the boulders leads to a loose breakdown chamber, while climbing down through the boulders leads to a 3m climb and another very unstable breakdown chamber. The main way on is along a low crawl immediately at the base of the First Pitch. A junction is soon reached. To the left is the Second Pitch (7m) which can be descended via two alternative holes to the Main Chamber. Back at the junction the right hand crawl leads to a wide complex bedding, Route 880.

Main Chamber

In the Main Chamber are three ways on. Descending the boulders in the floor of the chamber leads to the free-climbable Third Pitch (4m) and down through boulders to a small streamway, Upper Clough's Passage in Ease Gill Caverns. The water can be followed upstream for 40m to avens below the Main Chamber and downstream to two climbs down into Clough's Passage and the way on to Dismal Junction. Above Upper Clough's Passage and before the two climbs down is a low crawl leading to a series of rifts and sandy tunnels where the stream below can be heard. This is San Andreas Fault Passage.

Back in the Main Chamber the other two ways on are down the obvious rift at the other end of the chamber. This leads below the breakdown chambers at the base of the First Pitch and is liberally endowed with loose boulders. Just after entering the rift a loose climb up on the left leads through to the connection to Delicate Sound of Thunder and Luff's Passage (see County Pot description).

Route 880

Route 880 is a wide low bedding with several holes in the floor. It is easy to become disorientated and end up going round in circles. After about 10m a junction is reached; to the left is an obscure low crawl over a hole (4m Pitch) with a chamber below through to a large sand filled chamber, Newton's Wonder, with a fine set of gour pools and associated stalactites. The avens leading out of Newton's Wonder close down so do not climb the formations! A stream enters from the roof and is lost in the boulders in the floor. It is assumed to be the stream seen in Luff's Passage.

Back in Route 880 the main way on leads past three holes in the floor all of which have been descended to unstable boulder chambers. The main bedding narrows and becomes a flat out crawl to a narrow pitch head. Just before this climbing down the last hole breaks out into a large chamber with a rock bridge, Hanging Death Hall. At the far end of this are several sand choked crawls which are very close to Mancunian Way in Ease Gill Caverns and an aven dropping down from the narrow pitch head mentioned above. In the floor of this chamber the stream in Upper Clough's Passage, can be heard below.

Tackle

Pitch	Ladder	Belay	Lifeline
1st	20m	Bolt	50m
2nd	8m	2m	15m
3rd	free-climbable but short ladder useful		

All the holes in Route 880 can be descended with a 7m ladder and a 2m belay.

BOLT BELAYS – see Warning, page 13.

Permission – CNCC.

TOP SINK   **NGR SD 680811**   **Grade IV**
Alt. 349m   Length included in the Ease Gill Caverns total.
Explored 1952, NPC.

The furthest upstream entrance to the Ease Gill Caverns, situated in the right bank of the gill 67m up-valley from the sheepfold. A climb down leads into a tight passage which quickly reaches a junction with a short inlet on the left. From here the floor starts to cut down in a typical meandering canyon passage to the head of Walrus Pot. At the foot the passage doubles back underneath itself and continues as an awkward series of bends, hence the name 'πr^2' Passage. The passage finally starts to enlarge, and Penknife Pitch of 4.5m is reached, at the bottom of which is a junction with Wisdom Tooth Passage entering from the left. This can be followed via a short climb up into a high, winding streamway which eventually chokes.

At the larger inlet on the left a chimney on the right hand side can be climbed to an exposed step over the top of the waterfall. After a short distance holes in the roof of the stream passage lead up into Surprise Passage which continues upstream for about 50m to a choke. Back to the right a flat-out crawl continues above the holes in the floor. This is the far end of Dire Straits which connects via Danish Passage to the downstream end of Bradshaw's Passage (see below).

The combined waters at the foot of Penknife Pitch flow into the long, winding, hands and knees crawl of Bradshaw's Passage which eventually emerges at the complex Limerick Junction; a series of abandoned oxbows at various levels. If the upper level is followed for the last stretch of Bradshaw's Passage two passages lead off to the left and both soon join at the start of the CRG Extension, an old dry passage. Two climbs up lead into a high passage which requires traversing in places to a junction, with a climb down into a passage on the right. The other passage leads to a steep, loose boulder slope up into a sandy chamber from which a slit leads back and up a further slope to a low crawl. This emerges in Cobweb Chamber which has several choked inlets. Down the climb another passage can be reached, which eventually leads to a choke, while a hole down leads into the very tight Booth-Eyre Crawl.

If the lower level of Bradshaw's Passage is followed for the last section a point is reached where one can stand up and the passage turns sharp right. To the left a muddy slope of boulders rises up to a squeeze through a hole. The passage splits and to the left is Skywalker Passage, over 50m of muddy rift passage on a thin false floor with holes down into Bradshaw's Passage below. Care! To the right and down round a corner leads to Lower Molar Passage along a traverse to a junction and an oxbow. To the right up a 3m climb leads to Danish Passage, 100m of easy going to a chamber with climbs up to two choked inlets. Straight on at the junction leads to Upper Molar Passage. An awkward climb and traverse leads to a fine passage followed by a sudden drop into another chamber. At the far end a 4m climb up leads to

Dire Straits which starts as a narrow awkward rift to a flat-out crawl through to Upper Wisdom Tooth Passage (above).

From Limerick Junction two routes lead into Limerick Passage, and a traverse above the stream leads to a passage off on the right. This is Old Limerick Passage, and it can be followed along an abandoned route past several avens and chambers to a final crawl somewhere in the vicinity of Far East Passage. On upstream in Limerick Passage leads past several obstacles to choked inlets off on either side.

Downstream from Limerick Junction in the main passage takes one on with the stream through a chamber with a 5.5m pitch to a series of cascades to a complex collapse area, and an impassable bedding. At the upper level a traverse on loose material, The Bridge of Sighs, leads to a narrow rift section which emerges dramatically at the start of Nagasaki Cavern, and soon twin holes in the floor are encountered. These lead down to the stream again, and from here it can be followed down into Far East Passage to a 3m pitch, and the junction with another passage on the left which can be followed a short distance to a boulder chamber and inlet which becomes tight above a waterfall. The stream entering here is that last seen at the end of Booth-Eyre Crawl. Upstream in Far East Passage a route has been forced through calcite squeezes to Limerick Junction. From the boulder chamber holes up through dangerous boulders enter a well-decorated tunnel to an upward slot leading to the extensively choked Neutron Cavern.

Continuing on along Nagasaki Cavern the route is a series of climbs up and down over great heaps of collapse boulders in a very unstable area, to where the route funnels down into a smaller chamber at the far end of the Cavern. A large meandering passage leads on, past two holes in the floor, to a short drop into a large unstable chamber, The Assembly Hall. Almost opposite the point of entry into this chamber is the short climb up which leads into the beautiful Easter Grotto, from the far end of which a tight crawl runs to Gypsum Caverns, whilst a hole down through the boulder floor leads to a further climb down into the White Way, and Thackray's Passage, which contains the main stream. Upstream leads to an extensive and extremely dangerous boulder choke.

Downstream in Thackray's Passage is well decorated, but gradually the height decreases to a hands and knees crawl. At this point a crawl through a stalactite grill up a rock slope on the left is the only way on as the streamway is too low. A short section of larger passage leads back down to the stream, and a further section of easy going leads to Holbeck Junction. A climb up to the right here leads into the start of the large series of chambers comprising Gypsum Caverns, and it is possible to make a complete loop round in them. A further loop runs beneath Gypsum Caverns; starting near the climb, a sandy bedding plane leads to a chamber and a tight tube connects with the main streamway near the climb up to Easter Grotto.

Tackle

Pitch	Ladder	Belay	Lifeline
Walrus Pot	18m	3m	23m
Penknife Pitch	6m	3m	9m

BOLT BELAYS – see Warning, page 13.

Permission – CNCC.

WHITTLE HOLE   NGR SD 659799   Grade I
Alt. 204m   **Length 9m**

On left bank of Leck Beck 91m downstream of Leck Beck Head on limestone shelf. Short oxbow with a narrow active inlet.
Permission – CNCC.

WITCHES CAVE   NGR SD 660799   Grade I
Alt. 218m   **Length 550m**
Explored 1974-1990, CDG.

Obvious cave entrance in N bank of Ease Gill, below the Lower Kirk. In flood conditions this normally dry entrance resurges large volumes of water. Stooping height passage leads to step up into various blind boulder chambers on right. Straight ahead is choice of 8m sump to chamber floored by deep pool, or 5m climb up and 4m pitch back down to same point. In roof are choked tubes.

Nearer the entrance are two small floor rifts with sumps. These are connected underwater and lead to shaft emerging in roof of huge underwater passage. To W the passage quickly diminishes close to Leck Beck Head Flood Risings. To E is upstream in a large tunnel varying between 27m and 33m deep. Present limit of exploration is 475m from base.

Tackle

Pitch	Ladder	Belay	Lifeline
Climb up	6m of scaling ladder, or pole		
1st	8m	3m	9m

Permission – CNCC.

WRETCHED RABBIT ENTRANCE   NGR SD 676806
Grade III
Alt. 319m   **Length** – part of Ease Gill Caverns
Explored 1984, RRCPC.
WARNING – The low passage at the end of the Big Rift and the cascades beyond may become impassable in extreme flood.

The entrance is located in Ease Gill Beck immediately upstream of New Cave with which it is now connected and 30m down the gill from Slit Sinks. An oil drum marks the entrance. Once inside a short hands and knees crawl leads to the first of a series of short but awkward drops into the Big Rift. This first drop is rigged with a fixed rope belayed to a scaffolding bar at present.

At the bottom of this first climb are three ways on although only one is obvious at first. The obvious way on is down the Big Rift, descending the series of climbs mentioned above. At the bottom of these a high narrow passage continues for 20m to a chamber and the way on ahead leads on down Upper Wretched Rabbit Passage into the rest of the cave.

Upper Entrance Series
Back at the base of the first drop an inlet enters from the right. This can be

ascended along a high winding passage for over 15m to a choke of gritstone boulders with tree roots entering from the roof. This point is directly below the northern bank of Ease Gill below the obvious mountain ash tree. The third way on from the base of the first drop is a tight bedding on the eastern wall and can be followed for 5m to a 3m climb down into the Parallel Streamway.

The alternative way into the streamway is via an awkward 3m climb at the bottom of the Big Rift. The streamway can be followed upstream for 100m. It splits up into several inlets, most of which choke under Ease Gill Beck or become tight. At the end of the longest inlet is a tight muddy connection to New Cave.

The rest of the Entance Series lie mainly to the west of the Big Rift. The easiest way into these passages is via a climb up into a connecting crawl from the Parallel Streamway to the Big Rift located just downstream of the low connecting bedding at the base of the first climb down. The way on is along a low bedding plane crawl, the Cross-Over Passage, which heads north-west and crosses over the roof of the Big Rift at a large deep hole. At the hole a passage on the left can be climbed into and this leads back above the Big Rift as the large meandering High Level Oxbow to a point immediately above the second climb down in the Big Rift. Off the High Level Oxbow a tight low crawl meanders north-westwards for about 20m to a 3m pitch down to a chamber.

This pitch need not be descended as the chamber below can be reached much more easily from the passage at the far end of Cross-Over Passage. This passage breaks out into a high meandering streamway which can be followed upstream to a well decorated high level boulder chamber, Stalactite Chamber. About half way between the 2m climb and Stalactite Chamber is a small passage on the right which leads after a few metres to the chamber at the base of the 3m pitch mentioned above. The meandering streamway can be followed downstream via a 2m climb to the top of a 9m pitch which lands in the chamber at the bottom end of the Big Rift just before the continuation to the rest of the cave. Just before the 9m pitch is a junction. From here a narrow meandering passage can be followed until it becomes too narrow and is blocked with fill. A few metres back from here is a 4m climb up and the passage can be followed by traversing in the roof to two boulder chokes which need digging. At the top of the 4m climb is a bedding plane in the roof, Mud Inlet. This leads to a low wet inlet which draughts well and heads towards Corner Sink. It is possible to traverse for some distance downstream beyond the top of the 9m pitch at roof level.

Upper Wretched Rabbit Passage

Back at the downstream end of the Big Rift a hands and knees passage which quickly enlarges leads on into the rest of the cave. A meandering canyon passage which includes several short climbs leads after about 100m to holes in the floor above two waterfalls. By traversing over the holes to the right another stream passage is reached. Following this upstream leads to two ways on. A 2m climb on the right leads to a complex of passages above and parallel to the Wretched Rabbit streamway. To the left the stream continues to a slope up boulders on the left. At the top of the slope a squeeze and a chimney leads to Depot 1.5 and from there to Stop Pot. At the bottom of the slope the stream continues as a narrow passage for some distance eventually becoming too tight.

Lower Wretched Rabbit Passage

After traversing over the holes above the waterfalls the main way on descends a 3m wet cascade to a continuing stream passage, which is followed past a fine long stalactite and some oxbows. After 40m of twisting and turning passage several routes in the roof lead up into Four Ways Chamber where a route leads off in the roof to Stop Pot. Downstream is another 100m of mixed going including a traverse and a crawl to the junction with Lower Pierce's Passage in County Pot just short of Eureka Junction. The Four Ways Chamber route forms a useful escape route in wet weather if the lower route is too wet.

Tackle

15m of ladder or handline for the climbs in the Big Rift.

Permission – CNCC.

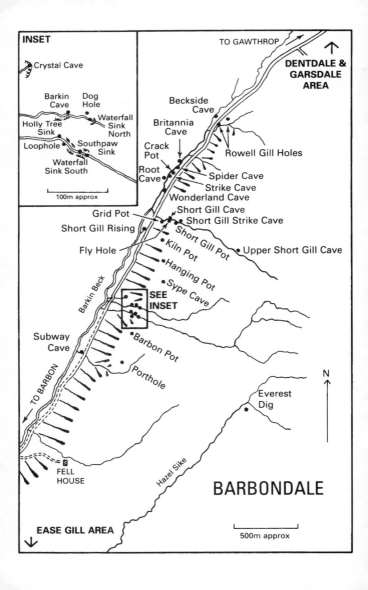

BARBONDALE

BARBON POT
NGR SD 666838
Grade IV

(Secret Pot)

Alt. 283m   **Length 320m**   **Depth 37m**

Descended 1952, NPC; extended 1963, GC; 1966, NSG.

Open shaft used as dump for dead sheep in line of shakeholes 137m S of Barkin Gills. Close to track up to fell from gate at roadside.

Entrance shaft is best laddered from ledge 4.5m down, reached by climb down E side (beware of loose rocks) and enters Main Chamber – 18m long with floor of mud-covered blocks. Crawl near foot of shaft descends to choked rift. At south end, climb down 3m between boulders into short crawl into Whoop Hall with aven inlet passage at far side. Keep to right in descent of unstable boulder slope into Main Passage, which is choked beneath Main Chamber. Hidden in narrow trench is small stream joined via mud chute 15m downstream. At first aven, a short, choked inlet contains delicate mud formations. 8m further is '63 Chamber where stream sinks.

Descend hole in floor to tight fissure passing beneath boulder choke. Over boulders on left is large aven and progress in Main Passage is made by crawling 3m above stream level. Where passage widens, an abandoned inlet leads back to slot at base of aven. Easy walking follows except where false floor forms two levels. Size increases beyond and boulder floor descends into '66 Chamber which contains fine straw stalactites. Stream sinks but is seen again in final bedding plane reached by a crawl and muddy descent from far end of chamber. Behind right wall are an aven inlet and a high phreatic passage 21m long.

Tackle

Pitch	Ladder	Belay	Lifeline
Entrance Climb	–	–	9m
1st	15m	4.5m	21m

Permission – Fell House, Barbondale.

BARKIN CAVE
NGR SD 666840
Grade III

Alt. 244m   **Length 64m**   **Depth 12m**

Obvious pothole in stream bed at foot of lower waterfall in North Barkin Gill. Best to enter through subsidiary hole and use lifeline for 4.5m climbable descent. Roomy passage for 11m to 2nd pitch, climbable with care after traversing to far side. Crawl from chamber below gets too tight but in opposite wall is squeeze through rift and tight drop into Hidden Stream Passage – a low tube carrying water from Holly Tree Sink* to Crystal Cave and sumped in each direction.

A climb up from entrance passage enters high rift running parallel for 18m.

Tackle

Pitch	Ladder	Belay	Lifeline
1st	–	–	9m
2nd	–	–	12m

Permission – Fell House, Barbondale.

BECKSIDE CAVE   NGR SD 674857   Grade II
Alt. 250m   Length 12m
Explored 1974, GC.

A small hole on E bank of stream. Downstream crawling to a constricted sump.

BRITANNIA CAVE   NGR SD 671852   Grade II
Alt. 226m   Length 107m
Explored 1953, RRCPC.

The only obvious cave on W bank of Barkin Beck. Where small stream emerges 512m upstream from Short Gill bridge. Mainly a narrow, twisting rift passage but with two low, wet, crawls in the first 30m. Stream passage follows steeply inclined bedding planes and ends in constricted fissures and sump.

CRACK POT   NGR SD 670851   Grade I
Alt. 221m   Length 6m   Depth 3m

A 2m deep rift between Barkin Beck and the road. Short crawl descends to stream in impossible low passage. The cave has been used as a dump for farm refuse.

CRYSTAL CAVE   NGR SD 666841   Grade IV
Alt. 221m   Length 290m   Vertical range 21m
Explored 1952, NPC; extended 1960, GC.

Open cave entrance where stream emerges below rock face 91m from road. The main drain for the Dog Hole system and the Barkin Gill sinks. Hands and knees crawling for 30m to short, flat-out crawl with stream – impassable in wet weather. Just beyond is a high chamber, The Hall, and above next section of streamway is a decorated roof passage, The Gallery, reached by a climb at two points. Above waterfall in Spout Chamber, stream passage continues for 52m to a duck with average air-space of 150mm.

Roof lifts beyond and straight ahead is a sumped inlet. Main stream enters under left wall and can be followed up Second and Third Waterfalls, both about 4.5m high and climbable with care. Above, the stream comes from a tube with little air-space which has been forced for at least 30m, in dry conditions, and may have been linked to Monsoon Chamber in Dog Hole. On left at top of Third Waterfall is dry North Passage, choked after 20m. Barker's Passage enters at foot of Third Waterfall and leads to an extremely tight connection with Hey's Passage in Dog Hole, passable only to very thin cavers. Permission – Fell House, Barbondale.

DOG HOLE
NGR SD 667840
Alt. 250m   Length 914m (excluding Crystal Cave)   Depth 24m

Near Series   **Grade III**
Explored 1950, GC; 1952, NPC.

A low opening in the N bank of North Barkin Gill, between two waterfalls.
The rocks at the entrance should be replaced afterwards to keep out animals.

A muddy descending crawl to the top of a wide rift, Bridge Chamber, which
descends in steps for 9m; care is required on the initial climb down. To the left
from foot of climb, a series of wide bedding-plane inlets leads back towards
the gill. Main way on is over a shelf into small Boulder Chamber. Hole by left
wall drops into Hey's Passage which takes a small stream in wet weather and
descends past calcite pools to head of pitch. Above on right is desperately tight
connection with Barker's Passage in Crystal Cave. 4.5m pitch is climbable
with care, constricted at top but wider below. Crawling follows to short drops
into Jet Chamber where stream runs away down a tube which gets too tight.
An old inlet rift can be followed up for a short distance.

Main Stream Series and South Passage   **Grade IV**
Explored 1966-67, GC.

**WARNING – A trip to South Passage should only be contemplated by an
experienced party after acquainting themselves with more details of the route
than it is possible to give in this description.**

A devious and unpleasant route from Boulder Chamber connects with the
main stream passage linking the inlets from the upper Barkin Gill sinks.
Beyond is South Passage which continues beneath Barbon High Fell for
0.4km.

The first section of the route passes through a complex area of breakdown
cavities and bedding planes named 'The Jungle'. It is easy to stray into unstable
parts, particularly when returning, so careful note must be made of one's
route. Several restricted inlets beneath the North Barkin Gill are passed
before the main stream is reached at Monsoon Chamber. Downstream is
impassable but South Gill Passage becomes easier upstream with a height of
1.2m on average.

A strong stream enters from Foreleg Passage which rises, beyond low
flooded inlets, to Gour Chamber after 24m. Rift above gets too narrow and
hole in floor leads to muddy crawl and very tight squeeze into a further
choked chamber. Next inlet is Hindleg Passage which quickly ascends and
branches to narrow avens beneath South Waterfall Sink.

Dry passage ends in breakdown but hole in floor enters lower bedding.
South Passage starts with a very tight downward crawl into cavern 2.4m high
and 4.5m wide which continues downstream for 91m with short crawls over
gravel banks and breakdown blocks. If not silted up, stream may be followed
through very low crawl 3m long, beneath blank wall at end. Phreatic passage
continues but after joint-controlled canal, stream commences to cut down in
deepening trench. Traverse on ledges in top part of rift to Breakdown Corner
where upper level swings right to choke and stalagmite grotto. A small inlet

joins stream in narrow, twisting rift passage beneath. Far South Passage continues for 61m to a sump beyond a duck.

Permission – Fell House, Barbondale.

EVEREST DIG   NGR SD 676832
Alt. 408m
Excavated RRCPC.

Shakehole high on left bank near top of Hazel Sike. Digging revealed narrow rift 6m deep blocked by large boulder at top. Shakehole side now slumped in. Water in nearby stream sink may flow N under watershed towards Dentdale.

FLY HOLE   NGR SD 670847   Grade II
Alt. 250m   Length 9m   Depth 8m
Explored 1970, GC.

Opposite Short Gill Cave is a concealed entrance behind embedded boulder in S bank of gill where walls recede.

A short, dirty, squeeze permits entry to an inclined bedding rift, blocked at the bottom.

GRID POT   NGR SD 669847   Grade III
Alt. 232m   Length 24m   Depth 9m
Explored 1966, NSG.

Obvious entrance in S bank at foot of Short Gill 91m from road. Cave quickly takes water when gill starts to flood. Scramble down into chamber with tight slot in floor at far end, covered by timbers to exclude debris from clean-washed flat crawl below. Crawl ends at a short drop onto a boulder slope in a cross rift formed on a vertical shale bed. Down slope is choked completely, but up slope leads to window in left wall, giving on to a climbable 2.5m descent to a large ledge with a 3m long choked passage running off. A further 1.2m step leads down to a low, wet crawl with a partial choke after 4.5m, preventing further progress.

HANGING POT   NGR SD 668844   Grade I
Alt. 259m   Depth 6m

In blind valley, mid-way between Short Gill and Crystal Cave. An excavated sink in shattered rock. The stream is next seen in Short Gill Cave.

Permission – Fell House, Barbondale.

HOLLY TREE SINK   NGR SD 666840   Grade III
Alt. 244m   Length 61m   Depth 12m
Explored 1968, GC.

In N bank of South Barkin Gill above a large fall with overhanging walls (normally dry).

Excavated entrance rift with crawl into parallel fissure. Two 3m chimney descents into stream passage. Roof lowers beyond further inlets and 21m crawl leads to pool with low air-space. Water reappears in Barkin Cave.
Permission – Fell House, Barbondale.

KILN POT   NGR SD 669846   Grade II
Alt. 267m   **Length 23m**   **Depth 8.5m**
Explored 1977, CPC.
WARNING – Beware of loose boulders.

Entrance in collapse area at bend in small stream above quarry. A steep boulder slope leads down into a low chamber with unstable roof and floor, and a choice of routes. To the right a nice phreatic tube ascends to a choke, while straight ahead it is possible to crawl under a tremendous dropped block to a short crawl and a hole, down which a small stream falls to sink in cobbles at the bottom. To the left is the last possible way on, and this leads to the lowest part of the pot via a highly dangerous loose boulder slope to the inevitable choke.

LOOPHOLE   NGR SD 666840   Grade II
Alt. 250m   **Length 9m**

Open entrance in left (S) wall of South Barkin Gill between two short walls. A short, clean, passage descends to a pool where daylight is seen. In wet weather, stream flows through cave and reappears to sink in dipping bedding cave on opposite side of gill.
Permission – Fell House, Barbondale.

PORTHOLE   NGR SD 666836   Grade III
Alt. 282m   **Depth 34m**
Explored 1977, RRCPC.

One of an indistinct line of shakeholes 274m S of Barbon Pot. Small hole in floor of shakehole leads directly onto 27m pitch into chamber with hading cross-rift. Downstream soon becomes tight and wet. Upstream rift widens but way barred by 'hanging death' block. Ledge on pitch has short passage to choke.

Tackle – 30m ladder; stake & sling belay; 37m lifeline.

ROOT CAVE   NGR SD 669851   Grade II
Alt. 224m   **Length 9m**
Explored 1981, GC.

Small hole in grassy W bank of Barkin Beck by minor resurgence. Dirty crawling to squeeze and low chamber with sump.

ROWELL GILL HOLES   NGR SD 674856   Grade I
Alt. 253m   **Length 6m**   **Depth 6m**
Two rock-walled shakeholes on N bank of Rowell Gill above sink. Another short, choked, crawl can be entered close to the stream.

SHORT GILL CAVE
NGR SD 670847   **Grade III**
Alt. 244m   **Length 549m**   **Depth 15m**
Explored 1966, NSG.

WARNING – Liable to flooding.

In the deep part of Short Gill 137m from the road. Approach by following stream bed. Pothole entrance at stream level beneath overhanging N wall.

Care needed on 5m climbable descent, awkward when returning. Rope advisable for second drop of 3m at end of short rift which bells out below. Wide, dry, passage runs northwards and is mainly low with mud and gravel floor for 73m. A series of well-developed and active gours, up to 1m deep, occupy next section of cave. Care should be taken to avoid damage. The wider, false-floored passage beyond is followed by a short, tight, stream trench dropping into the much larger Main Stream Passage, 229m long.

A strong stream enters from a constricted sump but can be followed down in a clean-washed streamway. Two sumped sections can be bypassed by climbing into a low, muddy roof passage but this is absent in the final length of cave descending to the third sump, dived to 24m where a bad constriction prevented further progress.

Flood Series

Below the entrance climbs, a stream channel on left of passage enters from narrow inlet and can be followed down a diverging crawl to join two constricted passages leading back under the gill in which water backs up in wet weather. One is a tight crawl ending in inlet rifts after 30m. The other is Reverse Passage which starts as descending fissure from hole in floor. Beyond a low gravelly crawl, a deep pool in a rift can be passed to a rising passage and choke.

SHORT GILL POT
NGR SD 670847   **Grade II**
Alt. 259m   **Length 46m**   **Depth 34m**
Explored 1950, CPC; 1958, KCC.

A wide rift in S bank of Gill above 6m fall, formed where vertical shale bed has been washed out.

A series of climbable rift descents between wider sections which extend beneath the stream bed. The third drop is difficult and constricted at the top.

Tackle – 9m lifeline.

SHORT GILL RISING
NGR SD 676846
Alt. 213m   **Length 10m**
Explored 1981-82, CDG.

WARNING – Many loose boulders.

Resurgence SW of Short Gill Bridge has no passages accessible to the non-diver. Exploration is still continuing and the flooded passage has been followed to a junction with a much larger passage, where a loose boulder slope is a considerable hazard.

SHORT GILL STRIKE CAVE   NGR SD 671847   Grade II
Alt. 259m   Length 15m

Entrance 50m along gorge above Short Gill Pot. Straight, dirty, crawl into N wall of gorge becomes too low.

SOUTHPAW SINK   NGR SD 667840   Grade IV
Alt. 253m   Length 85m   Depth 15m
Explored 1968, GC.

WARNING – The entrance can quickly become impassable in wet weather.

A narrow fissure in South Barkin Gill stream bed 18m below top of Gill.

A very tight squeeze from floor of 2.4m deep shaft enters a fissure passage descending to a 5m pitch. This is tight at first but is wide below and a ladder is advisable. Below is a short but complex system of shattered chambers and squalid crawls. Water from nearby sinks is seen in the cave before reappearing in Foreleg Passage in Dog Hole.

Tackle – 6m ladder; 2m belay; 9m lifeline.

Permission – Fell House, Barbondale.

SPIDER CAVE   NGR SD 670852   Grade II
Alt. 226m   Length 15m

Sink of Barkin Beck in left bank, 37m downstream of Britannia Cave. Narrow entrance behind blocks enters a complex low chamber. The stream sumps and roof-level crawls are choked. A secondary entrance just upstream enters a low chamber with stream and silted tube towards main cave.

STRIKE CAVE   NGR SD 670851   Grade II
Alt. 224m   Length 23m
Explored 1970, GC.

Narrow entrance in left bank of Barkin Beck at stream level 82m upstream from Wonderland Cave. Sideways crawling in tight fissure to small chamber where stream sumps after flowing from a low passage on left. Subject to flooding.

SUBWAY CAVE   NGR SD 663837   Grade II
Alt. 198m   Length 25m
Explored 1983, LCCC.

In gill to south of Barkin Gills and just below road. Irregular shaped passage with silt banks ends in block collapse with stream audible.

SYPE CAVE   NGR SD 669842   Grade III
Alt. 268m   Length 27m
Explored 1966, GC.

Resurgence in Yoredale limestone for a very small stream at head of shallow gully 120m ENE of Crystal Cave. Crawling with the stream until passage gets too tight. A cross-rift at 18m gives turning space.

UPPER SHORT GILL CAVE   NGR SD 675845   Grade III
Alt. 351m   **Length 66m**
Explored 1977, SWETC Caving Club.

Entrance in small outcrop on N bank of Short Gill, 350m upstream of main Short Gill sink. Flat out squeeze leads immediately to awkward squeeze into side of passage carrying small stream, Right, upstream, is crawl passage averaging 1m high and wide. Squeezes over boulders fallen from small avens impede progress until the 3m wide Pillar Chamber is reached after 40m. Two small passages lead on, both becoming too tight and awkward after 6m. The draught entering the right hand passage emerges from a small hole in a shakehole some 10m away.

WATERFALL SINK NORTH   NGR SD 667840   Grade II
Alt. 250m   **Length 12m**
Explored 1964, GC.

Sink of North Barkin Gill at foot of upper waterfall, 14m upstream of Dog Hole. A low bedding cave with stream sinking through boulders.

WATERFALL SINK SOUTH   NGR SD 667839   Grade III
Alt. 256m   **Length 8m**
Explored 1969, GC.

At foot of short waterfall at top of entrenched part of South Barkin Gill. A tight descending crawl soon chokes. Stream enters Hindleg Passage in Dog Hole.

WONDERLAND CAVE   NGR SD 669850   Grade II
Alt. 224m   **Length 76m**
Explored 1953, RRCPC.

Entrance in projecting rock spur on left bank of Barkin Beck, 274m N of Short Gill Bridge. Stream rises just below. Main Passage runs parallel to Beck with low crawl at stream level and dry passage above, 26m long. On right at first chamber is muddy abandoned inlet choked after 15m.

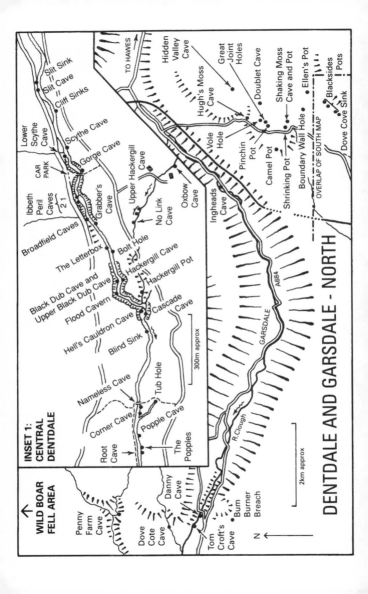

DENTDALE AND GARSDALE - NORTH

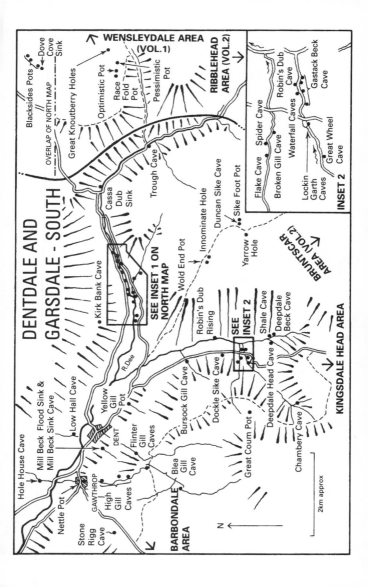

DENTDALE and GARSDALE

BLACK DUB CAVE NGR SD 737862 Grade IV
Alt. 168m **Length 183m**
Explored 1969, KCC.
WARNING – Whole cave fills completely and rapidly in flood.

GScL. Entrance at right hand end of large overhang by pool below waterfall at Black Dub. Tight crawl through flood debris to very tight squeeze followed by easier going to sloping chamber with vadose trenches across floor. From far end of chamber the main passage continues past two inlets on left and becomes a silted-up crawl which chokes beyond two avens. Both inlets divide and choke and both avens lead to short, sandy crawls which choke.

BLACKSIDES POTS NGR SD 792885 Grade II
Alt. 580m **Depths 4.5m to 22m**
ML. A row of small open pots in line of shakeholes on either side of the boundary wall. About 12 shafts are known; some are free-climbable but the deeper shafts need tackle. The deepest and largest are as follows:

Roaring Rift NGR SD 795886 Grade III
Alt. 587m **Depth 22m**
Explored 1983, DHSS.

The deepest of the Blackside Pots.

Small shakehole with narrow opening between limestone block and bedrock to head of 12m pitch. Short passage to 2m descent and forward under cemented boulder to very awkward 5m pitch with difficult take off. Below is 'T' junction and inlet stream reached by squeeze and 2m climb, but outlet is too tight. To right is further 2m drop and crawl forward into small chamber. The last drop is difficult to reverse.

Zygal Hole NGR SD 793885 Grade II
Alt. 585m **Length 30m** **Depth 10m**
Explored 1983, DHSS.

Just S of fence in the line of Blacksides Pots. Large shakehole with holes down into cave at south end. 2m climb down into nice passage ends with loose rubble in floor.

BLEA GILL CAVE NGR SD 692852 Grade IV
Alt. 412m **Length 1.8km** **Depth 52m**
Explored NSG; extended 1975, Lancs. Caving and Climbing Club.
WARNING – The entire system floods rapidly and completely; exploration

should only be considered during dry, settled weather. Parties should familiarise themselves with both ends of the system before a through trip is planned.

MdL. Excavated entrance 9m W of obvious sink in Blea Gill close to end of green lane. Short climb down enters narrow stream passage, normally dry, leading to junction downstream. Left ends in a choke while right continues for 40m, slightly enlarged, until a small chamber is reached. Straight ahead at roof level is the start of the upper series, a complex maze of inter-connecting tubes, often tight and awkward, and ending in constricted chokes.

From the chamber main way is left through static pool to junction; left chokes after short distance and right at roof level enters a small tube. This continues to hole in floor and drop down leads into low shingle crawl. Follow water to left and along section of low, wet passage with feeders entering at stream level and occasional breaks in the roof giving access to the Upper Series. Continue with the stream and the passage gradually enlarges at the start of the main drain, about 600m of streamway with alternating sections of low, wet crawls, and breakdown chambers which have highly unstable roofs. Eventually the passage decreases to a tight squeeze through loose blocks (care!) and continues downstream as a complex of enlarged joints. After 15m main stream is regained and downstream for 80m ends in large boulder complex. This choke lies 50m from resurgence and climb up through loose blocks to right emerges at lower entrance.

BLIND SINK   NGR SD 734861   Grade I
Alt. 155m   **Length 6m**
WARNING – Takes a considerable flow in flood.

GScL. Open slot against N bank of riverbed about 100m downstream of Hell's Cauldron. Climb down into rift leading to short crawl becoming narrow and partly choked. May connect with end inlet in Tub Holes.

BOLT HOLE   NGR SD 738863   Grade I
Alt. 175m   **Length 12m**
Explored 1970, KCC.
WARNING – Fills to roof in wet weather.

GScL. Low bedding in S bank of riverbed a few metres from drop down into Hackergill gorge. Flat crawl into passage which is heavily silted in both directions. Entrance is blocked by boulders and flood debris.

BOUNDARY WALL HOLE   NGR SD 791889   Grade II
Alt. 556m   **Length 9m**   **Depth 5m**
Explored 1966, KCC.

ML. Small pot 69m NW of wall in line of shakeholes. Easy climb to small chamber and squeeze into fissure which is too tight.

BROADFIELD CAVES   NGR SD 740864   Grade IV

Alt. 178m   **Length 670m**   Depth 23m

Explored 1969 and 1971, NSCC/BSA.

**WARNING – Entrance is submerged in flood and large sections of the cave
flood to the roof.**

GScL.   Oil drum entrance against N bank of riverbed just downstream of
tributary from N. Climb down and awkward squeeze into small passage leading
to 2.1m climb down into chamber and large bedding plane – the Old Link
Way. Crawl to right in this bedding has mud floor and emerges at the chamber
in Ibbeth Peril Cave 2 after 107m of crawl. To left from foot of 2.1m climb the
Old Link Way is a 67m flat crawl over a mud floor to emerge in the roof of
Problem Series. Opposite the foot of the 2.1m climb a trench leads into
Jordan's Passage. Awkward going to incline into lower bedding which gives
way to a crawl to a spiral climb down steps of 2.1m and 1.5m. Below, a wide
passage closes to a crawl, and a squeeze past blocks reaches a further spiral
climb down to a deep sump.

Problem Series

Upstream from Old Link Way a traverse in an oxbow is followed by
alternate walking and traversing for 107m to a high level main inlet splashing
down from the left. Main passage continues past two short inlets up on a shelf
to the left to reach an extensive choke with water entering from the riverbed
above. Just back from choke is way to unstable chamber on left, a former
entrance which was collapsed because of its instability.

Main inlet is short trench reducing to wide, low bedding plane. Three
awkward squeezes emerge at bottom of a climbable rift – The Clam Pit – now
choked at the top but formerly the entrance to Problem Series.

Downstream from Old Link Way leads to a large side passage at roof level,
diminishing to a crawl up and over a large gour to a static sump after 30m.
Main streamway continues past the side passage, meandering sharply to head
of 1.5m cascade, followed immediately by a 6m pitch, climbable with care but
tackle advisable. Pitch lands in Main Chamber, 21m long and 6m wide with
ascending boulder slope at far end. Way on is down small hole through
boulders under left wall near foot of ladder. Two squeezes lead to sandy
passages and pool followed by low crawl in stream in wide bedding narrowing
to small passage in shale bed. Short slope ends at deep, narrow sump 153m
from Main Chamber, which has been dived to a depth of 4m where it gets too
tight. Traverse over pool gains a sandy passage, and 3m up in left wall is small
passage choked after 6m. Ahead is a further small static sump which gets too
tight after 2m.

Tackle – 8m ladder; 6m belay; 12m lifeline.

BROKEN GILL CAVE   NGR SD 722839   Grade I

Alt. 259m   **Length 8m**

Explored 1975, UWFRA.

GScL.   Strong rising in S bank at foot of small outcrop is entered by awkward
flat crawl. Small tube leads to corner and silt bank.

BUM BURNER BREACH   NGR SD 696904   Grade II
Alt. 259m   **Length 18m**
Explored 1974, KCC.

GScL.   Large sink in second field up from road, almost due S of cattle grid. Very immature passage with several squeezes to small chamber. Outlet is too tight although water is presumed to drain to Danny Cave.

BURSOCK GILL CAVE   NGR SD 722850   Grade I
Alt. 236m   **Length 8m**
Explored 1972, BSA.

GScL.   Low bedding 12m from main Deepdale road at foot of small waterfall in tiny gill. Low crawl past oxbow into small stream becomes too tight.

CAMEL POT   NGR SD 783896   Grade II
Alt. 525m   **Depth 10m**
Explored 1978, DHSS.

ML.   Old car wedged in shaft top. 10m pitch onto rubble. All the cross rifts leading off are blind.

Tackle – 12m ladder; stake & sling belay; 20m lifeline.

CASCADE CAVE   NGR SD 736861   Grade I
Alt. 160m   **Length 6m**

GScL.   Obvious entrance with small stream emerging, high on S bank of river a short way down-valley of Hell's Cauldron. Narrow rift to sharp bend and 2m cascade with excessively tight passage above.

CASSA DUB SINK   NGR SD 762868   Grade I
Alt. 220m   **Length 9m**
Explored 1970, NSCC.

GScL.   Water from several sinks in the Cassa Dub area resurges close to Tub Holes nearly 3.2km away. One sink against N bank is now blocked by boulders and flood debris but was climb down into fissure passing right-angled bends and higher level oxbow before becoming too narrow.

CHAMBERY CAVE   NGR SD 711826   Grade II
Alt. 441m   **Length 153m**
Explored 1969, NSCC.

MdL.   High in the headwaters of Gastack Beck a small stream emerges from a triangular section, shale-floored crawl leading to several circular chambers where water has penetrated the full depth of the limestone. Awkward climb up final waterfall chamber emerges from upper sink entrance.
Permission – Hill Top Farm.

CLIFF SINKS   NGR SD 746865   Grade I
Alt. 189m
Explored 1969, KCC/BSA.

GScL.   Two obvious sinks at foot of shattered scar on S bank of river. Upstream sink is joint covered by boulder and dropping to wide bedding plane completely choked after 3m; other sink further along scar is almost identical.

CORNER CAVE   NGR SD 731862   Grade I
Alt. 150m   Length 9m

GScL.   At confluence of Tub Holes Valley with river Dee is open joint on S bank. Several surface holes lead into this small passage which is choked and is a possible old resurgence.

DANNY CAVE   NGR SD 697913   Grade II
Alt. 153m   Length 198m
Extended 1966, CDG.

GScL.   Obvious resurgence on S side of river Clough just downstream of Danny Bridge. Wet crawling leads to sump after 61m. Sump is 6m long and must not be free-dived as it contains a tight squeeze. Narrow walking size passage beyond is abandoned streamway with holes down to sumped zone, and zig-zags along joints to tight duck after 131m. Beyond duck is chamber and sump which is too low.

DEEPDALE BECK CAVE   NGR SD 727831   Grade I
Alt. 274m   Length 11m
Explored 1970, BSA.

GScL.   Bedding entrance on right bank of beck about 160m upstream of the farm has strong stream emerging. Flat crawl in water becomes too low.
Permission – Deepdale Head Farm.

DEEPDALE HEAD CAVE   NGR SD 725832   Grade II
Alt. 260m   Length 91m
Explored 1970, BSA.

GScL.   Tight rift entrance at foot of small waterfall in gill behind the farm. Small chamber at foot of 3.6m entrance climb has upstream passage commencing at a waterfall and leading through a chamber to another cascade, the way at the top being blocked by a thick tree root. Downstream a squeeze leads into a slightly larger collapse chamber with squeeze through boulders into passage. Inlet to right becomes too low after 12m near foot of entrance climb. Main downstream passage is walk to aven and sloping cascade, narrowing to sideways walking in meandering passage. Where dip changes the roof drops to a crawl and an impassable S-bend.
Permission – Deepdale Head Farm.

DOCKLE SIKE CAVE   NGR SD 722842   Grade I
Alt. 259m   **Length 33m**
Explored 1953, NPC; extended 1970, BSA.

GScL. A short way above the Deepdale road is minor resurgence below small scar. Tight, wet crawl ultimately gets too tight.

DOUBLET CAVE   NGR SD 793898   Grade I
Alt. 526m   **Length 55m**
Explored 1969, YURT.

WARNING – Liable to complete flooding.

ML. In eastern limb of double shakehole at head of Sikes Pits Gill. Slide down into roomy passage which passes loose boulders below second entrance and continues to aven chamber. Outlet crawl in stream becomes too low.

DOVE COTE CAVE   NGR SD 695919   Grade I
Alt. 200m   **Length 100m**

GScL. Obvious sink and resurgence entrances in Ringing Keld Gutter are connected by walking-size streamway with occasional lower sections. Several surface holes connect with the cave, one via a pitch. Cave is in steeply-dipping beds, close to Dent Fault and upper entrance is a waterfall down the dip. Permission – Dove Cote Farm.

DOVE COVE SINK   NGR SD 788881   Grade III
Alt. 575m   **Length 50m**   **Depth 18m**
Explored 1983, DHSS; extended 1991, DHSS.

ML. Impressive shakehole 10m deep. Water tested to Keld Beck Resurgence 1.6km distant. Best to use tackle on entrance climb of tight descent into rift. Water enters partway down but easiest way is to left into dry rift and through window to rejoin stream. At mud slope is way through boulders to tight crawl where water runs away to right. Easier dry passage leads to 2m climb down and very tight streamway.

Tackle – 10m ladder; stake & sling belay; 18m lifeline.

DUNCAN SIKE CAVE   NGR SD 753839   Grade II
Alt. 503m   **Length 153m**
Explored 1966, NPC; extended 1972, CPC.

UnL. Twin entrances where Duncan Sike sinks at small scar 46m SE of shooting box high on N slopes of Whernside. Narrow passage to wet 61m long crawl which enlarges to walking size after acute bend and reaches branch passage on right which is well decorated and emerges in another sink after a squeeze. Main passage continues downstream for 18m to where it splits into two levels, soon rejoining as a low crawl ending at impassable fissures. Lower section of cave floods severely.

ELLEN'S POT   NGR SD 795887   Grade II
Alt. 570m   **Depth 8m**

Explored 1988, DHSS.

ML.   8m blind shaft in open joint cutting across obvious exposed limestone.

Tackle – 10m ladder; bar belay; 18m lifeline.

FLAKE CAVE   NGR SD 721839   Grade I
Alt. 277m   **Length 6m**

Explored 1975, UWFRA.

GScL.   Sink in left bank of Broken Gill 37m upstream of Spider Cave. Low squeeze into small chamber with narrow outlet blocked by rock ribs. Water probably resurges at Spider Cave.

FLINTER GILL CAVES

Upper Cave   NGR SD 698865   Grade II
Alt. 324m   **Length 20m**   Depth 2.5m

Rediscovered 1993, ULSA/NPC.

SiL.   Boulder-covered rift entrance in true left bank of Flinter Gill, about 210m north of where the Green Lane track crosses the beck. A rift drops into a tortuously low bedding which has been followed with difficulty for about 15m. The water probably flows to the Lower Cave about 25m away.

Lower Cave   NGR SD 699869   Grade IV
Alt. 320m   **Length 304m**   Depth 15m

Explored 1977, Dent Caving Club; extended 1993, ULSA/NPC.

WARNING – The cave should not be entered if water is flowing down the entrance. Much of the cave is only passable during very low water conditions and exploration should only be considered during prolonged dry, settled weather.

SiL.   Dam surrounds slab-covered entrance (which may be obscured by flood debris) on true left side of Flinter Gill 30m downstream of Upper Cave. Drop into wet crawl that reaches a junction after 30m where the stream divides. Ahead is a too-tight passage to a sump but to the left is a small awkward passage that leads through a duck under flake to a wet crawl and a further duck. Beyond, the entertaining struggle continues with an awkward Z-bend followed by a well-decorated grotto (care!). The outlet is an enlarged squeeze and wet crawl to Spout Hall, a 7m long fault chamber where the stream sinks. Here a dry route through formations leads into another decorated chamber and a crawl that rejoins the water at Stream Junction with fine formations (care!).

Downstream the workout continues with The Long Flume, a sporting glide along a steeply-dipping, smooth-floored crawl with fast flowing water. This continues past several grottoes and a wet squeeze until a squeeze over a fallen boulder is reached. Beyond is a further tight squeeze into a continuing crawl where the way forward finally gets too low.

Upstream from Stream Junction is a crawl in water which soon breaks out into a short walking-sized chamber with good formations (care!). Water enters from two passages, the first too immature to follow, the other obvious way being a wet crawl that can be followed for 30m to a choke close to the sink in Spout Hall.

FLOOD CAVERN   NGR SD 737862   Grade II
Alt. 166m   Length 122m
Explored NSG.

WARNING – Takes large volume of water in flood and lower series fills to roof.

GScL. Just down-valley of Black Dub on N side of riverbed is large overhang with masses of flood debris. Towards left end of cliff face is route through debris into short passage and 2.1m climb down into wide, low passage leading into chamber 6m wide and 2.1m high, with extensive sand and silt blockages downstream. Upstream is easy crawl over boulders into second chamber with choked outlets and aven climb into short, sandy upper bedding.

GASTACK BECK CAVE   NGR SD 724838   Grade II
Alt. 220m   Length 153m
Explored 1963, HWCPC; extended 1969, BSA.

GScL. Entrance about 180m downstream of road bridge on shelf on right bank, just past rising from boulders. Passage 0.9m high leads for 30m to abandoned passage on right. This has many flowstone cascades and is 24m long to sandy chamber with tight exit over block to surface opposite Robin's Dub Cave. Main way continues to second passage on right which is a large oxbowed oxbow, very muddy in parts. Streamway is lowering crawl to shallow canal and final silty sump, dived for 2.5m to hopeless silt choke. A climb up out of the canal leads into a bouldery chamber with a route down to a dangerously loose choke or a 5m climb up a loose rift to the upper entrance. Permission – Deepdale Head Farm.

GORGE CAVE   NGR SD 741864   Grade I
Alt. 187m   Length 6m

GScL. In N wall of gorge just upstream of Penny Bridge is small rising with flat crawl becoming too low where floor rises.

GRABBERS CAVE   NGR SD 739863   Grade II
Alt. 178m   Length 55m
Explored 1987, NCC.

GScL. Low bedding entrance on rock shelf on left bank of river bed downstream of Ibbeth Peril. Tight crawl draughts strongly and intersects streamway. Downstream is 12m wet crawl to constriction, and upstream after 40m of wet crawling is low air-space.

GREAT COUM POT   NGR SD 709837   Grade II
Alt. 525m   Depth 7m
Explored 1976, South West Essex Tech. Coll. C.C.

UnL.   Dry shaft beside small quarry at end of scar is covered by lorry door.
Bottom is 3m wide and choked, although narrow rift drops further.

Tackle – 8m ladder; 2m belay; 12m lifeline.

GREAT JOINT HOLES   NGR SD 788898   Grade II
Alt. 532m   Depth 10m
Explored 1980, DHSS.

ML.   Large depression with four choked shafts. Water has been tested to
Hugh's Moss Cave.

GREAT KNOUTBERRY HOLES   NGR SD 794867
                                                     Grade II

Alt. 564m
Explored 1963, EPC.

ML.   In northernmost of large twin shakeholes 427m N of last wall corner at
summit of Arten Gill track.

1.   Length 6m   Depth 15m
Entrance under boulder bridge by small landslip at N end of shakehole is
unsafe and pot should not be descended. Pitch lands in high, choked rift with
descending boulder slope.

2.   Length 15m   Depth 18m
Tight entrance in gritstone boulders 8m SW of 1 opens into wide rift pitch.
At foot cross passage enters high parallel rift. Limestone is very rough –
gloves essential.

Tackle for either hole – 15m ladder; 6m belay; 18m lifeline.

GREAT WHEEL CAVE   NGR SD 720836   Grade II
Alt. 274m   **Length 76m**
Explored 1969, BSA.

GScL.   In S bank of Gastack Beck in collapse area upstream of road. Fissure
rising enters small chamber with alternative entrance hole under tree trunk
on bank. Upstream is 61m mostly crawling to very low section. Beyond is low
collapse chamber followed by duck into larger passage. Short inlet on right
ends in well-decorated chamber and main passage continues, to emerge from
upper entrance behind large boulder at sink.
Permission – Hill Top Farm.

HACKERGILL CAVE   NGR SD 737862   Grade I
Alt. 173m   **Length 113m**
GScL.   Bedding entrances at lower end of Hackergill gorge join an upstream
bedding plane with vadose trench. Easy crawl on scalloped floor to junction.

Left divides and chokes after 15m and right chokes after a similar distance. The passage ends are a few metres from badly-choked sinks in Hackergill.

HACKERGILL POT   NGR SD 737861   Grade II
Alt. 175m   **Depth 14m**
Explored 1969, BSA.

GScL. In right bank of Hackergill 46m above confluence with river Dee is joint entrance with pitch a few metres in. Awkward descent through constrictions ends in small, choked chamber. Floods completely in wet weather.

Tackle – 15m ladder; bar & sling belay; 21m lifeline.

HELL'S CAULDRON CAVE   NGR SD 736861   Grade I
Alt. 175m   **Length 14m**

GScL. On N side of river in large cliff at Hell's Cauldron. Easy climb into passage entering wide bedding crawl which steps down into further bedding ending in small chamber, heavily choked. Right of entrance is 3m climb up into rift which gets too tight.

Hell's Cauldron, the plunge pool in bed of River Dee, takes water from Hackergill but has no stream outlet in normal conditions. Divers have found the pool choked by cobbles at 4m depth.

HIDDEN VALLEY CAVE   NGR SD 795904   Grade II
Alt. 503m   **Length 91m**
Explored 1966, WRPC/CPC.

ML. Sink in large, blind depression 595m ENE of Doublet Cave. Entrance is blocked by boulders. Low winding crawl to duck into roomier going in canal passage ending at low air-space.

HIGH GILL CAVES
Upper Cave   NGR SD 694863   Grade II
Alt. 275m   **Length 244m**
Explored 1958, NPC.

SiL. Fissure entrance in E bank of gill just downstream of sheepfold. Short drop into passage 3m wide and 0.9m high lowering to wallow and easier going to chamber with good formations. Left is short inlet becoming too tight while downstream passage continues from opposite wall as crawl through blocks at floor level into easier crawling and further well decorated chamber (care!). At far end of this a short passage leads to smaller chamber and choke.

Middle Cave   NGR SD 694865   Grade II
Alt. 259m   **Length 91m**
Explored 1962, Sedbergh School Speleological Society.

HScL. Sink in shakehole E of gill leads down fissure to streamway entering small chamber after 33m. Large bedding to right gradually enlarges and has fine formations (care!). Varied going ends at solid choke.

Lower Cave   NGR SD 693868   Grade III
Alt. 227m   Length 441m
Extended 1958, NPC.

HScL.   Obvious entrance near farm where stream emerges high on E bank
of gill. Scramble over debris into chamber 2.4m high, walled half way across.
Easy walking gradually lowers to crawling into larger chamber about 15m
long and 8m high with waterfall entering at far end. Scaling gear is needed for
this and upstream is traversing over and through calcited blocks for 46m to
open passage. Walking with occasional crawls in streamway with thick shale
bed in floor and lower part of walls ends at choke with trickle of water
emerging. This is same choke which ends the Upper and Middle Caves.

Tackle – 8m of scaling gear for waterfall in Lower Cave.
Permission – High Gill Farm, Gawthrop.

HOLE HOUSE CAVE   NGR SD 693883   Grade III
Alt. 146m   Length 55m
Explored 1974, Worth Valley Caving Club.

GScL.   Small rising on E bank of gill beside lane to Hole House Farm, just
upstream of limekiln. Flat crawling for 15m to sharp bend and small chamber.
Low crawling in canal with one section only passable on one's back reaches
second small chamber at junction. Left is impassable almost immediately
while main passage becomes too low in wide bedding after 9m, just after
small branch ending in unstable boulders.
Permission – Hole House Farm.

HUGH'S MOSS CAVE   NGR SD 788901   Grade III
Alt. 503m   Length 1.1km
Explored 1968, YURT; main explorations 1981, DHSS,

WARNING – Extremely flood prone – loose boulders in some areas.

Furthest of the three resurgences has two entrances. Slide down into the
dry one and pass boulder choke on right via a squeeze into wet passage.
Passages on right run to wet entrance but to left is slope up to second squeeze
and Pellucid Passage and another squeeze into main stream on a higher level.

Downstream becomes tight close to resurgence and passages on left head
back towards the entrance. Upstream is canal and decorated chamber on
way to first breakdown chamber and two ways on into Nervous Breakdown
Chamber whose roof does not inspire confidence! Roomy varied going
upstream past parallel flooded rift to Dihedral Hall, 1m wide, 10m long and
12m high. Ahead is breakdown chamber with stream entering on right from
small passages. First is impassable but second is squeeze to wet crawl into
Frog Hall or more pleasant route via boulder scramble at end of breakdown
chamber. Way forward swings round to right with Long Inlet straight ahead –
100m of wet canal to twin sumps.

Main passage continues as large bedding to decorated chamber and squeeze
into Dog's Head Chamber (7m × 3m × 3m). Varied going for 70m to canal
and 'T' junction where right closes down. To left is Cacoethes Chamber with

formations and ahead is Canal Complex – a maze of wet passages with way out a crawl over and between boulders into the Rest Room. 15m ahead is way up into Upper Series and forward is maze with stream which becomes too tight.

Upper Series

Above 4m climb is ring bolt for rope. **Do not enter** passage to right which has delicate formations and ends in a choke above the stream.

The left passage to the south across a traverse is walking passage but reaching it is very awkward. Pass under poised block and past aven to a crawl back to the stream, which falls 3m into a tight rift. Upstream is walking and crawling under large boulders into chamber with tight inlet on left. The way forward is dry for a short distance and at a shattered area is large aven over to left (Bromley's Aven). This is very close to Great Joint Holes. A bolt route enters passage which becomes too tight.

Continuing streamway becomes a crawl close to end of Pinchin Pot and way on degenerates into a boulder choke with very low bedding to right and further boulder choke.

Tackle – 8m rope for climb to Upper Series.

IBBETH PERIL CAVE 1   NGR SD 741864   Grade III
Alt. 181m   **Length 1.2km**   **Depth 23m**

Total length of Ibbeth Peril 1 and 2 with Broadfield Caves is 2.65km.
Explored NSG; extended 1992, DHSS.

WARNING – When river Dee is in flood, entrance is completely sumped.

GScL. Entrance under overhang next to waterfall into large pool. Scramble over flood debris into passage which lowers to short crawl. Past this is choked inlet on left and man-made dam beyond which the floor cuts down to cascade into small chamber where water sinks and walk out into Main Chamber. Walls swing away and floor of silt and cobbles changes to massive fallen slabs sloping down into the chamber proper – 61m long, 30m wide and up to 14m high.

Along chamber wall 12m to the NW is slot down into So Low Series. A spiralling route through somewhat unstable chamber meets the water which sinks in the entrance passage. Both the water outlet and a bedding plane trending NW become impassable.

Near left wall of Main Chamber are fine formations (care!) and several small grottos, one with a short, choked passage. At far end of chamber is waterfall, overcome by a short climb to a further cascade, easily climbed into a large passage with formations on the left side. Floor lifts steadily to double bend and short oxbow on left. Pool and wet crawl end at upstream sump, dived but too tight after 21m.

Near foot of waterfall in Main Chamber are routes down through boulders into two series of passages. Left of fall is climb down into Mud Series: left leads to chokes below NW side of Main Chamber; ahead with the water leads past short, choked side passages to low air-space section, passable after drought to sump; and right are passages becoming low and muddy. This route passes

CAVES OF THE IBBETH PERIL AREA

Plan based on BSA/KCC/ULSA/DHSS and CDG surveys

0   100m

N

sump

Main Chamber

Jordan's Passage

Problem Series

Link Way

Old

pitch

IBBETH PERIL CAVES

BROADFIELD CAVES ENT

Upstream

Downstream Passage

R.Dee

Purgatory Passage

Pretties Passage

Paradise Passage

Hacker Gill

UPPER HACKERGILL CAVE ENTS

short branch on left to reach climbable drop and slope down into streamway where water from sump reappears and flows off into downstream sump.

Other series starts just right of waterfall and collects main flow. Large passage enters from right after a few metres, becoming low upstream at a duck where the Upstream Downstream link to Ibbeth Peril 2 emerges. Downstream to left is fine passage to junction beyond which the streamway gets too tight. Right at junction leads to two static sumps, one reached by a 5.4m pitch. Sumps have been dived into extensive flooded bedding planes which join below descending submerged rifts where a wide bedding has been followed to a junction 150m from base at −27m.

Tackle – 8m ladder; 3m belay; 12m lifeline.

IBBETH PERIL CAVE 2   NGR SD 741864   Grade III

Alt. 181m   **Length 780m**   **Depth 18m**

Explored 1967, NSG; extended 1992, DHSS.

WARNING – In high flood, water flows into entrance passage, which becomes impassable.

GScL.   Behind boulders at foot of scar 15m from Ibbeth Peril Cave 1. Short drop into flat crawl through pool and continuing through small chamber and past extensive bedding inlet area on left down small cascades to head of pitch with belay on right. Landing is to one side of Main Chamber from which several passages radiate including two opposite head of pitch, reached by climb up stal-covered boulder slope. At top of climb is short, wide passage blocked by stalagmite and with good formations (care!), while the other passage, reached by traverse across boulders, has small stream emerging and is awkward going with good formations past several squeezes for 24m to stalagmited partial choke.

Behind foot of ladder is easy 3m scramble up into wide, low passage with mud floor, giving way to collapsed blocks and crawl to left and junction with Pearl Chamber to the right. A tight muddy crawl on the left intersects Upstream Downstream Passage.

Downstream is a crawl, passing a roof inlet which is below Ibbeth Peril pool! A low passage on the right needs digging after 20m but following the stream down via a short bypass leads to a canal with variable air-space which emerges below the waterfall area of Ibbeth Peril Cave 1.

Upstream in Upstream Downstream is a mixture of crawling and walking past areas of loose breakdown until after 90m cobbles prevent progress.

Two routes from Main Chamber lead into downstream passage, which soon enlarges to walking size but quickly lowers where stream sinks under right wall and after 12m more is a choke, close to the Main Chamber in Ibbeth Peril Cave 1. Upstream from entry into streamway is the Old Link Way, starting as a trench in a wide bedding but becoming an uncomfortable crawl which eventually emerges, after several squeezes and muddy sections, in Broadfield Caves.

Tackle – 8m ladder; 3m belay; 12m lifeline.

INGHEADS CAVE   NGR SD 773907   Grade I
Alt. 271m   **Length 8m**
Explored 1977, GC.

HScL.   Flood rising on SE bank of Clough River 200m downstream of Ingheads Bridge. Entrance behind tree above resurgence, into joint passage with standing water. Sinks above bridge.

INNOMINATE HOLE   NGR SD 745845   Grade II
Alt. 494m   **Length 24m**
Explored 1974, KCC.

UnL.   Follow track up towards Whernside from near Whernside Manor. Just before walls end is small dry valley to S, in which is cave. A 1.5m drop and slide to left under large boulder leads to walking-size passage to partial choke. Beyond is more walking to final choke. Stream probably rises about 30m away.

KIRK BANK CAVE   NGR SD 731870   Grade IV
Alt. 326m   **Length 557m**   **Depth 21m**
Explored 1981, RRCPC.

Entrance is small stream sink on Kirk Bank, NE of Blue Bonnet Well. 5m of low tube leads to sharp left bend and crawl through pools to emerge in larger passage. Easy going for 125m passes a small inlet on left, which ends too tight after 60m, to a sudden side step where passage becomes a narrow meandering rift with crumbling chert ledges. After approximately 180m an area of collapse is met, and just beyond the stream is lost in a small crack on the right. The next 45m is a sideways crawl in a narrow rift, with a number of loose flakes.

At the end of this stretch the character changes completely, becoming a nice arched hands and knees crawl. Finally, the roof lowers and deeper water is encountered, until just beyond a rock bridge the passage ends at a froth-covered sump.

The resurgence, in Scotchergill Wood (NGR SD 724873), can be entered for 15m to a choke, and is approximately 200m from the sump.

THE LETTERBOX   NGR SD 738863   Grade I
Alt. 177m   **Depth 3m**
Explored 1970, BSA.

GScL.   Part way up N bank of river a few metres from head of Hackergill Gorge. Short crawl to tight drop, difficult to re-ascend. Too tight at bottom but there is a strong draught and small stream can be heard in wet weather.

LOCKIN GARTH CAVES   NGR SD 722837   Grade I
Alt. 177m   **Length 6m**
Explored 1970, BSA.

1.   GScL.   Small cave on left of pool below large waterfall beside road. Low crawl divides and becomes too tight.

2. GScL. Climb up to ledge at S side of pool reaches large entrance with steep slope down into chamber and impassable fissure.

LOW HALL CAVE   NGR SD 704876   Grade III
Alt. 144m   Length 300m
Extended 1980, Bedfordshire Rock Outdoor and Cave Club.

GScL. Twin entrances in E bank of Low Hall Beck, just behind farm, join in a few metres, and easy passage continues past short inlet on left to where roof lowers. A 5m long duck, which will sump rapidly in wet weather, brings one to a junction, with a small passage on the right which ends too tight just beyond a small aven. Ahead the main stream emerges from a cobble-floored bedding (which may require digging) and this gradually enlarges to give about 180m of pleasant streamway to where a low chamber is reached. A number of small inlets enter this, but all soon end in dangerous loose chokes.
Permission – Low Hall Farm.

LOWER SCYTHE CAVE   NGR SD 743865   Grade I
Alt. 188m   Length 6m
Explored 1971, BSA.

WARNING – In wet weather when river flows at entrance, cave fills to roof.

GScL. Boulder-covered entrance below small rock face on N bank 9m down-valley from side stream. Step down into low, wet bedding which is too low to left and probably connects with Scythe Cave. Downstream is narrow and blocked by mud slump from bedding on right.

MILL BECK FLOOD SINK   NGR SD 701869   Grade I
Alt. 157m   Length 10m   Depth 2m
GScL. A normally dry flood sink located at the end of a short dry stream bed 11m downstream of Mill Beck Sink Cave. Behind grill holding back flood debris is a crawl ending at a small chamber where water enters in wet conditions. The only outlet is a very low bedding choked by flood debris and an assortment of dead animals neatly packaged in polythene bags.
Permission – Millbeck, Dent (but permission is not normally given).

MILL BECK SINK CAVE   NGR SD 701869   Grade IV
Alt. 160m   Length 561m   Depth 28m
Entered circa 1983, persons unknown; explored 1993, ULSA & NPC.

WARNING – The entire cave fills to the roof during flood and it is only possible to enter during prolonged dry, settled conditions. The further reaches contain extensive and pungent slurry deposits that seep into the cave from the fields above – not for those with weak stomachs!

GScL. Entrance at sink of Mill Beck is capped by an iron grill which prevents access to the cave. A descent of 2.7m through boulders and water drops into a fissure passage entering a small bedding chamber. The outlet is a sporting mixture of sideways crawling and thrutching around several awkward bends in narrow, clean-washed passage. In low flow conditions the stream may sink into some impenetrable holes in the floor, however, these are liable to become choked in which case the water flows all the way to the first pitch. After 49m the floor cuts down to the head of first pitch, bypassed via a dry crawl and 5m climb on the right.

From the base of the pitch following the stream leads to a smooth-floored, flat-out crawl in water (where the water enters from a too-low bedding on the left if the stream is sinking in the entrance crawl). An enlarging trench then leads to the head of the second pitch which, although short, is a wet and awkward overhanging climb that is best laddered.

The landing is in an aven chamber with large flowstone formations. The stream cuts back under the pitch into a short canyon passage ending at The Fault, a shattered hading rift criss-crossed by calcite veins. Here the stream drops down a hole under the left wall into a wet bedding plane that soon gets very low; the main way forward is a dry crawl on a shelf ahead, a low and sharply scalloped bedding that passes through The Shredder, two very low thrutches over sharp scallops. Easier going is soon reached at an enlargement in a small bedding chamber and ahead a continuing crawl over cobbles enters an abandoned trench passage that regains the stream near a bedding chamber on the right.

Upstream, the water can be followed for 40m to where way forward gets unpleasantly low close to the stream outlet at The Fault. Downstream, a fine walking and stooping-sized streamway continues for 86m until the water is finally lost in a steeply dipping phreatic rift passage partially choked by pebbles and shingle.

To the right at the stream sink is a dry flood outlet, an easy hands and knees crawl over cobbles that eventually degenerates into a flat-out passage containing liberal quantities of vile-smelling slurry deposits. After another 110m a junction is reached where a slide up a cobble bank to the right enters an awkward flat-out crawl dissected by vertical chert beds and containing several noxious pools. Those with insensitive noses can continue for a further 65m of aromatic flat-out crawling to gain a final static sump and a well-earned tick for perseverence. A side passage on the right just before the sump can be followed for 10m to another static sump.

Tackle

Pitch	Ladder	Belay	Lifeline
1st	–	–	–
2nd	4m	2.5m	–

Permission – Millbeck, Dent (but permission not normally given).

NAMELESS CAVE   NGR SD 732862   Grade I
Alt. 153m   Length 30m
Explored 1969, BSA/NSCC.

GScL. In S bank just downstream of footbridge at Lenny's Leap is flat crawl with trickle of water emerging at foot of small scar. After 9m is junction with larger rift, choked to right but passable to left by traversing over obstacles to another choke.

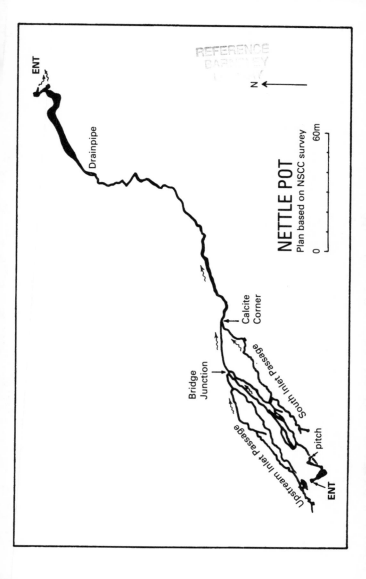

NETTLE POT

Plan based on NSCC survey

ENT

Drainpipe

Calcite Corner

Bridge Junction

South Inlet passage

Upstream Inlet passage

pitch

ENT

N

0   60m

NETTLE POT

NGR SD 693873

Grade III

Alt. 159m   **Length 0.8km**   Depth 30m

Discovered 1970, NSG; explored NSCC.

WARNING – In flood conditions entrance crawl may sump completely.

GScL.   In SE bank of Nettle Pot Gill 91m upstream of road bridge at Gawthrop*. Obvious entrance into small chamber with crawl to left to head of pitch with bolt belay. Below is stooping-height passage to slight enlargement and complex junction with several other passages, but main route continues ahead to join main streamway at Bridge Junction. Left passage at complex junction turns back parallel to main passage for 30m and has tight oxbow; right at complex junction are three ways into another parallel passage leading left to another junction. Left here is alternative route to Bridge Junction while ahead enters the small South Inlet Passage, leading right to an aven chamber with choked beddings above, and left to join the main streamway at Calcite Corner.

Main Stream Passage

Upstream from Bridge Junction the passage divides after 11m. Upstream Inlet Passage to right is smaller and starts with a chert wall on the right. After 107m, having passed a small inlet on the left, an aven chamber is reached and a rift leads to an inlet bedding which is too tight. Larger way from junction ends very close to the aven chamber.

Downstream from Bridge Junction a well-decorated streamway (care!) leads to Calcite Corner, where South Inlet Passage enters. On downstream is Cascade Alley, a finely-decorated walking passage with a thick shale bed at floor level. Passage eventually reduces to crawl and long pool; to right is the Drainpipe and to left Coward's Oxbow, rejoining at a wet crawl which sumps in wet weather. Final flat-out crawl leads into concrete culvert, 40m long, to emerge at the rising below the Dent-Sedbergh road at NGR SD 696875.

Tackle – 8m ladder; short spreader; 12m lifeline.

(*N.B. Park cars in village, not at bridge.)

NO LINK CAVE

NGR SD 740862

Grade I

Alt. 189m   **Length 9m**

Explored 1975, UWFRA.

GScL.   About 55m downstream of Upper Hackergill Cave is small covered entrance in N bank which can only be entered feet first as below 1.2m drop just inside is sideways crawl with no room to turn. End is tight corner with impassable slot and vocal connection to main streamway in Upper Hackergill Cave.

Permission – Hacker Gill Head.

OPTIMISTIC POT

NGR SD 789864

Grade II

Alt. 575m   Depth 18m

Extended 1990, DHSS.

ML.   Tight slot lands on small ledge at 2m. Bolt belay for next 15m drop in a tight shaft onto debris and a squeeze into an aven with daylight above. Forward is 2m climb where digging is in progress.

Tackle – 15m ladder; short spreader; 22m lifeline.

OXBOW CAVE   NGR SD 743860   Grade II
Alt. 219m   **Length 15m**
Explored 1969, BSA.

GScL.   In S bank of Hackergill 122m upstream of farm is narrow rift joining muddy, flat crawl at 'T' junction. Muddy wallow emerges from bedding entrance concealed behind nettles.
Permission – Hacker Gill Head.

PENNY FARM CAVE   NGR SD 731862   Grade I
Alt. 213m   **Length 30m**

GScL.   Obvious entrance on S side of beck on corner upstream of junction with Nor Gill. Short, roomy cave very close to Dent Fault ends in collapse.
Permission – Hebblethwaite Hall, Sedbergh.

PESSIMISTIC POT   NGR SD 792865   Grade II
Alt. 580m   **Depth 22m**
Extended 1983, DHSS.

WARNING – Top of main pitch is rather loose.

ML.   Tight 4m drop leads into spectacular shaft. Belay ladder on surface (15m belay) for 17m drop. From debris climb up 3m and squeeze into parallel shaft dropping to lower level and a confusion of small passages.

Tackle – 22m ladder; 15m belay; 25m lifeline.

PINCHIN POT   NGR SD 788898   Grade II
Alt. 534m   **Depth 15m**
Explored 1980, DHSS.

ML.   Pitch of 5m lands in cross rift with descent over boulders onto 8m pitch in circular shaft with delicate boulders in roof (care!). Crawl through narrow passage into parallel shaft and fissure. Water emerges in Hugh's Moss Cave which is extremely close.

Tackle

Pitch	Ladder	Belay	Lifeline
1st	6m	Bar & spreader	10m
2nd	9m	3m	14m

THE POPPLES   NGR SD 730861
Alt. 148m   **Length 55m**
Explored 1990-1992, CDG.

GScL.   The all weather resurgence for the caves of the Upper Dentdale System which drains all of the upper part of the valley. Water rises from several low beddings on the south side of the River Dee but there is no enterable passage for the non-diver. The larger, more easterly rising has been entered by divers who have followed a very low bedding plane to a point about 50m from base.

POPPLE CAVE   NGR SD 731862   Grade II
Alt. 149m   Length 153m
Extended 1971, KCC; and 1972, CDG.

WARNING – Cave is connected to main water flow and floods rapidly and completely in wet weather.

GScL. Obvious bedding entrance at foot of small scar on S side of river Dee 64m up-valley of main rising (The Popples). Low crawl to 2m step down into larger passage. Downstream is completely choked and upstream leads to pool and junction with crawl up on shelf to left. This continues over mud floor to small chamber with static sump. Main route leads through deepening pool to widen into chamber and impressive sump, dived for about 17m to where a lowering of the roof prevents access to an apparently large submerged passage.

Just back from sump in right wall is muddy crawl to collapse area and further crawling to impenetrable inlet, 6m past which is small sump.

RACE FOLD POT   NGR SD 787864   Grade III
Alt. 570m   Depth 18m
Explored 1983, DHSS.

ML. Stream in decent sized valley falls down narrow rift beneath huge gritstone boulder. 3m belay required for 18m of ladder. First 5m are **very** tight and stirrup is useful on return. There is a ledge at 8m and take bedding to left to regain ladder below a flake. This is very tricky to reverse! Roomy shaft lands on boulders and tight crawl ends in blank wall. Water emerges at Cross Wold Rising 0.4km distant.

ROBIN'S DUB CAVE   NGR SD 724838   Grade III
Alt. 229m   Length 426m
Explored 1968, BSA and NSCC.

WARNING – Tight crawl near entrance may sump in wet weather.

GScL. Joint entrance in N bank of Gastack Beck a short way below road bridge. Crawl to low bedding; upstream to left a wet crawl gets too tight after 18m. Downstream passage enlarges after squeeze and cuts down below well-decorated bedding (care!). Canyon continues, with small cascades, past several roof-level inlets; largest of these is 24m long passage to silt choke.

Main passage reaches climbable waterfall, spanned by rock arch, dropping into well-decorated chamber. Smaller outlet with some impassable inlets becomes crawl with flowstone on walls (care!) to cascades down chert ribs, the last being down a 2.4m high chert sheet. Easy traverse and climb down enters chamber and hands and knees crawl passing small abandoned outlet

on left. Beyond, the main way forward quickly reaches a mud-choked oxbow on the right whilst ahead the water flows into a flat-out crawl, a wet and very low bedding forced through shingle and cobbles to an impassable bedrock squeeze after another 8m. Water reappears at Robin's Dub Rising.
Permission – Deepdale Head Farm.

ROBIN'S DUB RISING   NGR SD 726844   Grade III
Alt. 185m   Length 25m
Explored 1978, CDG.

WARNING – The cave is extremely flood liable. The passage beyond the sump can only be reached by non-divers in low flow conditions.

GScL.   A large rising situated on the true right bank of Deepdale Beck. The rising carries water from Robin's Dub Cave and from sinks in Deepdale Beck which are evident only in low water conditions.

A slide over a slab at the entrance reaches a duck and a short wet crawl ending at a 2.5m long sump situated under the left wall. The sump is not suitable for free-diving due to an abundance of sharp roof pendants which may hinder progress; in very dry conditions it can be passed as a low air-space duck to a further 20m of low, watery and gloomy bedding plane where all ways forward finally get too low over shingle deposits.

ROOT CAVE   NGR SD 729862   Grade I
Alt. 148m   Length 37m
WARNING – Fills to the roof in wet weather.

GScL.   About 64m down-valley from main risings (The Popples) is small channel entering river from S. Up this is low entrance in small scar. Flat crawl to silt bank and roots in roof; beyond is pool and easier crawl to climb up and over large boulders to choke.

SCYTHE CAVE   NGR SD 743865   Grade II
Alt. 188m   Length 18m
WARNING – Fills to roof when river is flowing past.

GScL.   On S bank below rock shelf nearly opposite small gill entering from N. Obvious entrance into low streamway; upstream to left divides and becomes impenetrable after 6m. Downstream is flat, wet crawl to duck which can be passed in dry weather to partial shingle and debris choke.

SHAKING MOSS CAVE   NGR SD 788893   Grade II
Alt. 536m   Length 33m
Explored 1966, KCC.

ML.   On Shaking Moss where small stream sinks at end of small gorge above Dent-Garsdale road. Low, wet entrance to cross joints and alternative entrance via 4.8m pot in next shakehole. Downstream leads to portcullis and chamber below 6m pot. Passage beyond gets smaller and stream runs into choked rift.

SHAKING MOSS POT   NGR SD 788893   Grade II
Alt. 536m   **Depth 14m**
Explored 1966, KCC.

ML. In large shakehole 27m SW of Shaking Moss Cave. Single pitch into large chamber with no exit.

Tackle – 15m ladder; stake & sling belay; 18m lifeline.

SHALE CAVE   NGR SD 726833   Grade I
Alt. 247m   **Length 33m**
Explored 1970, BSA.

GScL. Upstream of top footbridge at farm is entrance behind large boulder on shelf on W bank of Deepdale Beck. Easy crawl with upper part in shale bed rises until floor is also shale. Flat crawling and two short joint-determined sections ends in choked bedding.
Permission – Deepdale Head Farm.

SHRINKING POT   NGR SD 787893   Grade II
Alt. 536m   **Depth 9m**
Explored 1971, YURT.

ML. In small shakehole E of Coal Road, 183m N of Cowgill Head. Hole into rift pitch with much shattered rock. Fissure beyond blocks at foot is too tight.

Tackle – 9m ladder; stake & sling belay; 12m lifeline.

SIKE FOOT POT   NGR SD 754839   Grade II
Alt. 503m   **Length 6m**   **Depth 6m**
Explored 1972, CPC.

UnL. In shakehole just E of entrance to Duncan Sike Cave by shooting box. Straight pitch to crawl which chokes.

Tackle – 8m ladder; stake & sling belay; 12m lifeline.

SLIT CAVE   NGR SD 746866   Grade III
Alt. 192m   **Length 107m**   **Depth 6m**
Explored 1970, NSCC.

WARNING – Floods rapidly and completely in wet weather.

GScL. About 30m down-valley from Slit Sink is excavated hole under scar, blocked with boulders and flood debris. Climb down into low, wide bedding plane. Upstream soon reaches extensive choke and vocal connection to Slit Sink. Downstream wet crawling, broken by step down, ends at a choke.

SLIT SINK   NGR SD 746866   Grade II
Alt. 189m   **Depth 6m**

WARNING – Floods rapidly and completely when river starts to flow past.

GScL. Obvious entrance in small scar below road, in N bank. Awkward pitch to rock-floored bedding, heavily choked in each direction. Entrance now sealed.

Tackle – 8m ladder; sling belay; 12m lifeline.

SPIDER CAVE   NGR SD 721839   Grade I
Alt. 265m   **Length 9m**
Explored 1975, UWFRA.

GScL.   Obvious resurgence entrance on N bank of Broken Gill just upstream of footbridge. Spacious passage to crawl up cobbles into flat crawl which becomes too tight.

STONE RIGG CAVE   NGR SD 682866   Grade II
Alt. 290m   **Length 30m**
Explored 1970, NSCC.

Where small stream sinks by wall W of Stone Rigg on the Dentdale-Barbondale watershed is low elliptical passage running S at shallow depth. Entrance filled in again at farmer's request.

TOM CROFT'S CAVE   NGR SD 695915   Grade II
Alt. 153m   **Length 18m**
GScL.   On S bank of river about 91m downstream of Danny Cave is large entrance closing to small hole. Narrow crawls and climbs reach small chamber with tight rift dropping to sump.

TROUGH CAVE   NGR SD 772858   Grade I
Alt. 256m   **Length 36m**
Explored 1969, KCC.

GScL.   Obvious, partly-walled entrance on W side of riverbed just below junction with Great Blake Beck. Low crawl to streamway after 4m; downstream is too tight and flat crawl upstream becomes too low after about 30m.

TUB HOLE   NGR SD 732861   Grade III
Alt. 153m   **Length 1km**   **Vertical range 45m**
Explored 1924, YRC; extended 1959, NPC; 1974, CDG; 1992-3, ULSA/NPC.

WARNING – This is the main flood vent for the Upper Dentdale System which carries all the water sinking higher up the dale. It floods completely and extremely rapidly.

GScL.   The entrance is located below a small scar at the head of a normally dry side valley to the south of the River Dee. A scramble down over boulders leads into wide bedding cave floored by a pool. An easy crawl soon enlarges to a stooping-height passage that passes some roof inlets including a short passage that can be followed to a too-tight rift where water enters. The impressive main passage continues past a flood outlet on the right, a 12m crawl ending at the Oxbow Sump, a 10m long tight dive that connects with a side passage just inside the entrance.

After 91m a climb up out of the water enters a collapse chamber of standing height with a descent back to water at the far end. This is the First Pool, a 15m long static sump bypassed via an arched rift passage on the left. Beyond is a large walking-sized bedding cave containing extensive shingle deposits. This soon lowers to a crawl ending at the Second Pool, a 10m long sump. The sump can be bypassed via a pool and low duck on the right of the passage or by climbing up into the roof just before the pool to enter a short dry bedding crawl that passes over the sump.

Both bypass routes reunite at the upstream side of the Second Pool where a bouldery, walking-sized bedding cave leads to the Third Pool, the main sump in the cave. This has been dived for 5m to a three-way junction. From here South Passage is a low bedding followed for 90m and continuing; North Passage is a 25m dive to a too-tight squeeze between boulders. The main way forward is East Passage, a huge and complex submerged bedding that descends to 18m depth and a chamber after 125m; beyond here is a massive submerged bedding that attains a maximum depth of 38m and which has been followed up-valley to the present limit of exploration at 34m depth and 405m from base.

The dry cave continues beyond the Third Pool as a smaller bedding located on the right side of the passage. Easy progress over boulders leads a route down to the undived Fourth Pool on the left whilst ahead a crawl continues through a series of rifts and low bedding planes containing extensive deposits of shingle and flood debris. After 170m a slide over a cobble bank on the right leads to a crawl and static pool. Beyond is an upward slope to a wriggle between blocks into a bedding chamber where a stream is encountered sinking on the left.

Following the water upstream through a block-strewn crawl reaches a duck followed by a thrutch up a clean-washed rift to a junction. Ahead a draughting crawl in the water can be followed to where the way ahead becomes too low over fallen slabs. To the left at the junction are a series of dry crawls in an extensive bedding plane; one of these can be followed for 30m to a clean-washed draughting choke that is believed to lie just below the dry stream bed of the River Dee. In normal conditions the water in this final section of cave is believed to come from a sink in the bed of the River Dee a few metres downstream of Cascade Cave.

Permission – Tub Hole Farm.

UPPER BLACK DUB CAVE   NGR SD 737862   Grade I
Alt. 174m   **Length 23m**
Explored 1969, KCC.

GScL.   On opposite side of gorge to Hackergill Cave is bedding entrance leading to 'T' junction. Left is easy crawl to chimney down into entrance overhang of Black Dub Cave. Right is crawl becoming too low after 18m.

UPPER HACKERGILL CAVE NGR SD 740861 Grade III
Alt. 192m   **Length 823m**
Explored 1969, BSA.

GScL. In NE bank of gill about 153m downstream of bridge at the farm. Two entrances about 24m apart start as crawls, then cut down as narrow canyons to join main streamway. Downstream to left is Paradise Passage, a 6m high meandering passage to climb over stalagmited blocks. Easy crawl beyond passes short inlet on left and lowers to squeeze and flat crawl. Floor cuts down to trench and roomier section followed by canal. Stream again cuts down, only to sink in impassable bedding to left. Ahead is silt choke a few metres from S bank of river Dee.

Upstream from entrance passages the main streamway is a meandering canyon, with occasional crawls, to collapse area with narrow inlet from right just beyond. Inlet is 24m long to dangerous choke, passed by tight squeeze into 30m of narrow canyon to final choke. Main streamway continues to larger well-decorated section with squeezes and oxbows which help to avoid the formations. Roof lowers to crawl over cobbles and flat crawl reaches two small cascades. Higher passage with mud floor leads to inlets which get too low or choke. Main route ends at chokes after three-way junction beyond chert barriers.

Permission – Hacker Gill Head.

VOLE HOLE   NGR SD 789898   Grade III
Alt. 530m   **Length 60m**   **Depth 22m**
Explored 1980, DHSS.

ML. In massive long rocky shakehole SW of Hugh's Moss Cave. Fissure in west wall leads to top of 8m pitch onto roomy boulder slope. Second 8m drop is down steep boulders and a single 16m ladder is used for both pitches.

Narrow rift drops to junction complex and straight ahead is aven with daylight visible above. To left is crawl emerging in large passage leading to 3m climb down to a small stream. Soon becomes impassable in both directions.

Tackle – 16m ladder; 5m belay; 22m lifeline.

WATERFALL CAVES   NGR SD 724838   Grade I
Alt. 221m   **Length 30m**
Explored 1969, BSA.

GScL. Two entrances in washed out shale bed 165m downstream of road bridge. Right entrance is small rising and is too low after a few metres. Left entrance is easy crawl with larger stream, leading to impassable inlet on right. Roof lowers and crawl passes waterfall spouting from roof, to reach small chamber. Above awkward climb up cascade the passage splits and becomes too narrow.

WOLD END POT   NGR SD 744846   Grade II
Alt. 494m   **Depth 6m**

UnL.   Sink just S of track across Great Wold, near old kiln. Small, choked shaft.

Tackle – 8m ladder; stake & sling belay; 12m lifeline.

YARROW HOLE   NGR SD 750837   Grade I
Alt. 543m   **Length 9m**
Explored 1972, CPC.

ML.   Prominent sink with small waterfall about 0.4km SW of shooting box. Narrow passage to complete choke at side of collapsed shakehole.

YELLOW GILL POT   NGR SD712864   Grade III
Alt. 180m   **Length 200m**   **Depth 15m**
Explored 1983, Lancs. Caving and Climbing Club.

WARNING – The low passages below the pitch may flood to the roof in wet weather, and the three squeezes are impossible for those of above average build.

GScL.   Small, covered entrance in gill just above the road leads to a 2m drop and calcited squeeze. Beyond, small passage and further squeeze at a corner encounters junction. Ahead soon chokes, whilst to right allows better going to a 9m pitch.

From foot a low bedding with a tight, wet squeeze enlarges slightly to end at a silt choke beyond two small breakdown chambers in the roof. Entrance blocked at present.

Tackle – 10m ladder; 5m belay; 12m lifeline.

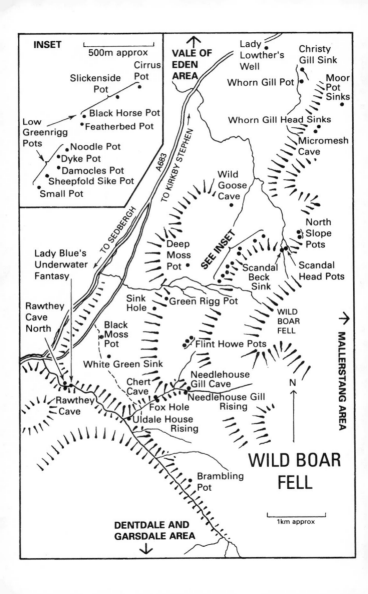

WILD BOAR FELL

BLACK MOSS POT
NGR SD 724982   **Grade I**
Alt. 320m   **Length 10m**   Depth 4.5m
Explored NPC.

GScL. Small entrance above packwall in side of large shakehole on E side of road to Needle House. Crawl to head of 3.6m climbable drop. Stream enters at foot in wet weather and disappears in choked floor. Climb up of 4m into mud choked passage.

BRAMBLING POT
NGR SD 739955   **Grade II**
Alt. 366m   Depth 6m
Explored 1982, GC.

ML. On limestone bench above the Rawthey. Slabbed-over pothole at W end of sink depression; tackle needed for descent into small chamber.

Tackle – 7m ladder; stake & sling belay; 11m lifeline.

CHERT CAVE
NGR SD 734972   **Grade III**
Alt. 335m   **Length 479m**
Explored 1966, NPC.

Small entrance on NW side of Needlehouse Gill 0.4km upstream of bridge. Low passage into bedding plane running along the strike of a bed dipping at about 30°. The going improves and after two canals a chamber is reached. Stream emerges from sump but short climb into high level passage provides by-pass into larger streamway beyond. Upstream continues to climb and crawl dropping into a pool at a junction. Right is a sump, dived for 3m to very low section, but left a crawl enters a large, dry chamber. Crawl to left here ends in a boulder choke while right the way leads over boulders as a crawl to an aven with impenetrable passage 3m up.

CHRISTY GILL SINK
NGR NY 761031   **Grade II**
Alt. 311m   **Length 15m**   Depth 11m
Explored NPC.

WARNING – Avoid in wet weather; water backs up in the lower reaches.

GScL. At foot of blind valley on Wharton Fell, 0.8km S of Birkett Common road. Entrance in rock face only takes water in flood. Crawl 6m long to head of 4.5m pitch, climbable with care, approach feet first and use lifeline. At foot is hole in floor to constricted, descending crawl which chokes with inwashed gravel and meets complete mud and boulder choke after 6m.

Tackle – 15m lifeline for climb.

DEEP MOSS POT   NGR SD 740995   Grade I
Alt. 427m
Excavated NPC.

Long, rocky shakehole in dry valley 183m N of Clouds Gill. Stream sinks near 3m long bouldery cave which becomes too small and dig at other end of shakehole is 3m deep in boulders. Large shakehole to N has draughting, bouldery hole.

FLINT HOWE POTS   NGR SD 741982/3   Grade I-II
Alt. 490m
Explored GC.

In line of deep shakeholes commencing 1km SW of Small Pot (see Low Greenrigg Pots).

1.   Peat Pot   Depth 4m
At S end of long sink depression, short passage in peat drops into small choked chamber in limestone.

2.   Trouser Pot   Depth 8m
Covered hole in shallow shake 50m SW of 1. 4.5m pitch to platform between two legs. Left leg now largely infilled with debris from right leg which drops to fissure with minute stream outlet.

Tackle – 6m ladder; stake & sling belay; 10m lifeline.

3.   Ogee Pot   Length 5m
Covered hole in E bank of very deep shakehole. Tight squeeze into low passage with soft orange mud.

4.   Depth 5m
In next deep shakehole with very small stream. A short crawl to climb down into chamber below poised blocks.

5.   Depth 5m
Covered hole in grassy shakehole close to fenced sheep fold. Descend through unstable blocks, now filled in.

FOX HOLE   NGR SD 734972   Grade I
Alt. 350m   **Length 61m**
Explored 1975, KCC.

Small hole in SE bank of Needlehouse Gill about 137m downstream from main rising by top corner of plantation. Entrance drops into 30m of walking-size passage leading downwards along the strike. At far end way closes down and is heavily choked by gravel banks. Just before the crawl a climb in the roof leads to very small tube, followed for about 18m. Fox footprints found here were going one way only! Cave is thought to be parallel to Uldale House system, and an earlier development. Entrance blocked at present.

GREEN RIGG POT   NGR SD 736989   Grade III
Alt. 404m   **Length 180m**   **Depth 17m**

Explored 1966, NPC; extended 1993, ULSA/NPC.

Entrance in Smiddy Lmst, main passage in Peghorn Lmst.

An interesting cave which appears to be a remnant of a large pre-glacial fossil trunk route. Follow Doven Gill up from road and where gill forks climb out of stream valley to south and follow obvious line of shakeholes. Entrance is located in third shakehole, about 274m south of gill.

Entrance pitch (bolt belay) is 2.4m descent to ledge followed by 10m descent landing on cone of animal skeletons in the 1st Chamber, a large fossil passage littered with breakdown. To the north and behind the ladder the passage is blocked by fill and here a low crawl at roof level becomes too low after 8m. 6m from the bottom of pitch a route behind a large boulder near the left wall leads down to an unstable undercut and a diversion of routes; left leads to a large aven, whilst ahead is a streamway choked almost immediately by glacial fill.

To the south from the bottom of the ladder the large passage becomes blocked by fill and breakdown. A crawl at roof level reaches the 2nd Chamber, the outlet for which is another crawl at roof level leading to the 3rd Chamber which contains a large stalagmite boss. At the far end a short section of walking-size passage reaches a run-in of black cobbles where a stream enters and a short passage and squeeze on the right gains a large aven. Ahead the main passage degenerates into a flat-out crawl in water ending at two shingled ducks beyond which the way forward finally becomes too low.

A stream on the surface above the end of the cave has been tested to Needlehouse Gill.

Tackle – 14m ladder; bolt belay; 18m lifeline.

BOLT BELAYS – see Warning, page 13.

LADY BLUE'S UNDERWATER FANTASY
NGR SD 718973

Alt. 229m   **Length 450m**

Explored 1976/76, KCC; extended 1987, CDG.

GScL.   There is no passable cave for non-divers. Entrance is in plunge pool below waterfall in river Rawthey, about 18m upstream from Rawthey Cave. It is impossible to enter in times of moderate to heavy flood.

Low, submerged bedding passage (Sump 1) leads to air after 15m, and a low crawl meets Sump 2 after 15m. This is 158m long and reaches a depth of 12m, being very large and varying from 1.5m × 6m to a tube 4.5m in diameter. At the far end, surface is reached in Dog Dirt Aven, a chamber 18m high and 9m across. Continuing large passage can be followed to abandoned sump in another large chamber, but by-pass reached via climb on shelf to left rejoins stream, and just beyond a small waterfall is start of Sump 3.

This final sump is 100m long and goes down to 15m, with several low sections, before finally emerging in Colonel Comer's Party, a stooping-size passage which ends in a boulder choke after 30m. An alternative roof-level crawl also ends at same choke, where dangerous route rejoins abandoned main passage. 46m of walking ends at Sump 4 dived for 30m to an underwater choke.

The whole of the cave explored to date runs fairly straight NE, and is believed to be main drainage route for most of the streams sinking along W side of Wild Boar Fell.

Permission – Uldale House or Eller Hill.

LADY LOWTHER'S WELL   NGR NY 754034
Alt. 300m   **Length 10m**
Explored 1993, CDG.

Rising on Ravenstonedale Common, 200m below Kirkby Stephen-Sedbergh road. Below water, divers have followed a low passage to a partial choke after 10m.

LOW GREENRIGG POTS
Alt. c 520m
Explored 1979-1984, GC; except for Featherbed Pot.

ML.   Holes on limestone outcrop between Scandal Head and Clouds Gill, listed from north to south.

1.   Cirrus Pot   NGR SD 754993   Grade III
Depth 15m

At NE end of Low Greenrigg near stream sink in broad depression. Very tight opening beside large boulders onto 9m ladder pitch, followed by gully descent with squeeze, to narrow rifts.

2.   Slickenside Pot   NGR SD 753999   Grade II
Depth 5m

DANGER – Unstable blocks.

In shallow shakehole on terrace above sheepfold; sealed entrance to pitch into shattered chamber.

3.   Black Horse Pot   NGR SD 750998   Grade II
Depth 12m

Slabbed entrance at N end of deep shakehole. 9m ladder pitch and short climb in rift with loose blocks.

4.   Featherbed Pot   NGR SD 750998   Grade I
Length 25m   Depth 8m
Explored NPC.

Open cave with short climb down into roomy passage ending in mud choke; low branch enters rift in floor.

5.   Noodle Pot   NGR SD 748995   Grade I
Length 9m   Depth 4.5m
Climb down into short passage with right branch into parallel fissure.

6. Bike Pot   NGR SD 747995   Grade I
Length 5m

In shakehole just N of old conduit. Two short fissures.

7. Damocles Pot   NGR SD 747995   Grade II
Depth 9m

In third shakehole S of old conduit. Covered hole requires 5m ladder to platform of jammed blocks, with climb down narrow rift below.

8. Sheepfold Sike Pot   NGR SD 746995   Grade II
Length 35m   Depth 14m

Entrance high on bank between two shakeholes W of fenced sheepfold. 13m pitch (3m belay) bells out into an aven chamber with rift to NE ending in tight crawl and rift to SW in aven with unstable blocks; from pitch a low descending tube passable for 11m through tight wet squeeze to loose blockfall.

9. Small Pot   NGR SD 746993   Grade I
Depth 5m

An open climbable rift.

MICROMESH CAVE   NGR NY 763019   Grade II
Alt. 415m   Length 25m
Explored 1983, GC.

UL. On Wharton Fell, in immature sink 100m SSW of Whorn Gill Head Sinks. Constricted tubular crawl with even tighter tubes to sides, ends too tight.

MOOR POT SINKS   NGR NY 767024   Grade II
Alt. 390m   Length 10m
Explored GC.

UL. On Wharton Fell, in large depression just W of wall running S to Little Fell.

North Sink

Squeeze beneath blocks to low descending passage and choke.

South Sink

Dug squeeze into low tube to awkward bend and drop into rift, then too tight.

NEEDLEHOUSE GILL CAVE NGR SD 740973 Grade III
Alt. 402m   Length 400m
Explored 1979-1980, GC.

WARNING – Avoid in wet weather. After rain Surge Series fills rapidly, and overflows through Flush Series. Unstable rock in parts.

ML. On N bank of Gill just above highest exposure of limestone, 30m SE of boulder-choked Flood Rising. Covered hole. 2.2m climb down through constriction into joint network. Most obvious crawl, beneath stream bed, to Shower Chamber, blockfall chamber with nine passages leading off. To north is Flush System, various downstream routes to Stall Chamber where squeezes to left bypass choke and lead via canal passage to Aquarius Chamber and then increasingly unstable passage close to Flood Rising. Two routes (the left hand the easier) to east of Shower Chamber into Surge Series, a complex of passages which variously end in unstable chokes, tight inlets and sumped fissures.

NEEDLEHOUSE GILL RISING   Grade II
NGR SD 739972
Alt. 390m   **Length 20m**
Explored 1966, NPC.

ML.   Resurgence on S side of Gill about 0.8km upstream of bridge. Crawl over collapsed blocks to squeeze into stream passage with numerous fallen blocks, ending in mass of unstable boulders. Short joint cave in scar 35m to W.

NORTH SLOPE POTS   NGR SD 763001   Grade II
Alt. 525m

ML.   On highest part of Main Limestone outcrop, over the watershed from Little Wold.

1.   **Depth 6m**
   Under scar in wide sink depression is narrow fissure descent in clean rock.

2.   **Depth 9m**
   In shakehole near 1. Entrance through gritstone blocks then climb down limestone pot.

RAWTHEY CAVE   NGR SD 718973   Grade I
Alt. 229m   **Length 107m**
Extended 1974/75, KCC.

   Entrance down boulder slope above rising on S bank of river Rawthey near mouth of gorge. Roomy passage to Sump 1 after 9m, and water outlet on right. Sump is 18m to airbell, with Sump 2, also 18m long, following immediately. Larger passage with aven inlet ends after 12m at Sump 3, dived for about 21m to area of silt banks rising close to roof. Roof at entrance to sump is unstable. Small side passage between Sumps 2 and 3 also sumps. Aven has been scaled for 6m to bedding which becomes too low; a roof passage parallels the main route and rejoins it by Sump 3.

RAWTHEY CAVE NORTH   NGR SD 718973   Grade II
Alt. 229m   **Length 15m**
Explored 1973, GC.

   In N wall of gorge opposite Rawthey Cave is flat crawl in bedding which narrows to small sump.

SCANDAL BECK SINK   NGR SD 757997   Grade II
Alt. 488m   **Depth 9m**
Explored NPC.

ML.   A straight shaft taking the stream, choked at the bottom.

Tackle – 9m ladder; stake & sling belay; 12m lifeline.

SCANDAL HEAD POTS   NGR SD 758998   Grade I
Alt. 490m

1.   **Length 5m**

By choked sink at head of shallow dry gorge; two short excavated holes.

2.   **Depth 5m**

Stream sinks into short cave with skylight entrance on bank; now largely silted up.

SINK HOLE   NGR SD 734987   Grade I
Alt. 400m   **Length 6m**   **Depth 2m**
Explored 1993, ULSA/NPC.

SmL.   Elongated shakehole 150m SW of Green Rigg Pot takes a large stream in wet conditions. A descending clean-washed crawl gets too low over cobbles after 6m.

ULDALE HOUSE RISING   NGR SD 729968
Alt. 259m   **Length 329m**   **Rises 37m**
Explored 1974, KCC.

Small pool below Uldale House emits strong flow which runs into river Rawthey 18m away. At a depth of 1.5m a narrow slot leads into a very silty submerged passage 43m long. Sump ends at strike-orientated passage which is comfortable walking in a well-decorated streamway past several boulder obstructions to the top sump. All this part of the cave is dead straight. Top sump has been dived for 30m to within a few metres of air-space, but stirred-up silt prevented proper exit being found. Now silted up completely.

No accessible cave for non-divers.

WHITE GREEN SINK   NGR SD 725977   Grade I
Alt. 313m   **Length 5m**   **Depth 1.5m**
Explored 1993, ULSA/NPC.

SiL.   Obvious sink at W end of White Green Pasture. A former dig through blocks (now filled in) gained the stream in an unstable boulder choke. Short crawl amongst very loose blocks ended where the water disappeared into a chaos of large shattered blocks. Water probably flows to Eller Hill Rising.

WHORN GILL HEAD SINKS   NGR NY 763020   Grade I
Alt. 411m

UL.   On Wharton Fell. Sinkhole 600m SW of Moor Pot. W side has fissure becoming too tight, with 3m fragment of phreatic tube above.

WHORN GILL POT   NGR NY 760028   Grade II
Alt. 320m   **Depth 9m**
Explored NPC.

GScL.   In shakehole on E side of Whorn Gill, downstream of main sink. A choked shaft in dangerously shattered rock.

Tackle – 9m ladder; stake & sling belay; 12m lifeline.

WILD GOOSE CAVE   NGR NY 748006   Grade II
Alt. 427m   **Length 5m**
Explored GC.

Shallow rocky sink in valley between Low and High Whiterigg. Short fissure passage to shallow blind pot.

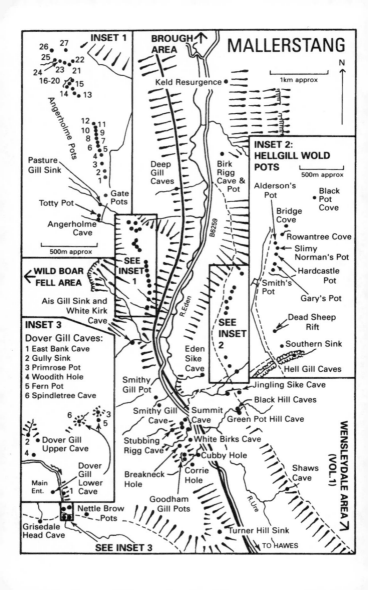

MALLERSTANG

AISGILL SINK   NGR SD 769975   Grade II
Alt. 420m   **Length 12m**
Explored GC.

Fissure sink by S bank of Ais Gill, 5m from head of White Kirk Gorge. Explorable only in dry conditions. Under slabs, short drop to descending tube ending too tight where waterfall audible. Replace slabs over entrance.

ANGERHOLME CAVE   NGR SD 771982   Grade IV
Alt. 405m   **Length 580m**
Explored 1977-80, GC.

WARNING – Very tight squeezes and crawls, dangerous loose boulders, liable to severe and rapid flooding.

Entrance by small sink in shallow gully above Angerholme Gill Head. Wriggle down between blocks into crawl and squeeze; after second small chamber very narrow fissure may require gravel clearance, before squeeze into stream. Downstream 30m of low passage. Upstream varied going, with tight crawls (one bypassed by Leapfrog Rift at higher level) and long oxbow on the right, beyond which easier going, with blockfall chamber (The Crematorium) on left; after further blockfall 45m long inlet on right. Main upstream passage has further squeezes and boulder obstacles; where walking height passage resumes, very dangerous loose wall on left. After bends and impassable oxbow on left, passage divides into two uncomfortable crawls reuniting at Pedestal Junction, then easier going again past main stream entering from impassable inlets on left, to sharp 'U' bend to squeeze, crawl and final choke.

ANGERHOLME POTS   Grades I-III
NGR SD 772986-768996

ML. Line of pots extending for 0.8km along E flank of Wild Boar Fell. There are two groups of pots, separated by a series of shakeholes and walk-down coves. Numbering is from the S.

Southern Series
Alt. 442m-463m

1. Stump Pot   NGR SD 772986   **Depth 18m**
Explored GC.

Climbable 6m descent into open pot; short climbable pitch at S end, walled passage at N end to 8m ladder pitch with squeezes into two aven shafts below.

2. Secret Pot   **NGR SD 772986**   **Depth 17m**
Explored GC.

Open pot has wedged block over easy slope to tall rift. Under W wall of shakehole constricted descending crawl to 16m ladder pitch, to short passage ending too tight.

3. 6m easy pot next to silted sink.

4. High Bank Pots   **NGR SD 772988**   **Depth 12m & 10m**

Two parallel rifts requiring tackle. E pot has pitches of 8m and 4.5m, W pot is 9m pitch to short passage.

5. 5m deep hading rift, climbable at S end.

6. Trident Pot   **NGR SD 771988**   **Grade III**
Extended 1965 & 1977, GC.   **Depth 26m**

Three shafts in one depression, outer ones blind (E 8m deep, W 4.5m deep). Central hole climbable in gully at S end; pitches of 5m and 8m follow, with loose slope between, then 2m climb to showerbath and outlet tube too narrow after 12m.

7. Small fissure pot with tight entrance, 4.5m deep.

8. Window Pot   **NGR SD 771989**   **Grade III**
                                                                        Depth 12m

A series of inter-connecting shafts and rifts below two shallow surface pots. Stream sinks in N hole and reappears in chamber below, reached by 5m pitch from muddy cave entrance in side of S hole. Adjacent pitch drops into connecting rift to a roofed shaft on W side with window to S hole and two short entrance pitches via N hole.

9. J Pot   **NGR SD 771989**   **Depth 6m**
Open 'J'-shaped rift, climbable at S end.

10. Sett Pot   **NGR SD 771990**   **Depth 14m**
Explored GC.

Wide rock-walled shakehole has tight entrance on N to narrow rift pitch.

11. Depth 6m; walk down to 3m climb into choked rift.

12. Poly Pot   **NGR SD 771990**   **Depth 12m**
Explored GC.

Squeeze past boulder then chimney down rift to 8m pitch.

Northern Series
13.   **Depth 6m**

Open shaft with rowan tree in first shakehole SE of Cove Pot.

14. Cove Pot   **NGR SD 769993**   **Depth 18m**

A long E-W rift is deepest at W end where small stream falls and sinks in choked fissure. Easiest descent is by 4.5m pitch from wedged block into cross-rift, then scrambling. E end chokes at 12m depth in narrow rift.

15.   **Depth 17m**

Dry shaft with pitches of 11m and 6m.

16.   Nab Pot   **NGR SD 769994**   **Depth 11m**

Wide pot with floor sloping down to choked sink. 4m pitch where stream enters needs long belay.

17.   **Depth 12m**

In adjacent shakehole, just S of path. Rift pot with 9m pitch and narrow fissure down to choke.

18.   **Depth 6m**

Slope down to cave with 4.5m climbable pitch to choke.

18a.   **Depth 4.5m**

Small climbable pot taking bog drainage.

19.   Vein Pot   **NGR SD 769994**   **Depth 20m**
Explored 1981, GC.

WARNING – Unsafe and best avoided.

Sink on mineralised fault line. Small muddy hole under boulder on S side to series of climbable pitches over precarious boulder piles; stream sinks in choked fissures.

20.   **Depth 8m**

On line of vein to NE, narrow pot needing ladder.

21.   Beacon Hill Pot   **NGR SD 769994**   **Grade II**
Extended 1970, CPC.   **Depth 27m**

On highest plateau of Angerholme Wold. Fine pitch in wide shaft followed by narrow 2nd pitch to gravel floor.

Tackle

Pitch	Ladder	Belay	Lifeline
1st	15m	4.5m	21m
2nd	12m	3m	15m

22.   **Depth 9m**

Straight shaft, a few metres SE of Beacon Hill Pot.

23.   **Depth 9m**

Choked rift just NW of Beacon Hill Pot.

24a.   **Depth 4m**

A choked gully sink.

24b.   **Depth 3m**

Another choked sink.

25.   Main Sink   **NGR SD 768996**   **Depth 8m**

Big rock-walled sink with floor of collapsed blocks through which stream sinks. Climbable gully in SE side.

26.　　　　　　　　　　　　　　　　　　　　　　　**Depth 6m**

Narrow climbable pot.

27.　　　　　　　　　　　　　　　　　　　　　　　**Depth 4m**

Choked sink with tree on Little Wold.

Tackle – most shafts can be explored with two 8m ladders; stake & sling belay; and 25m lifeline.

BIRK RIGG CAVE　　　NGR NY 785008　　　Grade II
Alt. 296m　　　　　**Length 21m**
Explored 1973, GC.

ML.　Entrance covered by sheets, in deep sinkhole 91m ESE of Birk Rigg Farm, near Outhgill. Approach by following fell wall from Thrang Bridge. Debris slope leads to low streamway. Downstream becomes a tight, descending rift with traverse over constrictions and boulder blockages. Flat crawling with stream follows, to a chamber and massive collapse.

BIRK RIGG POT　　　NGR NY 785009　　　Grade II
Alt. 296m　　　　　　　　　　　　　　　　　　**Depth 9m**

ML.　Climbable descent into roomy rift chamber, floor of which is several metres deep in bones, spiced with old iron and broken bottles!

BLACK HILL CAVES　　　NGR NY 788963　　　Grade III
Alt. 400m
Explored 1979, MSG.

GL.　Two caves on opposite side of gorge of infant Ure to Green Pot Hill Cave.

1.　　　　　　　　　　　　**Length 10m**

Active rising. Bedding crawl to choke.

2.　　　　　　　　　　　　**Length 30m**

Bedding entrance a few metres E of 1. Inside entrance right fork chokes after 5m, left fork crawl for 8m to dug-out squeeze, then continuing crawl through technical duck with minimal air-space, ending in choked bedding.

BREAKNECK HOLE　　　NGR NY 777957　　　Grade I
Alt. 393m　　　　　**Length 8m**　　　　　**Depth 4.5m**
Explored 1976, YURT.

ML.　On shoulder of gill S of waterfall E of White Birks Cave. Hole covered by rocks is climb down into zig-zag rift ending at blank wall after muddy squeeze.

CORRIE HOLE　　　NGR SD 779953　　　Grade I
Alt. 412m　　　　　**Length 9m**
Explored 1972, YURT.

ML.　In shallow depression 91m S of Goodham Gill. Through cave with stream flowing in impenetrable joints below.

CUBBY HOLE   NGR SD 731955   Grade I
Alt. 372m   **Length 4.5m**
Explored 1972, YURT.

UnL. Entrance behind rocks on S side of beck in small gorge. Crawl to sump below mud blockage. Possible old resurgence.

DEEP GILL CAVES   NGR SD 777003   Grade I
Alt. 350m   **Length 5m**
ML. Several small caves in shallow gorge just above railway.

DOVER GILL CAVES   Grades II-III
Alt. c 410m
Explored 1982-4, GC.

ML. This series of caves associated with Dover Gill, a tributary of Grisedale Beck, includes Dover Gill Lower and Upper Caves. Smaller caves in the group not passably linked to these are listed below; there are other small caves in the area, none more than 8m long.

East Bank Cave   Length 30m
Small walled entrance opposite resurgence. Crawling to joint fissure doubling back to stream bank, but too tight to emerge.

Fern Pot   (Length and depth – see Dover Gill Lower Cave)
Abandoned sink hole in dry valley below Primrose Pot. Alternative entrance to Dover Gill Lower Cave.

Gully Sink   Depth 8m
10m NW of entrance to Dover Gill Upper Cave. A few metres of steeply-descending passage to choke; water reappears in Upper Cave.

Primrose Pot   Depth 5m
The active sink for Dover Gill Lower Cave. Climbable surface shaft to short rift passage and unroofed aven; second small shaft at top of surface waterfall, to choked chamber.

Woodith Hole   Length 47m
Midway between Gully Sink and the Lower Cave, 4m from the stream bed. 4m deep draughting fissure into breakdown chamber and short sumped streamway, between Upper and Lower Caves.

DOVER GILL LOWER CAVE NGR SD 757944 Grade III
Length 376m
Explored 1982-4, GC.

WARNING – First section floods rapidly to roof, ducks beyond only passable in dry conditions.

ML. Main entrance above resurgence, where tight fissure drops into wet bedding. Other entrances are Fern Pot, abandoned sink in dry valley leading up to Primrose Pot, and Spindletree Cave, 30m SW of Primrose Pot, in enticing sink with tree that may be Spindle or Purging Buckthorn. Main entrance is wet crawl; after Bar Chamber 40m long low inlet on left, from surface stream sink. Main passage improves to stooping height, but after impassable inlet from Upper Cave, lowers again to duck, then higher section with choked high-level passage. After sharp bends, tight tube at right angles on left is link to Spindletree Cave. Main passage subdivides; main left branch ends where daylight can be seen from Primrose Pot, right branch to exit (for the slim), via 8m climb and two tight squeezes, into Fern Pot.

DOVER GILL UPPER CAVE NGR SD 757945 Grade III
Length 514m

Explored 1982-84, GC.

ML. Awkward entrance through boulders in shakehole, through squeeze to 3m drop into roomy streamway. Blockfall downstream, but upstream varied going to large cross passage in roof. Further upstream fine canyon passage; sumped inlet just beyond stalagmite column, then lowering crawl to choke very close to stream bank. Roof passage reached by 4m climb; Old South Series has some good formations. Crystal Palace is boulder chamber; should not be crossed as passages beyond are short and end near surface. To north roof passage is traverse, and complex of joint passages and awkward entry into Elbow Inlet ending in sump and small inlet.

EDEN SIKE CAVE   NGR SD 782970   Grade III
Alt. 397m   Length 772m

Explored 1960, NPC; extended 1975 and 1982, CDG.

ML. Entrance in small shakehole 0.4km NW of Hell Gill Farm, 91m from rising, which is very tight. Downstream passage is crawl with low airspace but upstream is walking, crawling and traversing along increasingly sharp-walled passages to 'T'-junction. Left is canal followed by drier going to a sump while right a fissure can be followed to a chamber with water entering 3.6m up. Sump is 9m long in small passage, to 15m of passage becoming tight.

Above 3.6m climb is short crawl to aven and 150m of sharp rift passage (Bacon Slicer Rift). Beyond another aven is short climb and wet crawl into Candlestick Grotto and low rift to an awkward tight duck to 75m of wet crawl until the air-space is minimal.

GATE POTS   NGR SD 772984   Grade II
Alt. 415m   Depth 11m

Explored GC.

Near gate in wall, partly sheeted shaft into shattered chamber requires 6m ladder, with climbable rift descending further. In E bank of nearby grassy shakehole is small entrance to mud slope and blind pitch.

Tackle – 6m ladder; stake & sling belay; 10m lifeline.

GOODHAM GILL POTS   NGR SD 778955   Grade I
Alt. 412m

Explored 1972, YURT.

ML.   Two small pots N of head of gorge of Goodham Gill.

1.   Length 9m

Open pot-like sink near ruined building is impenetrable but in adjoining shake a slot drops into crawl connecting with low streamway. Water enters from sumped joint and flows off down inclined crawl partly blocked by cobbles.

2.   Length 36m   Depth 4.5m

Open pot 91m N of 1 close to wall corner at N end of line of shakes. Drop into chamber with downstream crawl blocked by cobbles. Upstream over collapsed block to aven with daylight at top, then down slit into stream again. Crawling past another aven and under fallen blocks to Soft Stal Chamber where large slab has fallen and blocked the way on.

GREEN POT HILL CAVE   NGR NY 789963   Grade II
Alt. 400m   **Length 60m**

Explored 1968/1979, MSG.

ML.   Obvious rising on S side of gorge of infant Ure. Wet crawl with side passages too low or sumped, through duck to end too tight.

GRISEDALE HEAD CAVE   NGR SD 752942   Grade II
Alt. 418m   **Length 35m**

500m WSW of Dover Gill Caves. Small stream, drops 2.5m into pot; narrow joint passage blocked beneath another surface shake.

HELL GILL CAVES   NGR SD 788969   Grades I-III
Alt. 415m

ML.   The narrow gorge of Hell Gill contains ten small caves near its upper end. The largest is Corrie's Cave, an intersected phreas on the N side of the gorge, 1m above beck level, consisting of a 30m long loop with a low air-space duck – which may be partly shingled up – midway along. There are four 10m long caves and three more that are 7m long, situated at various heights above the beck in the gorge side.

HELLGILL WOLD POTS   Grades I-III
NGR SD 786970-790988
Alt. 420m-460m

ML.   Long line of shakeholes stretching N along bench from Hell Gill for 2km, contains several small caves and potholes. The main ones are listed below, starting at the S end. For those of the pots that need tackle, other than Alderson's Pot, that listed at the end should be sufficient. Replace the covering over any of the holes.

Southern Sink   NGR SD 786970
Alt. 420m   **Length 5m**

About 200m N of Hell Gill Bridge is sink into crawl ending at fallen block.

Dead Sheep Rift   NGR SD 785973
Alt. 425m   **Length 3m**

A straightforward rift, becoming too tight. Stream sinks a few metres to E in roomy pot with overhangs all round at top. It appears to be choked about 5m down, and would need ladder for descent.

Smith's Pot   NGR SD 785979
Alt. 440m   **Length 8m**   **Depth 5m**

Letterbox entrance covered by metal sheet in shakehole N of Joseph's Gill drops 2m onto false floor, then 3m to another 2m pitch (care as ledges crumble), then back 3m to below entrance to clefts containing formations. Local flooding may have blocked the entrance.

Gary's Pot   NGR SD 785980
Alt. 445m   **Depth 14m**

In shakehole with deeply dissected clints, about 150m N of Joseph's Gill and just N of Long Cove – a long, multiple shakehole. On SW side of boulder-floored 'pot' is small entrance to ladder pitch. Initial short drop is followed by larger drop to rift running back under entrance to choke. At foot of continued descent is squeeze with excessively tight descending rift beyond.

Hardcastle Pot   NGR SD 786982
Alt. 445m   **Depth 12m**

Drop down into rift then forward under boulders to a 7m pitch with a further 3m pitch to right and left. Left leads to a very tight rift which continues down; right is choked.

Alderson's Pot   NGR SD 785982
Alt. 445m   **Depth 23m**

Deepest of the pots. In shallow shakehole slightly to W of main line of shakeholes, E of last junction of field walls before moor wall turns down the fell. Entrance covered by metal sheets to avoid loss of animals and people. In bottom of shakehole drop down onto a block wedged across the rift, then straight onto a 20m free-hanging pitch. Bolt belays. Digging continues and fumes take a long time to clear. Please refrain from entry until digging complete.

Tackle – 25m ladder; 30m lifeline.

BOLT BELAYS – see Warning, page 13.

Slimy Norman's Pot NGR SD 785983
Alt. 445m   **Length 8m**

In deep shakehole to the SE of Alderson's Pot. Tight entry into a low red muddy crawl for 8m.

Rowantree Cove   NGR SD 786983
Alt. 448m   Depth 12m

About 100m NE of Alderson's Pot is sink in large shakehole with rowan tree growing over the central and deepest one of three shafts. To W is another shaft with mass of rusty fencing wire in top. Stream sinks in largest and easternmost hole, containing a bird cherry tree, with descent in SE corner and very narrow 'window' at floor level to central shaft. All three pots are choked at the foot and need tackle; there is a shortage of good natural belay points.

Bridge Cove   NGR SD 787984
Alt. 450m   Depth 12m

Northwards from Rowantree Cove there are no shakeholes for about 120m. The next hole to be met contains deeply fissured limestone, with rose bushes growing in wide fissure. At SE side descent is possible without tackle down boulders, between razor sharp walls, and under rock bridge. Fissure to S side of main rift is choked 5m lower. In next shakehole but one to N is 5m climb down narrow rift to excessively tight fissure. Next large shakehole N again has 6m climb down narrow, choked fissure.

Black Pot Cove   NGR SD 789987
Alt. 460m   Depth 8m

Last shakehole that has much limestone exposed, near N end of line of shakes. Climb down boulders at middle of N fissure to choked floor with small stream dropping down pot from surface to E, and fissure to S becoming too narrow. Several shakeholes to S, beyond a boggy area, is shakehole with bottom slumping into 5m long choked cave with poised block over entrance.

Tackle – any hole except Alderson's Pot:
15m ladder; stake and selection of belays; 25m lifeline.

JINGLING SIKE CAVE   NGR NY 787966   Grade III
Alt. 396m   Length 305m
Explored 1966, NPC.
WARNING – Avoid in wet weather.

ML.   Entrances at obvious resurgence at foot of limestone bench c250m S of Hell Gill and sink 150m to E. Sink entrance drops to flat crawl and 2m waterfall; 15m crawl to Easy Street, 30m of walking passage, then long wet crawl, angling along joints, with easy duck 30m before daylight is thankfully regained at the Lower Entrance.

KELD RESURGENCE   NGR NY 786022   Grade I
Alt. 300m   Length 20m
A short resurgence cave situated near Castlethwaite Farm. A hands and knees crawl rises to stooping height and ends at a sump. Dived to a calcited mud bank after 4m.

NETTLE BROW POTS   NGR SD 761945   Grade II
Alt. 425m
Explored GC.
ML.   In line of sinks and shakes behind a scar with two risings and a limekiln.

1.   **Depth 5m**
   In the eastern of the two largest depressions; small hole joins stream in climbable rift.

2.
   Several holes behind blocks at upper end of the next big depression enter linked fissures and a chamber.

3.   **Depth 5m**
   Second small shakehole W of 2; has slabbed entrance to pot, with squeeze to stream sinking in narrow fissures.

4.
   Small sink behind W rising has climbable pot and short passage.

PASTURE GILL SINK   NGR SD 772983   Grade I
Alt. 410m   **Length 6m**
Explored GC.
   Covered hole on S bank of stream just upstream of track; low passage under stream to impassable fissures.

SHAWS CAVE   NGR SD 798948   Grade I
Alt. 427m   **Length 6m**
ML.   Entrance in S side of gorge behind Shaws, about 90m downstream of bridleway. Roomy opening into wide, blind chamber. There are various other short caves in the gill.

SMITHY GILL CAVE   NGR SD 773794   Grade II
Alt. 395m   **Length 8m**
WARNING – Loose blocks are a hazard.
ML.   On S side of gill is shakehole with entrance under old cars and large and potentially unstable slipped block (care!) into wide bedding, then right into fissure with loose blocks and no way on.

SMITHY GILL POT   NGR SD 773964   Grade II
Alt. 395m   **Length 12m**   **Depth 5m**
Explored 1986, YURT.
ML.   In small shakehole on N side of Smithy Gill. Short drop, then hole to one side leads to top of roomy fissure. Both ends are choked by blockfall, and small inlet becomes too tight. Fissure in side of gill has excessively tight aural connection to pot.

STUBBING RIGG CAVE   NGR SD 776959   Grade II
Alt. 393m   **Length 156m**
Explored 1970/73, YURT.

WARNING – Entrance crawl floods.

ML.   Follow up stream which feeds Stubbing Rigg Inlet of Summit Cave.
Left branch emerges from low entrance with rock bridge outside. Flat crawling
in stream for 12m to easy crawling upstream, becoming walking size and
ending where stream emerges from 5cm high inlet. Narrow rift on left before
end enters ochreous collapsed aven. On surface behind cave are several
shallow pots which are the sinks.

SUMMIT CAVE   NGR SD 779961   Grade III
Alt. 360m   **Length 549m**
Explored 1970/74, YURT.

WARNING – Liable to flooding.

UnL.   Resurgence in pasture W of Hawes-Kirkby Stephen road just S of
county boundary. A number of inlets on a single streamway to give a variety
of through trips.
   Water emerges from a bouldery passage which becomes a crawl with main
stream entering from a flat crawl to the right. More obvious way is dry
passage which develops into a bedding plane and after 24m this chokes.
Upstream leads into canal passage to junction with dry passage ahead and the
water comes from the left. The dry passage is easier way in via a series of
crawls from opening to right of wet entrance. The main streamway is a higher
passage to Cascades Junction.
   Main stream comes from crawl to left and continues to a collapse block,
with way over into higher passage which becomes a wet, flat-out crawl for
76m to junction with a dry passage on the right. This leads out to the surface
in a small shakehole near the sink. Main streamway is flat crawl to emerge
at sink.
   Other passage from Cascades Junction leads up into blockfall area where
crawling to right under large slabs regains solid passage emerging in shakehole.
Across this the water flows out of a low bedding plane – Stubbing Rigg Inlet –
which becomes higher until two cascades are reached. Beyond these the way
continues past inlet on left until, after a squeeze, the way on becomes too
narrow. Inlet above the cascades is wholly crawling for 61m to the foot of a
small pot where one can emerge.

TOTTY POT   NGR SD 771982   Grade I
Alt. 410m   **Depth 4m**
Explored GC.
   Shattered sink in gully N of Angerholme Cave, into which it feeds.

TURNER HILL SINK   NGR SD 784941   Grade I
Alt. 442m   **Length 8m**
ML.   Stream sink on S side of wall which runs up fell from near the end of

the track to Lunds, just below crest of ridge. Water flows into low, wide entrance and can be followed down rift passage to sink in joints at foot of pot where it is possible to emerge.

WHITE BIRKS CAVE   NGR SD 779958   Grade I
Alt. 375m   Length 46m
Explored 1972, YURT.

UnL. In next pasture S of Summit Cave, 46m S of wall, in line of shakes. Entrance hole covered by grassed-over timbers is short drop onto rusting metal. Downstream crawl along tube with stream in trench below. Straight ahead chokes and way on back to left is too tight. Upstream from entrance is canal ending at an impenetrable inlet from the right. Crawl continues and splits, one way chokes and the other is too low.

WHITE KIRK CAVE   NGR SD 770975   Grade II
Alt. 395m   Length 8m
Explored GC.

   Entrance 4m above stream and 15m from rising. Crawl to choked fissure and low bedding to blockfall.

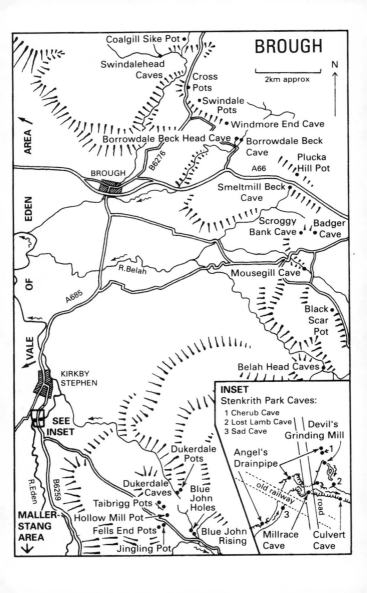

BROUGH

THE ANGEL'S DRAINPIPE NGR NY 773074 Grade III
Alt. 183m **Length 425m**
Full exploration & survey 1982, MSG.

WARNING – Flushed by frequent floods! Even when the cave is accessible there may be dangerously strong currents in the constricted passages.

Brockram. Enter Stenkrith Park on N side of Eden and E side of road; Lower Entrance 25m N of lower entrance to Devil's Grinding Mill, to right of Cherub Cave. Middle Entrance, often blocked by flood debris, on N bank of Eden 10m upstream of corner in cliff (and sinks for Devil's Grinding Mill); Top Entrance in river bank 120m further upstream, beyond site of old railway bridge.

Stream is met inside Top Entrance; varied crawling, past impassable daylight connections, to clamber down Fish Trap Falls and mixed walking and crawling in narrow jagged passages, with various short oxbows and inlets, to 'T'-junction. Right is Block Chamber with tight connection to downstream series, and on right easy crawl to Middle Entrance. Downstream of 'T'- junction is Shelf Chamber; straight ahead are oxbows (one shingled up and one with sump) linking with Downstream Canals but easiest route is right down crawl to junction with hading rift. Right is tight link back to Block Chamber, left to Downstream Canals, chest-deep wading in narrow rifts, to final thrutch over boulder and exit from Lower Entrance.

BADGER CAVE NGR NY 858132 Grade I
Alt. 336m **Length 11m**
Explored 1975, MSG.

GL. In prominent cliff 73m W of impenetrable rising. Low, dirty crawl turning left and becoming too tight.

BELAH HEAD CAVES NGR NY 858089 Grade I
Alt. 381m
Explored 1972, MSG.

GL. In gorge at head of river Belah, just below confluence of Bleaberry Beck and Potter Sike.

1. Length 6m
Obvious low entrance on W side of gorge. To right, crawl over boulder to impassable slot; straight ahead narrow crawl becoming too tight.

2.   Length 8m

High entrance at head of gorge on W side. Roomy, dry cave running parallel with side of gorge ends in choke with daylight visible.

3.   Length 3m

On N bank of Potter Sike 46m above head of gorge, 9m above stream level. Awkward squeeze down into small chamber closing to impassable rift.

Other small caves in the gorge all become too tight or choked.

BLACK SCAR POT   NGR NY 861107   Grade II
Alt. 473m   **Depth 6m**

GL.   Small, silt-choked pot in upper corner of large shakehole just W of Tan Hill-Barras road, on moor planted with conifers.

Tackle – 6m ladder; stake & sling belay; 8m lifeline.

BLUE JOHN HOLES   NGR NY 818038   Grade I
Alt. 472m

1.   Length 61m   Depth 9m

ML.   Obvious sinkhole with trees, up dry valley beyond sheepfold. Large entrance to roomy streamway passing under daylight holes after 12m and continuing to sump, completely choked 3m in at 1.5m depth. Climb above sump enters small aven.

2.   Length 23m   Depth 11m

ML.   Entrance 37m E of 1. Slide down mud slope to foot of 8m circular shaft from surface, and drop into stream, entering from sump on right which is near choked sump in 1. Downstream is hands and knees crawl for 18m lowering to second sump, too low after about 3m.

BLUE JOHN RISING   NGR NY 819037
Alt. 458m   **Length 21m**
Explored 1976, CDG.

ML.   Water from Blue John Holes rises from joints in shakehole, flows into pool and emerges from pool in adjacent shakehole. Indirect flooded passage connects the pools. No passage for the non-diver.

BORROWDALE BECK CAVE   Grade I
NGR NY 834160
Alt. 342m   **Length 26m**
Extended 1978, MSG.

GL.   Resurgence on W side of Borrowdale Beck just below waterfall. Hands and knees crawl to chamber and cascade; low section above to easier crawl, but then lowers to impassable bedding.

BORROWDALE BECK HEAD CAVE   Grade IV
NGR NY 833160
Alt. 340m   **Length c 500m**

Explored DCC; extended 1968, MSG.

WARNING – Floods badly after heavy rain. Tight, arduous and jagged passages.

GL.   Obvious rising from small cliff above Borrowdale House Farm. Tight wet crawl where stream emerges, turning left alongside unstable boulder; streamway becomes too tight 50m in but dry passage on left, with squeezes, small decorated chambers, and long oxbow, eventually rejoins stream; wet and dry passages beyond end in chokes, probably close to sink. A poised slab, The Guillotine, just after the stream is first left, fell c 1980, and the cave is blocked at this point.

COALGILL SIKE POT   NGR NY 818191   Grade II
Alt. 465m   **Depth 9m**

GL.   A few metres from the W bank of Coalgill Sike, near where the stream normally sinks in its bed. Straight pitch into choked rift.

Tackle – 9m ladder; 3m belay; 15m lifeline.

CROSS POTS   NGR NY 818177   Grade III
Alt. 427m

GL.   Obvious rocky depression E of road contains 2 at its N end. Stream sink adjoining to E is 1; 3 is under timbers in the rubbish tip on the opposite side of the road.

1.   Length 91m   Depth 23m
Extended 1968/74, MSG.

WARNING – Floods severely after heavy rain, and contains some very tight sections.

Climb down stream course into open pot. Squeeze above obvious flood sink in corner of open hole leads into blind aven. Narrow slot in side of open hole drops into small chamber, then 2.4m drop into aven chamber. Tight 3.6m drop leads off, followed by very tight squeeze and second 3.6m drop. To left here crawl to low bedding chamber and choked sink of water entering from another aven, where 3.6m climb up leads into higher aven and impassably-narrow rift where faint daylight can be glimpsed from the open pot. Right leads to squeeze over block to Starfish Junction; right here is Shrimp Passage, 15m crawl to a choke. Ways ahead and to right are crawls through squeezes to impassable beddings.

2.   Length 36m   Depth 17m
Two small entrances, use that to S. Climbable descent, tight at top (rope useful) into chamber, then further climb down into rift passage, ending choked.

3. Length 9m **Depth 8m**

Descending rift heading towards 2, ending in a choke, the only noteworthy feature being a 1.2m high stalagmite.

CULVERT CAVE   NGR NY 774074   Grade II
Alt. 183m **Length 76m**

Explored YRC & GC.

Brockram. In Stenkrith Park, on S bank of Eden 80m downstream of Devil's Grinding Mill. Entry is slab-roofed culvert under railway embankment, opening after 25m into natural upstream passage. Joint fissure to very low stream inlet on left and tight crawl ahead becoming too narrow.

DEVIL'S GRINDING MILL   NGR NY 773076   Grade I
(Stenkrith Cave)
Alt. 183m **Length 223m** **Depth 6m**

Brockram. Main entrance at rising from small cliff in Stenkrith Park on NE side of road bridge over river Eden. Interesting and sporting little cave taking part of river through a network of joint passages. Main fissure is walking obstructed by dams of flood debris to upper entrance, partially choked by vegetation like all the inlets. Two passages to left before choke lead into parallel fissure with canals in fast-flowing stream. Downstream are two outlets on right which can be followed down rapids into high passage. Traverse to right towards daylight gains access to inlet from right and dropping down from traverse, exit can be made into pool in lower end of gorge by swimming.

DUKERDALE CAVE   NGR NY 812050   Grade II
Alt. 457m **Length 15m**

ML. At foot of cliffs on N side of Dukerdale, near usually dry waterfall at valley head. Two small entrances above rising, connected by easy dry passage, with tight crawl on left to a choke.

DUKERDALE POTS   NGR NY 813051   Grade II
Alt. 488m

Explored 1967, GC.

ML. Two small pots just N of the head of Dukerdale.

1. **Depth 11m**

In deep shakehole near sink of Rigg Beck. Squeeze under rock bridge to 4.5m pitch into small rift chamber, from which a further pitch of 6m descends to a choke.

2. A few shakeholes N of 1 is a choked 9m pitch.

Tackle for either pot – 12m ladder; stake & sling belay; 15m lifeline.

FELLS END POTS   NGR NY 808040   Grade II
Alt. 503m
Main pot   **Depth 38m**

ML.   Entrance in shakehole adjoining main stream sink to E. First pitch into large rift, ladder best belayed from rock spike 3m down. Rift descends to choke, but second pitch through small hole on left at foot of ladder enters small, dry chamber. Third pitch follows immediately, and has tight take off, into blind shaft.

Tackle

Pitch	Ladder	Belay	Lifeline
1st	9m	1.5m	18m
2nd	8m	3m	12m
3rd	18m	3m	21m

Pot 2   **Depth 12m**

ML.   Several shakeholes to W of Main Pot is shaft descending to choked rift.

Tackle – 12m ladder; stake & sling belay; 18m lifeline.

HOLLOW MILL POT   NGR NY 811043   Grade II
Alt. 488m   **Depth 30m**
Explored 1929, YRC; extended 1959, CPC.

ML.   Stream sink just S of obvious open shaft (see Tailbrigg Pots). Open pot 6m deep, then chute down onto main pitch at foot of which stream sinks in choked rift. Alternative entrance 4.5m W of open pot, narrow 4.5m fissure and then 15m pitch, followed by tight crawl opening half way down main pitch.

Tackle

Pitch	Ladder	Belay	Lifeline
Open Pot	8m	3m	9m
Main Pitch	24m	3m	30m

JINGLING POT   NGR NY 810041   Grade II
Alt. 510m   **Depth 9m**

ML.   To S end of Keld-Kirkby Stephen road, further E than Fells End Pots. An obvious open shaft choked at the bottom.

Tackle – 9m ladder; 3m belay; 12m lifeline.

MILLRACE CAVE   NGR NY 773076   Grade II
Alt. 183m   **Length 110m**
Explored 1975, MSG.

Brockram.   Rising 3m above river opposite gorge entrance to Devil's Grinding Mill. Low bedding crawl in stream to tubular passage, then narrower crawl. Oxbow on right by-passes duck in streamway and rejoins stream at small chamber, beyond which the passage becomes a canal with deep water and sumps.

MOUSEGILL CAVE   NGR NY 853119   Grade III
Alt. 425m   **Length 150m**
Explored 1981-86, MSG.

GL. Lower Entrance is obvious rising on S side of gorge; Upper Entrance on step half way up normally dry waterfall. Lower Entrance leads through Wet Whiskers Wallow, a winding canal, to junction after 27m; left is boulder choke close to surface stream, right goes to choked tubes, straight ahead is sideways crawl (Near Squeak) into bouldery chamber and junction; left is squeeze to rift with very tight squeeze (Far Squeak) up to Upper Entrance, and continuing tube to fallen block. Right to easier crawling; ends too tight but before this branch on left through tight squeeze into 1986 extension, more crawling to possible dig.

PLUCKA HILL POT   NGR NY 850149   Grade II
Alt. 366m   **Depth 8m**
Explored 1968, MSG.

GL. In shakehole at rear of limestone bench is choked shaft covered by timbers.

Tackle – 9m ladder; stake & sling belay; 12m lifeline.

SCROGGY BANK CAVE   NGR NY 856131   Grade I
Alt. 336m   **Length 18m**
GL. In scar S of Rampson farm. Small dry cave, easy going to two small avens, and then crawl, ending too tight.

SMELTMILL BECK CAVE   NGR NY 849146   Grade II
Alt. 336m   **Length 1.9km**
Explored 1967/70, MSG.

WARNING – After heavy rain the entrance series rapidly sumps.

GL. Entrance in scar on W side of Smeltmill Beck, follow stream up from Light Trees farm. A long vadose system, showing remarkable joint control and with good formations. Two low entrances – enter that nearer the surface stream. Inside is a 3m high rift, and then a low wet bedding plane. Left runs back to the other entrance, and beyond to a series of wet crawls leading to Crab Grotto, and ending too low.

To the right, low wet passages lead to a higher section, with waist-deep water, then a final short low section, with two ducks, leads into a high rift streamway, with fine formations. Easy walking to Cairn Chamber, 0.4km in, 15m beyond which is Hollow Way on the right, a 46m long inlet crawl to a sump. Easy going continues through the well-decorated Hanging Gardens along a lengthy fissure which doubles back past Shrimp Inlet – a tight 36m crawl on the left. Narrower rift passage through Cascade Rift and Red Deer Rift, with two small waterfalls. Beyond the rifts the passage widens again, and easy going passes tight 18m long inlet on right, near oxbow on left, to reach Main Junction.

Right is Keyhole Passage, 137m of crawl, becoming tight, and ending in a

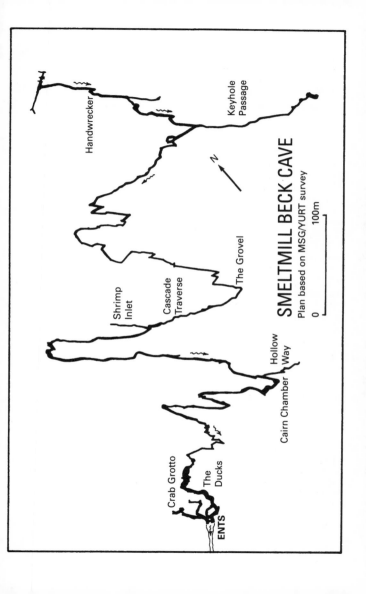

SMELTMILL BECK CAVE

Plan based on MSG/YURT survey

0   100m

N

Handwrecker

Keyhole Passage

Shrimp Inlet

Cascade Traverse

The Grovel

Hollow Way

Crab Grotto

The Ducks

Cairn Chamber

ENTS

small choked aven. To the left easy passage continues to chamber, and small hole on the right into Handwrecker Series. Hands and knees crawling, with side passage on right ending in a silted choke, to final junction with Hallowe'en Passage. To the left is a short sump into a small choked chamber, to the right a tight wet rift which closes down to impassable fissures.

Permission – Mr. Lord, Hewigill House, Winton, Kirkby Stephen.

STENKRITH PARK CAVES   NGR NY 773074   Grade I-II
Alt. 183m

Brockram.   Several small caves in the gorge of the Eden; easiest access on E side of road N of river.

1.   Cherub Cave   Length 20m

By small rising 25m N of Lower Entrance to Devil's Grinding Mill; the smaller and wetter hole to the right is the Lower Entrance of the Angel's Drainpipe. Easy crawl to where small stream enters from sump and sinks into tight rift and sinks.

2.   Lost Lamb Cave   Length 15m
Explored 1982, MSG.

Follow stream course down from Lower Entrance of Angel's Drainpipe, to impenetrable sink; entrance in bank of Eden about 50m beyond. Awkward crawl with wriggle through into parallel rift, ends in choke.

3.   Sad Cave   Length 10m

On the E side of the river, just upstream of the road bridge, is a 10m long cave ending in a shingle choke, only accessible by wading or swimming.

There are several other short caves in and around Stenkrith Park.

SWINDALEHEAD CAVES   NGR NY 815188   Grade II
Alt. 427m
Explored DCC.

GL.   In small gorge on Tarn Gill.

1.   Length 122m

Entrance on N side of stream, on ledge above obvious rising, drops into streamway. Short crawl and then easier going to two decorated chambers, stream rising from narrow fissures on right before first chamber. In second chamber easy 3m climb into upper passage with many straw stalactites, lowering to crawl, and wide bedding plane, rejoining stream which sinks into a choke. Upstream passage rapidly lowers and becomes impassable.

2.   Length 15m

A few metres upstream of 1 across small tributary. Small rising, passage lowers to wet crawl. Sink is nearby in bed of small tributary.

SWINDALE POTS   NGR NY 823172   Grade II
Alt. 419m
Explored 1922, YRC.

GL.   A group of pots associated with two stream sinks at rear of limestone bench. Follow walled lane from Brough-Middleton road and where lane turns left go straight ahead through gate.

1. West Pot   Depth 15m

In shakehole SW of main stream sink, taking water from recent gripping. Roomy shaft to ledge then narrower rift down to where water sinks in impenetrable fissures.

2. West Sink   Length 6m   Depth 3.6m

A few metres W of main stream sink, tight drop to crawl ending in gravel-choked bedding.

3. Blackbone Pot   Length 15m   Depth 20m
WARNING – A major collapse of the boulder ruckle in 1981 has left this pot in an unstable condition. Take care!

Two shakeholes S of West Sink. There is a chamber beneath the boulders of the shake floor, but pot is entered by squeeze over boulder on E side of depression. Rift descends to 9m pitch, take-off over dubious chockstone, into high chamber, 2m climb up to window onto 4.5m pitch (ladder can be pulled across from 1st pitch). Very narrow fissure at base becomes too tight after a few metres, where running water is audible ahead.

4. Gate Pot   Length 8m   Depth 17m

Next shake S of Blackbone Pot. Easy scramble down open pot then 7.2m pitch into rift; small hole drops down to a choke.

5. East Sink   Length 30m   Depth 18m

Beside the eastern of the two sinks. Two slot entrances against E wall of shake are each 9m pitches into a rift passage, with holes in floor. Chute beneath N entrance shaft is safest route down into the Main Chamber, exits from which are too tight or choked.

6. Blackbird Pot   Length 12m   Depth 15m

A few metres S of East Sink in small shake adjoining a larger bouldery depression. Two small entrances drop 3m into a chamber, followed by 10m pitch. Short passage at foot soon closes down.

There are a few smaller holes in the area, none of any great extent.

Tackle for any pot – 18m ladder; stake & sling belay; 24m lifeline.

TAILBRIGG POTS   NGR NY 810045   Grade II
Alt. 510m   Depths to 23m
Explored 1929, YRC.

ML.   Several potholes at rear of limestone area N of Keld-Kirkby Stephen road, including Hollow Mill Pot. Depths 9m to 12m except for the hole a few metres N of Hollow Mill Pot, which is a large open shaft 23m deep, choked at the bottom. Tackle listed is for any of the pots.

Tackle – 24m ladder; 6m belay; 30m lifeline.

WINDMORE END CAVE　　　NGR NY 828165　　Grade II
Alt. 381m　　　　　　　　**Length 192m**　　　　　　　**Depth 12m**
Extended DCC.

GL.　Entrance is small hole covered by slabs in field E of Windmore End farm, in depression just below the crest of the slope, near E wall of the field. A phreatic rift system. The entrance leads directly into Main Rift. First side passage on right, over small drystone wall, is tight descending rift, turning left to a squeeze up into a chamber. High level passage above wedged boulders in this chamber ends after a few metres. Main Rift continues, past two 9m tight side passages on left, to end in a small chamber, and a slippery 3.6m chimney down into a short section of rift ending too tight at the top of a mud slope.

Opposite second side passage on the left, turning right leads to Clarty Gap, a 6m long tight crawl into a small chamber; straight ahead another very tight crawl leading to two short choked rifts. Right in the chamber, up a stalagmite slope, leads into New Series, a rift, with several easy climbs up and down and some formations. Rift eventually ends in a choked chamber, and a 5.4m climb down to a blind rift, lowest part of cave.

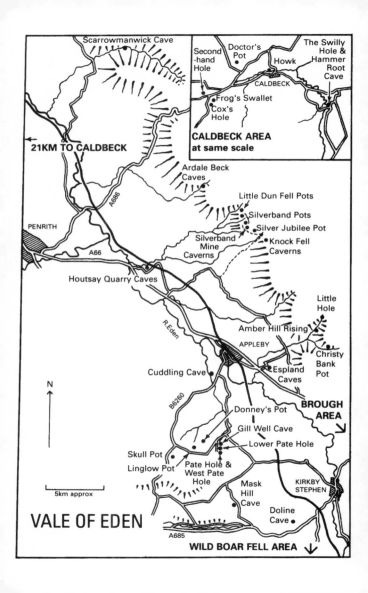

Scarrowmanwick Cave

21KM TO CALDBECK

PENRITH

Ardale Beck Caves

Little Dun Fell Pots
Silverband Pots
Silver Jubilee Pot
Silverband Mine Caverns
Knock Fell Caverns

Houtsay Quarry Caves

R. Eden

Little Hole

Amber Hill Rising

APPLEBY

Christy Bank Pot

Cuddling Cave

Espland Caves

BROUGH AREA

Donney's Pot

Gill Well Cave

Lower Pate Hole

Skull Pot

Linglow Pot

Pate Hole & West Pate Hole

Mask Hill Cave

KIRKBY STEPHEN

Doline Cave

N

5km approx

VALE OF EDEN

A685

WILD BOAR FELL AREA

CALDBECK AREA at same scale

Second-hand Hole

Doctor's Pot

The Swilly Hole & Hammer Root Cave

Howk

CALDBECK

Frog's Swallet

Cox's Hole

VALE OF EDEN

AMBER HILL RISING   NGR NY 761222   Grade I
Alt. 417m   **Length 6m**
Excavated 1965, CPC.

MSL. Important rising on S side of Scordale. Water from Christy Bank Pot emerges from massive landslip area. Has been excavated for about 6m to the underground stream, but not into solid rock.

ARDALE BECK CAVES   NGR NY 665352   Grade I
Alt. 530m
Explored 1991, Coventry Polytechnic Caving Society.

From Kirkland follow track to Crossfell. Looking down into Ardale, drop into the valley when you can see the waterfalls at the head, and make towards the waterfalls, which are in a S tributary of Ardale Beck. On the N fork of the tributary, the entrances are on the S side of the stream.

1. Length 5m   **Depth 3m**
Obvious large entrance, 4m from waterfall. Descend through boulders in floor, continue down and forward until stream can be heard flowing around you at current end of the cave, but stream passage cannot be reached.

2. Length 6m
Low narrow entrance 3m away from 1. Continues tight; possibly longer.

CHRISTY BANK POT   NGR NY 769206   Grade II
Alt. 472m   **Depth 6m**
Explored 1965, CPC.

MSL. Where Siss Gill sinks in small gorge under Christy Bank at head of Swindale. Excavated to about 6m into short horizontal passage, at present filled with flood debris. Water emerges at Amber Hill Rising.

COX'S HOLE   NGR NY 273369   Grade I
Alt. 314m   **Length 6m**   **Depth 3m**
Excavated 1968, FSWOAG.

In depression on Mickle Rigg about 0.8km SSE of junction of Orthwaite and Uldale roads. Trapdoor leads to shored shaft giving access to sloping bedding plane with short side passage. Dig at lowest point tends to fill with water.

CUDDLING CAVE   NGR NY 672185   Grade I
Alt. 134m   **Length 4.5m**

About 46m downstream of Cuddling Hole (a recess in the cliff face) on opposite (W) side of the river, 0.8km N of Hoff. Cave in river bank at water level is 1.2m high. Inside the passage splits; left closes down and right ends in fallen rocks.

DOCTOR'S POT   NGR NY 291407   Grade II
Alt. 320m   **Depth 8m**
Dug, 1970, FSWOAG.

On Faulds Brow about 0.8km ESE of lodge at summit of avenue on Westward-Faulds road. Entrance at base of small cliff in NE corner of largest of a complex of depressions. Marshy area drains into 8m shaft with unstable boulders at bottom.

Tackle – 9m ladder; stake & sling belay; 12m lifeline.

DOLINE CAVE   NGR NY 737057   Grade II
Alt. 340m   **Length 14m**   **Depth 4m**
Explored 1990, BPC.

Located in most westerly shakehole near large depression by Rasett Hill on Ash Fell. Entrance drops into narrow awkward tube for 10m to a fallen slab.

DONNEY'S POT   NGR NY 665127   Grade II
Alt.   m   **Depth 14m**
Explored 1989, CPC.

Located in shakehole 100m S of bend just after cattle grid on Great Asby to Halligill Farm road. Entrance between wedged boulders of Shap granite. Please replace wire mesh cover. Belay (5m) to trees. Through slot leads onto first pitch (8m). Second pitch is through rock window (5m, bolt belay). At foot of second pitch a short crawl leads to small chamber with dig in floor. At foot of first pitch there was a further 5m drop to floor, now filled with digging debris.

ESPLAND CAVES   NGR NY 718189   Grade I
Alt. 153m

Penrith Sandstone.   Two small caves beside beck at S side of Appleby golf course, SW of track to Espland farm.

1.   Length 6m

In red sandstone cliff is 3m wide opening to roomy rock shelter ending in wall pierced by small eroded tubes.

2.   Length 4.5m

91m to NW is hole in grassy bank into 1.5m diameter tubular passage ending at blank wall.

FROG'S SWALLET   NGR NY 274373   Grade I
Alt. 297m   Length 9m   Depth 6m
Dug 1969/70, FSWOAG.

Entrance at bottom of depression into which small stream flows, 91m NE of Cox's Hole. Complex system of passages between large boulders with tantalising glimpses of larger passages. Extremely unstable and entrance has now collapsed.

GILL WELL CAVE   NGR NY 678128   Grade I
Alt. 185m   Length 20m
Explored 1989, CPC.

A low entrance in true right bank of Asby Beck – liable to flooding and silting. 5m inside, way splits, left way rising and becoming too low after 10m, right way low and descending until too low after 5m. Both ways have mud and cobble floors, easily dug but constricted.

HAMMER ROOT CAVE   NGR NY 367367   Grade III
Alt. 158m
Explored and linked to The Swilly Hole 1990, Haymarket Caving Club.

Entrance 50m downstream of The Swilly Hole on E bank of the river Caldew.

A hammered squeeze down between boulders leads to a low wet passage heading back to the river, with outlets on the right. A tight squeeze in the right wall just below the entrance leads into a rift which increases in size until a boulder collapse, with chamber above, halts progress. Small oxbows and short sections of passage become tight, but following stream leads into main passage of The Swilly Hole.

HOUTSAY QUARRY CAVES   NGR NY 618279   Grade II
Alt. 85m
Explored 1988, MSG/Haymarket Caving Club.

Gypsum.   In active gypsum quarry near Newbiggin.

1.   North Cave   Length 100m
Large entrance in E side of quarry leads through series of chambers and crawls to loose choke and second smaller entrance.

2.   South Cave   Length 26m
Tubular passage 70m S of main entrance to North Cave. After 16m 4.3m aven opens onto quarry bench above, passage beyond ends in a choke.

3.   South-West Cave Length 10m
In quarry face 30m SW of South Cave, Loose entrance into crawl along tube to choke.

The first gypsum caves to be described in the British Isles; now believed to have been removed by quarrying.

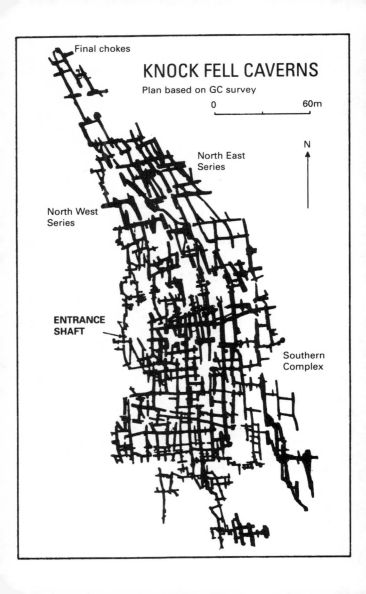

HOWK   NGR NY 319397

A number of small caves on either side of the gorge of Cald Beck, 275m W of the village.

1.   Alt. 180m   **Length 9m**   **Grade I**

On N bank of beck just below footbridge is roomy, dry through cave partly blocked by boulders at its upper end.

2.   Alt. 180m   **Length 4.5m**   **Grade I**

Short fissure close to lower end of 1 narrows and is clay choked.

3.   Alt. 176m   **Length 12m**   **Grade I**

Opening about 1.5m above beck level between 1 and ruined mill can only be seen from the stream. Straightforward crawl in resurgence cave which eventually becomes too small to follow.

4.   Alt. 176m   **Length 9m**   **Grade III**
Discovered 1970.

On S side of beck just upstream of old bobbin mill. Extremely narrow fissure about 2.4m above the stream becomes too constricted. Only for the very slim.

KNOCK FELL CAVERNS   NGR NY 720307   Grade III
Alt. 762m   **Length over 4.5km**
Explored 1979-84, GC.

WARNING – Extremely complex cave. Survey and compass essential. Considerable areas of passage with unstable boulders and loose rock. Shakehole normally blocked by snow December–April.

GL.   In shakehole 50m W of Pennine Way on crest of Knock Fell; 7m pitch (ladder required); rift passages to north (tight) and south both link to cross-joint maze of passages and collapse chambers, with occasional good formations, occupying area 320m by 120m. Near north end is climb down into Inferiority Complex, very dense network of muddy passages.

Tackle – 8m ladder; stake & sling belay; 12m lifeline.

This cave is an S.S.S.I.; please take great care throughout. Knock Fell lies within the Moor House Nature Reserve; permission to visit must be sought from the Regional Land Agent (North West), English Nature, Blackwell, Bowness-on-Windermere, Cumbria LA23 3JR.

LINGLOW POT   NGR NY 651120   Grade I
Alt. 320m   **Length 4.5m**   **Depth 6m**

On NE side of Great Asby-Orton road near tumuli 0.8km ESE of The Bungalow. Shallow depression in line of shakes has climbable blind pitch, covered over and occupied by putrescent carcasses.

LITTLE DUN FELL POTS   Grade II
Alt. 720m
Explored 1991, Coventry Polytechnic Caving Society.

1.   NGR NY 698330   **Length 5m**   **Depth 8m**

In large dry shakehole, 20m diameter and 10m deep, grassy with stones. Descend 3m then go along a rift for 4m, then descend a further 5m to reach present end of cave.

2.   NGR NY 698329   **Length 2m**   **Depth 4m**

WARNING – Loose rock, also danger of 'dam' collapsing.

30m SE of 1 in the side of 10m diameter flooded shakehole is 4m descent. Water from shakehole disappearing through hole.

Tackle – handline advisable in 2.
Permission – English Nature, by permit – see Knock Fell Caverns for details.

LITTLE HOLE   NGR NY 764236   Grade I
Alt. 473m   **Length 18m**
Explored 1963, Northern Cavern & Mine Research Society.

On E side of valley above largest waterfall at head of Hilton Beck. Low, wet crawl enlarges but soon chokes with boulders on left and becomes too low straight ahead.

LOWER PATE HOLE   NGR NY 678125   Grade I
Alt. 189m   **Length 24m**

On W bank of beck midway between Pate Hole and Great Asby. Wide entrance at foot of scar soon lowers and narrows to flat crawling over gours and
rock floor, quickly becoming too low.

MASK HILL CAVE   NGR NY 694072   Grade II
Alt. 287m   **Length 9m**
Explored 1975, Northern Dales Speleological Group.

Tight entrance covered with boulders on W side of Newbiggin-Great Asby road. Small bedding leads past unstable blocks to crawl ending at sand choke with strong draught. Water sinks in fissure to left.

PATE HOLE   NGR NY 678121   Grade III
Alt. 195m   **Length 970m**   **Vertical range 33m**
Explored 1975-77 & 1983-85, CDG; 1993, ULSA/NPC.

WARNING – Liable to complete and unpredictable flooding from main upstream sump, when it becomes an impressive resurgence. Should only be entered in dry, settled weather.

The entrance is situated on the E side of a normally dry stream bed about 1km S of Great Asby and is reached by following a public footpath running upstream on the E side of the beck.

Main Passage

Wide entrance below small scar leads into Main Passage, an impressive stooping-height tunnel with a short choked crawl on the left at the first corner. The main way continues down-dip over large gour dams passing a passage on the left (North Passage) and, a short way beyond, another passage on the left which is a short flat-out crawl connecting with Oxbow Passage.

Ahead, a wade through a pool ends at a scramble up into a tall cross rift where a descent at the far end reaches a broad sump pool. The pool is 6m deep and a way out underwater leads to an elliptical rift dropping into a chamber at −22m and a large submerged passage descending to −27m. Beyond, the sump passes through a low area before reaching a junction in a rift at 225m where both ways ahead soon become constricted.

Oxbow Passage

From the sump pool a canal passage on the left soon gains a low air-space section (which sumps in wet weather) with a submerged stream outlet under the right wall. Easier going follows past a flat-out crawl on the left which connects with Main Passage. Ahead, Oxbow Passage continues easily through pools to reach a junction with North Passage where a short crawl to the left regains Main Passage.

North Passage

This passage is more easily gained by entering the first side passage off Main Passage. An easy hands and knees crawl soon reaches a junction with Oxbow Passage on the right. Ahead, North Passage is initially a hands and knees crawl which lowers after about 100m. Beyond here an arduous and occasionally constricted flat-out crawl over shingle continues for a further 200m before the passage enlarges to stooping-height proportions. Ahead is a deepening canal which can be followed for a further 50m to gain a final static sump.

SCARROWMANWICK CAVE NGR NY 601481 Grade II
Alt. 290m   **Length 12m**
Explored 1972, YURT.

Scl.   Small entrance in S bank of Croglin Water, 2.8km upstream of village and just beyond waterfalls at head of gorge in Whin Sill. Resurgence in metamorphosed limestone is flat crawl becoming very narrow and awkward.

SECOND-HAND HOLE   NGR NY 265377   Grade I
Alt. 275m   **Length 6m**
Dug 1969, FSWOAG.

On Aughertree Fell about 18m N of Caldbeck-Uldale road. Increasingly constricted passage at bottom of small stream sink. Now collapsed.

SILVERBAND MINE CAVERNS   NGR NY 702317
Alt. 701m   Length 1.6km
Explored c1849 by lead miners.

GL.   An extensive network of phreatic caverns 0.8km into the mine and now inaccessible due to extensive collapse of the workings. In another part of the mine 0.8km of cave was enlarged slightly and used as part of the workings.

SILVERBAND POTS   NGR NY 704322   Grade II
Alt. 716m

GL.   In line of shakeholes above old hush.

1.   Stream sink, has very tight 4.5m pitch, now choked.

2.   Length 219m   **Depth 18m**
    Fluted shaft to boulder floor then further 2m descent to narrow, down-stream fissure passage trending N along a straight joint. Height increases and passage splits into parallel high-level rifts with open cross-joints, all ending in mud and gravel chokes. The small stream flows away down a narrow fissure beneath.

Tackle – 12m ladder; stake & sling belay; 15m lifeline.

3.   On Little Dun Fell 0.4km further NW, at the same level, beyond stream is large shakehole at NGR NY 703325. Climbable 11m descent amongst loose boulders to a choked rift.

SILVER JUBILEE POT   NGR NY 710316   Grade II
Alt. 768m   Length 75m   Depth 10.7m
Explored 1977, MSG.

GL.   Not easy to find; oval hole high in side of shakehole c800m ESE of Silverband Mine. 6m pitch requires tackle and belay stake, then step across blind 6m pit into series of phreatic passages with many blind shafts in floor, and some formations.
Permission – English Nature: see Knock Fell Caverns for details.

THE SWILLY HOLE   NGR NY 367367   Grade III
(Haltcliff Bridge Cave)
Alt. 158m   Length 832m   Depth 15m
Extended 1970, FSWOAG; extended 1990/91, Haymarket Caving Club and linked to Hammer Root Cave.

WARNING – The boulder chokes need a great deal of care when passing. The entire cave floods rapidly with little or no warning.

    The entrance lies at the foot of an exposed limestone face, on E bank of river Caldew, downstream of Haltcliff Bridge.
    A drop down into small chamber with three outlets, one of which is short flat-out crawl leading to another small chamber. The way ahead chokes, but to the left a tight rift between blocks leads to a high cross rift with ways NW

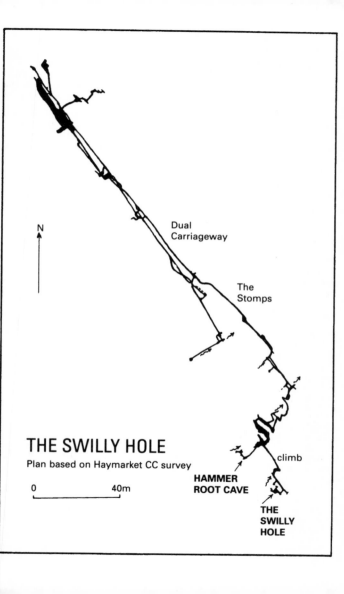

N

Dual
Carriageway

The
Stomps

climb

THE SWILLY HOLE

Plan based on Haymarket CC survey

0   40m

**HAMMER
ROOT CAVE**

**THE
SWILLY
HOLE**

and SE. Way to SE becomes blocked with mud, but the NW route leads to a chamber with pool in the floor, past small inlets on left side of passage.

It is possible to continue at a high and low level, the high route being driest and easiest, The high level starts above boulders, left through a squeeze and after a short distance a climb down regains the stream, which is followed to a collapse area, with stream entering on the left.

This stream leads to the second entrance (Hammer Root) by stooping left under boulders. Various ways on through boulders lead to a small section of larger passage. A stoop under the right wall, following the stream, enters a further collapse chamber; wet ways to the right lead through boulders back to the main passage, near where the Hammer Root enters. A few metres before the NW end of the chamber, awkward contortions lead into the main chamber (5m long, 2m wide and high) with various exits: a low crawl opposite point of entry becomes too tight; following stream to a dry exit on left, gains an oxbow (Lone Oxbow).

The oxbow rejoins main stream, beginning and ending with tight sections of rift. Two further exits, one at stream level and one above, rejoin the main streamway, which enters from under the right wall.

The way on follows the stream, mostly dipping rapidly past the Lone Oxbow on left, one tight squeeze, and short oxbows on right before becoming too small and wet (where the Caldew goes?). Some 5m back up the passage, a cross rift, at roof level can be entered in two places, heading NW, both unite, and the main way leads past a flake on the left, to enter another cross rift carrying a stream, entering from the left. To the left becomes tight with way on, also left, which joins main passage back at flake, and possible roof passage, too tight to enter. To the right, the stream is lost, but a climb up and left, or crawl under wall enters a dry section of cave, both ways meeting at the alcove.

From here virtually all of the cave is easier going, with sections of crawling. The first junction is met (after 55m approx); the start of the Dual Carriage Way. To the left a cross roads is met, ahead becomes tight, but a tight climb down gains a passage entering from the Dual Carriage Way.

To the right at crossroads is the start of the left hand lane of the Dual Carriage Way, following this a crawl back to left is the start of the passage entered from above, back at crossroads. This passage leads to a healthy stream, entering from the right. Upstream becomes muddy and tight, downstream becomes too tight, with short oxbows, above stream.

Forward along the Dual Carriage Way leads to the four ways junction past a small tube on the left, leading to right hand lane. Straight ahead across junction, the passage eventually doubles back on itself, sloping upwards with two outlets; one quickly becomes tight, the second carries on eventually becoming too tight, at a small bedding on the right.

At four ways junction, the left outlet is flat-out over mud, steeply climbing past bends until it chokes with mud and soil. The right hand passage is the main way on, it quickly divides and rejoins, until a second divide starts the Dual Carriage Way again. Both left and right hand passages lead to the 1990 choke, a low passage partly choked with blocks.

A short low section opens up slightly and by following the right hand wall up through blocks a chamber is entered. A climb up through blocks leads to a small mud choked chamber close to the surface. Following the right hand wall leads to three passages.

Straight ahead divides becoming small, the left hand branch can be followed past tight squeezes for a further 20m before becoming too tight, but with a good draught, the right hand branch enters a shale roofed chamber (very unstable) with fallen blocks barring the way on.

A climb up to the right enters the North East Rift series, easy walking passage descends to the first rift (6m high). This can be entered via a window or short crawl to the right. The second smaller rift is entered by crossing a mud pool and stooping opposite the point of entry, through a short arched passage. The obvious way on ends in small tight constricted tubes with a draught.

The third passage is tight tube which leads back under the right hand wall and can be pushed back into chamber near 1990 choke.

By climbing up into chamber left through blocks, a mud slope leads into the continuation of the chamber, an easy walking passage up to 4m square. This closes down to a tight rift, where a squeeze under the right hand wall enters a small alcove where it is just possible to stand up.

Note. A shale band can be seen in this faulted area of the cave, and a small chamber collapsed when disturbed.

WEST PATE HOLE   NGR NY 678121   Grade III
Alt. 195m   **Length 90m**
Explored 1970, YURT; extended 1970, RRCPC.

WARNING – Liable to complete and unpredictable flooding, apparently becoming a resurgence. Should only be visited in dry, settled weather.

Entrance is small crater at foot of low cliff opposite Pate Hole and is usually blocked by rocks, which should be replaced. Flat crawl rising steadily over and through muddy gours eases only slightly at the end, where a small stream emerges from a mud blockage and falls down a narrow 4m pot to a small sump. Cave may be a flood outlet for part of the Pate Hole drainage and it seems likely that water rises rapidly up the pot and overflows down the cave, to sump the entrance almost immediately. Fissure aven above pot has roots visible at top, and is the only part of the cave that might – or might not – extend above flood level. Bar belay and rope may be useful for ascending pot, as no natural belay available.

BOWLAND

For location of these caves see key map on front endpaper.

ARTHUR'S CAVE   NGR SD 797487   Grade I
Alt. 91m   **Length 30m**

Walk down lane to Fooden farm. Through farmyard the track continues and bridges stream. Follow stream down to river and walk downriver for 183m. Small stream resurges from obvious cave entrance 2m high in a scar.

Cave contains numerous rockfalls and lefthand passage round first fall meets stream which can then be followed past various collapses to final choke. Probable sink 0.4km N.

DINKLING GREEN MINE CAVE   Grade III
NGR SD 644475
Alt. 214m   **Length 9m**

In quarry midway between Whitmore Pot and road to S are small mine workings known locally as calamine pit. Lowest entrance, at foot of quarry face, leads down into a chamber with remains of a natural aven to one side. Awkward ascending traverse gains a small, natural passage to a clay choke.

FAIRY HOLES   NGR SD 656468   Grade I
Alt. 153m

On opposite side of river to Whitewell, S of wooded spur to E of New Laund Hill and about 15m lower than top of wood. Three entrances in small scar among trees high above river.

1.   Length 19.5m

Largest opening is 2.7m high entrance chamber with 7m aven at first corner. Muddy passage continues to end in calcited clay and boulder choke in roof and wall. Archaeological investigations in 1946 revealed Bronze Age potsherds.

2.   Length 14m

Low opening to right of main cave is undulating crawl becoming too low and having vocal link with 1.

3.   Length 5.5m

Opening to left of 1, and slightly higher, is crawl into steeply ascending rift which climbs 3m to a choked bedding plane floored with earth and twigs.

HELL HOLE

NGR SD 670469   **Grade III**

Alt. 214m   **Depth 38m**

Extended 1976, VCC.

Open shaft E of Whitewell Cave in small wood. Entrance pitch laddered from tree on W side passes ledge 8m down to reach floor. Pitch is free-climbable down flake below ledge. From ledge, entrance pitch ladder can be lowered down blind rift to old dig; rift can be traversed to SW but becomes too tight.

At foot of main shaft descend 4.5m stempled hole (care!) into Breakthrough Rift and 2nd Pitch, down first hole in floor. Ladder is belayed to buttress and passes ledge 6m down, from which traverse over pitch and climb up gains right continuation of Breakthrough Rift. At foot of pitch is short passage to pool. Squeeze forward at roof level enters 6m high aven and continuing passage which is being dug.

Tackle

Pitch	Ladder	Belay	Lifeline
Entrance	14m	6m	18m
2nd	15m	1.5m	18m

In shakehole 46m SW of Hell Hole is small sink in boulder-filled fissure. Next to fissure is a rift 4.5m long and 2.4m deep.

Permission – Duchy of Lancaster Estate Office, Forton, Preston.

WHITEWELL CAVE

NGR SD 667469   **Grade II**

Alt. 183m   **Length 81m**   **Depth 33m**

Extended 1986, LUSS.

On N side of Cow Ark-Whitewell road 91m along a track, opposite a quarry and limekiln 0.8km from Whitewell. Stream sinks near cave entrance in prominent scar amongst trees.

Small entrance to larger, sloping passage carrying small stream entering from right. Down through smelly debris to 3m drop into large passage and descent to chamber. Smaller crawl to abrupt drop into chamber with three exits. To south is decorated section to chamber and aven. The largest exit ends at boulder run in from an aven and last exit is small hole 1m up wall. It leads to another chamber and two further chokes. Downstream is mud floored pool – The Hodder Fodder.

Permission – Duchy of Lancaster Estate Office, Forton, Preston.

WHITEWELL POT

NGR SD 663469   **Grade III**

Alt. 159m   **Length 137m**   **Depth 41m**

Explored NPC.

Blocked entrance in hollow in small wood 0.4km from Whitewell on S side of Cow Ark road. Hole down into brick wall into steeply-descending low chamber with holes down into rift leading to 1st pitch. Low passage to 2nd pitch, a series of rope pitches down through three small chambers descending 24m to chamber with sinuous crawl to sump.

Next to sump is squeeze into larger passage and higher sandy chamber on left. Passage ascends steadily and divides into upper and lower ways. Upper route leads to aven and 18m climb up to choked rift. Lower way divides into two excessively-tight inlets but before these a muddy passage on right encounters a further inlet stream flowing into constricted passage. Upstream the way passes under two small avens and becomes too tight.

Tackle

Pitch	Ladder	Belay	Lifeline
1st	9m	3m	12m
2nd (rope)	–	–	36m belayed to foot of ladder

WHITEWELL RESURGENCE   NGR SD 661470
Alt. 107m   **Length 21m**   **Depth 16m**
Explored 1975, CDG.

Stream rises in pool below small cliff just NW of Cow Ark road 180m NE of road junction. Boulder floor 3m below surface of pool with passage leading into larger section which meets a rift. Up the rift is a small airbell and no way on. Downwards the rift widens after an initial narrow section and has been followed to a depth of 16m at 36m from base. No passages for the non-diver. Entrance blocked at present.

Permission – Forestry Commission, Kendal.

WHITMORE POT   NGR SD 645476   Grade II
Alt. 229m   **Length 27m**   **Depth 18m**
Explored 1972, VCC.

In top corner of wood NE of Dinkling Green Mine Cave is large shakehole with stream sinking near rift entrance. Short slope down to constriction at which rope can be belayed. Crawl to head of 4.5m rope pitch in large chamber. Way out enters small chamber with aven inlet and short, unstable passage on right. On left in floor is small pot from which a short rift leads to final chamber containing blocked side passages and unstable dig.

Tackle – 15m rope for pitch.
Permission – Duchy of Lancaster Estate Office, Forton, Preston.

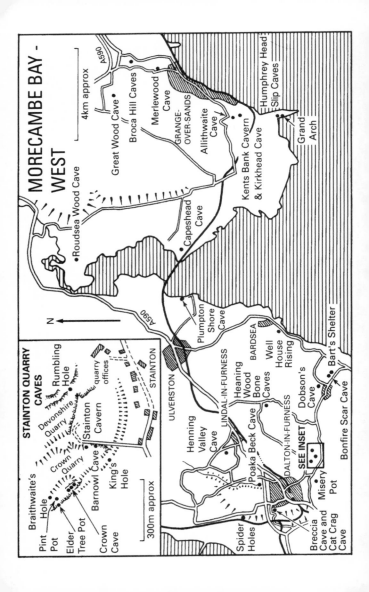

MORECAMBE BAY - WEST

N

4km approx

A590

- Roudsea Wood Cave
- Great Wood Cave
- Broca Hill Caves
- Merlewood Cave
- GRANGE-OVER-SANDS
- Allithwaite Cave
- Capeshead Cave
- Kents Bank Cavern & Kirkhead Cave
- Humphrey Head
- Slip Caves
- Grand Arch
- Plumpton Shore Cave

STAINTON QUARRY CAVES

300m approx

- Rumbling Hole
- Devonshire Quarry
- quarry offices
- STAINTON
- Braithwaite's Hole
- Pint Pot
- Elder Tree Pot
- Crown Quarry
- Barnowl Cave
- Stainton Cavern
- King's Hole
- Crown Cave

- ULVERSTON
- Henning Valley Cave
- LINDAL-IN-FURNESS
- Heaning Wood Bone Caves
- BARDSEA
- Well House Rising
- Poaka Beck Cave
- DALTON-IN-FURNESS
- Dobson's Cave
- Bart's Shelter
- SEE INSET
- Spider Holes
- Breccia Cave and Cat Crag Cave
- Misery Pot
- Bonfire Scar Cave

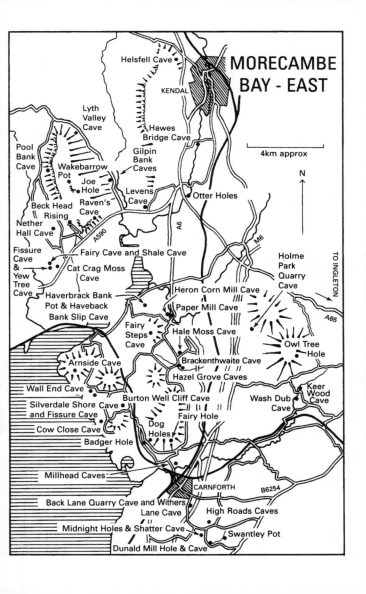

MORECAMBE BAY

ALLITHWAITE CAVE NGR SD 390759 Grade II
(Whittons Cave)
Alt. 40m **Length 18m**
Explored 1971, LCMRS.

UL. In escarpment 300m N of Kirkhead Cave.
Prominent rift on N side of steep-sided gully. Recent archaeological excavations have considerably enlarged the cave. Entrance rift is 5m high and 8m long. Human skull was found in floor deposits. Passage on right enters small chamber, then short crawl to final chamber where flowstone covers blockage.

ARNSIDE CAVE NGR SD 447770 Grade II
(Heathwaite Cave)
Alt. 60m **Length 23m**
Explored 1844, J. Ruthven.

PL. Follow track running W from main road opposite Arnside Tower (NGR SD 456771) for 0.8km to where wall crosses track. Turn left for 150m to crossroads. Turn left to where wall crosses path. Cave entrance 35m to W. Climb down holes in floor near entrance leads to lower passage ending in crawl into final chamber.

BACKLANE QUARRY CAVE NGR SD 505696 Grade III
(Dingle Pot Hole)
Alt. 38m **Length 58m**
Explored 1951, Morecambe Rock Climbing and Potholing Club.

PL. Follow road E from Carnforth towards Over Kellet. Turn right towards Nether Kellet just before M6 motorway. Cave entrance in depression immediately adjacent to motorway in wood on left of road. 4m crawl to junction with stream passage. Downstream sumps after 18m, but in dry weather a boulder choke can be reached. Upstream for 40m through two ducks to a third duck or sump, beyond which is an aven and further sump. Entrance now blocked.

BADGER HOLE NGR SD 482728 Grade I
Alt. 30m **Length 4m**
Explored 1911, J.W. Jackson.
DB. Archaeological site.

BART'S SHELTER   NGR SD 278721   Grade I
Alt. 84m   **Length 22m**

Confusingly called Bonfire Scar in some literature. In the same field as Bonfire Scar Cave but 200m to the SE. Entrance in small cliff. Drop down and immediately there are two ways on. Left has been dug for 6m till it closes down. Right passage also excavated for 15m. All cave is scene of ongoing archaeological dig. Do not disturb.

BECK HEAD RISING   NGR SD 446846
Alt. 25m   **Length 130m**   **Depth 8m**
Explored 1994, CDG.

A picturesque rising located at base of a small cliff: there is no enterable cave for the non-diver. At right end of cliff low passage leads to 0.6m high and 1m wide submerged bedding. Upstream is a squeeze at 90m, and a partial choke at 130m.

BONFIRE SCAR CAVE   NGR SD 277723   Grade I
Alt. 82m   **Length 5m**

Prominent earthwork leads up to small cave entrance in small cliff. Cave has been excavated archaeologically, and now consists of a single chamber 3m across by 5m deep.

BRACKENTHWAITE CAVE   NGR SD 498770   Grade II
Alt. 25m   **Length 113m**
Explored 1954, RRCPC.

UL. In scar by road immediately N of bridge over Leighton Beck. Network cave with several connecting entrances.

BRECCIA CAVE   NGR SD 224744   Grade I
Alt. 40m   **Length 6m**

Obvious entrance in small scar on slope below Cat Crag. A single sloping chamber.

BROCA HILL CAVES   NGR SD 417801   Grade II
Alt. 8m
Explored 1962, FSG.

UL. Entrances visible in cliff to W of Lindale-Grange road.

1. Length 6m

2. Length 30m
Permission – Broca Cottage.

BURTON WELL CLIFF CAVE   NGR SD 471750   Grade I
Alt. 30m   **Length 20m**
Explored 1965, E.G. Holland.

UL. In cliffs 65m S of Burton Well. Cave formed by collapse of limestone cliff.

CAPESHEAD CAVE   NGR SD 333781   Grade I
Alt. 15m   **Length 20m**

Excavated 18—, Duke of Devonshire.

PL.   Obvious entrance in cliff on W side of Old Park Wood, 300m N of railway. Archaeological site.

CAT CRAG CAVE   NGR SD 224744   Grade II
Alt. 49m   **Length 152m**

Walk up St Thomas Valley from lane by Brown Cow Inn. After 640m path on right just before hedge leads up through wood to entrances 21m apart at foot of cliff, that to right with short fixed ladder. Fairly linear cave except for complex of oxbows in between the entrances; muddy passages, some crawls, largely dug out. Main route ends in choke of clay fill.

CATCRAG MOSS CAVE   NGR SD 439823   Grade II
Alt. 7m   **Length 15m**

Explored 1983, MSG.

RHB.   Follow main road from Levens towards Lindale. Turn into petrol station on NW side of road at NGR SD 439823. Obvious cave entrance immediately behind garage. Uninspiring crawl in phreatic passage.

COW CLOSE CAVE   NGR SD 459739   Grade I
Alt. 18m   **Length 9m**

Explored 1965, FSG.

UL.   Follow path running N from Jack Scout Cove parallel to cliffs for 120m. Fork left for 45m. Cave entrance on right.

DOBSON'S CAVE   NGR SD 275724   Grade II
Alt. 61m   **Length 30m**   **Depth 20m**

Explored 1890, Barrow Naturalists Field Club.

Archaeological cave, to N of Scales village, in first field on left of Baycliffe road as it climbs out of Scales. Entrance covered over c 1925 and exact location now uncertain.

DOG HOLES   NGR SD 483730   Grade I
Alt. 53m   **Length 55m**

PL.   From Black Bull public house in centre of Warton village, follow road up hill to gate on right-hand side of road at NGR SD 481730. Through gate for 200m along structural valley. The two cave entrances are located in a limestone pavement. Easy passage from N entrance to collapsed shaft 6m deep connecting with surface. Passage continues for 27m, becoming too tight. Upper passage entered from top of shaft. Lower fissure entered from base of shaft. Archaeological site.

DUNALD MILL HOLE – DUNALD MILL CAVE
NGR SD 515676   Grade III
Alt. 76m   Length 309m

WARNING – Crawls in Dunald Mill Hole sump during floods. Pollution by sewage.

UL.   Follow road from Over Kellet towards Nether Kellet. Turn left at NGR SD 513685. Turn left immediately after quarries for 330m to Dunald Mill Cottage. Obvious entrance in semi-blind valley immediately left of road.

Follow stream from cave entrance along Dunald Mill Hole through four short crawls to reach Far Chamber and terminal sump. Possible to continue beyond this point into Pool Chamber under dry conditions. Cave beyond Pool Chamber accessible only to divers. 4m long, boulder-filled bedding plane leads to large passage with an airbell and the present limit of exploration.

Entrance to Dunald Mill Cave on left inside entrance to Dunald Mill Hole. Short crawl to junction. Left soon becomes tight. Right leads down inactive streamway to 5m climb down. Passage at foot of climb soon becomes too tight. Permission – Dunald Mill Cottage.

FAIRY CAVE   NGR SD 434826   Grade II
Alt. 9m   Length 165m

MaL.   Turn off Witherslack-High Newton road at NGR SD 426840 along track to Slate Hill Farm. Turn left at 'T'-junction and right at base of hill. Follow path for 1.3km. Cave entrances visible in cliff; Fairy Cave is second entrance. Muddy, stooping-size stream passage ends in mud sump.

FAIRY HOLE   NGR SD 496729   Grade I
Alt. 82m   Length 16m   Depth 5m

Excavated 1954-62, RRCPC.

PL.   From Black Bull public house in centre of Warton village, follow road up hill. After 200m, turn into abandoned quarry on right. Take path on W side of quarry and follow this northwards alongside stone wall for 250m to junction of stone walls. Continue N alongside the same stone wall for 90m to point where wall turns NE. At this point, leave the wall and continue N for 200m. Cave may be recognised by large spoil heap outside entrance. From large entrance passage a climb leads to a large lower-level passage.

FAIRY STEPS CAVES   NGR SD 487789   Grade I

UL.   Follow road SW from Beetham to Slack Head. At NGR SD 493790, turn right along public footpath. Follow this for 0.5km to junction. Turn left and follow path for 0.4km to steps descending cliff. Caves in base of cliff to left of steps. Caves formed by collapse of limestone cliff.

1.	Alt. 100m	Length 4m
2.	Alt. 100m	Length 5m
3.	Alt. 100m	Length 5m

FISSURE CAVE　　　　NGR SD 455755　　　　Grade I
Alt. 5m　　　　　　**Length 15m**

PL.　Follow marine cliff N from Silverdale Cove for 100m. Cave is obvious rift-like entrance at base of cliffs. Easy passage soon becomes too tight.

FISSURE CAVE (Lyth)　　　NGR SD 434824　　　Grade II
Alt. 9m　　　　　　**Length 20m**
Explored 1977, D. Baldwin.

MaL.　Entrance in base of cliffs 200m S of entrance to Fairy Cave. Narrow entrance drops into fissure which becomes too narrow.

GILPIN BANK CAVES　　　NGR SD 46-87-　　　Grade II
(Badger Hill Caves) (Lyth Valley Caves)
Alt. 8m　　　　　　**Length 60m**
Explored 1967, North Lonsdale Speleological Society.

UL.　Numerous entrances to short caves located at moss level around limestone knolls of High Heads and Low Heads.

GRAND ARCH　　　　NGR SD 390738　　　　Grade I
(Edgar's Chapel) (Fairy Church)
Alt. 34m　　　　　**Length 12m**　　　　　　**Depth 11m**
UL.　Obvious entrance in cliffs on W side of Humphrey Head 90m S of Holy Well. Can be entered either by climbing up to foot of cliffs or by descending pitch, whose entrance is found on top of the hill just above the cliff. The latter approach is, however, unnecessary. Cave consists of single chamber with short phreatic inlet.

GREAT WOOD CAVE　　　NGR SD 401807　　　Grade II
(Headech Cave)
Alt. 120m　　　　　**Length 35m**
Excavated 1951-67, H. Headech.

UL.　Follow road NW from junction at NGR SD 405809 for 60m. Turn left through gate and cross field to gate at bottom. Pass through this and cross field to pylon. Cross stile beyond pylon. Follow edge of wood and pass through gate into next field. Follow edge of wood for a further 74m beyond gate. Cave entrance 21m into wood at base of small scar. Muddy crawl to small chamber.

HALE MOSS CAVE　　　NGR SD 500775　　　Grade III
(Fox Holes) (Boggart's Hole) (Amazon) (White Moss Cave)
Alt. 26m　　　　　**Length 213m**
Explored 1954, RRCPC; extended 1963, KCC, and 1970, LCMRS.

UL.　Turn W off main road from Carnforth to Milnthorpe at NGR SD 509778. Follow road to 'T'-junction. Turn left here for 0.4km. Obvious entrances in low cliff on NW side of road, just beyond track on right-hand side of road. Main entrance is obvious. Entrance series consists of a network of passages, but the main route always follows the largest passage. Once beyond the network, the cave forms a single passage of hands and knees crawling dimensions, which after 104m ends at 1.5m sump. Beyond is a further 3m sump, and 6m of passage to an undived sump.

HAVERBRACK BANK POT   NGR SD 482802   Grade II
(Fairy Cave) (Dog Hole) (Haverbrack Cave)
Alt. 60m   **Depth 12m**
Excavated 1912, J.W. Jackson, and 1956-62, D. Benson and K. Bland.

UL.   Follow road from Storth to Beetham. At bend in road at top of hill (NGR SD 484799), cross stile on N side of road and follow path for 4m. Take path on left and follow for 35m to a junction. Turn left here for 80m to a fork. Bear right here for 100m to cave entrance on right-hand side of the path. Cave consists of a single vertical shaft with little horizontal development at the base. Archaeological site.

Tackle – 5m ladder; 4m belay; 9m lifeline.

HAVERBRACK BANK SLIP CAVE   Grade I
NGR SD 482801
Alt. 60m   **Length 8m**
UL.   In low cliff 75m S of Haverbrack Bank Pot. Cave formed by collapse of limestone cliff.

HAWES BRIDGE CAVE   NGR SD 511890   Grade II
Alt. 30m   **Length 6m**
Explored KCC.

DB.   Several entrances in bank of River Kent immediately S of Hawes Bridge (NGR SD 511891). Cave is undercut subterranean course of River Kent. Only accessible under drought conditions.

HAZEL GROVE CAVES
Main Cave   NGR SD 499770   Grade IV
Alt. 27m   **Length 450m**
Explored 1965-68, RRCPC; extended 1983, CDG.

UL.   Follow road SW from Brackenthwaite Cave across bridge over Leighton Beck. Take path on left through wood. Follow path alongside the beck and across the footbridge over the beck. Go through the gate and up the field. Main entrance is in the small scar under the wall running down to the footbridge.
   Entrance developed in enlarged gryke. 10m crawl to First Chamber. At W end is sump, which has been dived a short distance through a sediment-filled

passage. At E end a short crawl leads to Second Chamber. A further low crawl leads to Third Chamber, where daylight can be seen. At the foot of the boulder slope in the Third Chamber is the entrance to the wide bedding plane of the M6 Crawlway. Several crawls lead off this to form a network. At the top of the boulder slope, a window leads into a high passage running above the M6 Crawlway to Six Ways Chamber. The main passage continues for 45m until it becomes too tight.

8m beyond Six Ways Chamber, a cross-joint allows access back into the M6 Crawlway. A short crawl along here leads to Bridge Chamber, where a rock bridge must be crossed. A further, longer crawl leads to the base of a 3m deep collapsed shaft where daylight enters. On the right-hand side of the shaft, a low entrance leads into a rift, which becomes too tight, However, a window on the left of the rift leads into a parallel rift which can be followed to a continuation of the M6 Crawlway. This becomes choked by collapse after 15m.

East Cave   NGR SD 501772   Grade I
Alt. 27m   Length 55m
Explored 1965, RRCPC.
UL.   Easy crawl along former eastern continuation of Main Cave. Now quarried away,
Permission – Hall More Farm.

HEANING WOOD BONE CAVE   Grade II
NGR SD 267748
Alt. 53m   Length 12m
   Rift entrance in old quarry on E of drive to private house. Narrow rift to tight squeeze up into Bone Chamber, more easily reached by excavated 4.3m shaft from surface. Archaeological deposits must not be disturbed.
Permission – Mr. Redshaw, Heaning Wood, Great Urswick.

HELSFELL CAVE   NGR SD 501936   Grade II
Alt. 152m   Length 32m
Excavated c1880-85, J. Beecham.
DB.   Follow Windermere road out of Kendal to Hallgarth Farm (NGR SD 504939). Cross fields for 0.4km to wooded cliff visible on hillside to SW of road. Cave is obvious entrance at N end of base of scar. Entrance crawl turns sharply right into rift passage 23m long. Midway along, side passage on left blocked by stalagmite after 9m.

HENNING VALLEY CAVE   NGR SD 247764   Grade III
Alt. 91m   Length 213m   Depth 15m
Extended 1958, FSG and RRCPC.
   Entrance on ledge at S end of old quarry partly walled with oil-drum inserted. Roomy passage, with constricted Knee-bone Passage to right, to hole up into bedding chamber and then squeeze down into 0.3m high bedding

opening into larger passage, leading to Mud Chamber with awkward pitch into Edmund's Chamber with dangerous mining deads; various side passages, mostly constricted.

Tackle – 9m ladder; 6m belay and stake; 11m lifeline.

HERON CORN MILL CAVE   NGR SD 496799   Grade I
Alt. 15m   **Length 50m**
Explored 1976, RRCPC.

PL.   Obvious entrance by weir on W side of River Bela at Heron Corn Mill, Beetham. Main passage is active subterranean meander of river. Two smaller passages lead off the main passage to three small entrances.

HEYSHAM BEACH CAVE   NGR SD 407617   Grade I
Alt. 5m   **Length 11m**
St Bees Sandstone.   Follow base of marine cliff W from St Patrick's Chapel (NGR SD 408616) in Lower Heysham. Obvious entrance in cliff just beyond first headland. Marine cave aligned along joints in sandstone.

HIGH ROADS CAVE 1   NGR SD 515688   Grade III
Alt. 90m   **Length 137m**
Explored 1968, LCMRS.

UL.   In N face of High Roads Quarry. Largely-phreatic abandoned passages developed on two levels. Now quarried away.

HIGH ROADS CAVE 2   NGR SD 514688   Grade II
Alt. 90m   **Length 70m**
Explored 1968, LCMRS.

UL.   In N face of High Roads Quarry. Cave consists of three parallel rift passages connected by bedding-plane crawls. Now quarried away.

HOLME PARK QUARRY CAVE   Grade II
NGR SD 535787
Alt. 90m   **Length 70m**   **Depth 7m**
Explored 1993.

Hole in floor of working quarry is now sealed. 5m pitch lead to 12m wide chamber. Water sinks in floor, and passages along fault were forced for 15m and 45m.

HUMPHREY HEAD SLIP CAVES   Grade I
UL.   Base of cliffs on W side of Humphrey Wood. Caves formed by collapse of limestone cliff.

1.	Alt. 8m	NGR SD 390741	Length 13m
2.	Alt. 8m	NGR SD 390741	Length 6m
3.	Alt. 8m	NGR SD 390736	Length 16m

JOE HOLE   NGR SD 453865   Grade II
Alt. 122m   Length 6m
Explored 1961, KCC.

UL.   Follow track around foot of White Scar (NGR SD 46-85-) to 180m S of Rawsons Farm. Turn left here and follow track uphill to NGR SD 454858. Fork right here and follow this path over a wall and into a structural valley, at end of which, 0.5km beyond the wall, the cave entrance is clearly visible in the cliff to the right of the path. Cave is a bedding plane crawl.
Permission – Forestry Commission, Grizedale, Hawkeshead, Cumbria.

KEER WOOD CAVE   NGR SD 562755   Grade I
Alt. 90m   Length 20m
Explored 1969, LCMRS.

RM.   Follow E bank of River Keer N from bridge at NGR SD 561752 for 0.3km. Short hands and knees crawl in passage developed along minor anticlinal fold in Upper Carboniferous shales.

KENTS BANK CAVERN   NGR SD 391758   Grade I
Alt. 40m   Length 24m
Explored 1992, Morecambe Bay Archaeological Research Society.

   On S side of steep gully opposite Allithwaite Cave. Cave has been revealed by archaeological excavation. Two small entrances connect inside and lead to two downward leading small phreatic tubes, blocked by deposits.
   Ongoing archaeological excavation. Do not disturb.
Permission – Tel: 05395-35426.

KIRKHEAD CAVE   NGR SD 391756   Grade I
Alt. 34m   Length 13m
UL.   From Blenket Farm in Allithwaite (NGR SD 386761), pass through the farmyard along the public footpath until a gate across the track is reached. Passing through the gate, continue E across the fields to base of the wooded cliff forming the W side of Kirkhead. Follow the edge of the woods S for 200m. At this point, turn into the wood and go directly upslope. The large cave entrance is at the base of the cliffs. The cave consists of a single, large chamber. Archaeological site.
Permission – Lane Side Farm.

LEVENS CAVE   NGR SD 484857   Grade II
Alt. 8m   **Length 27m**
Explored 1955, KCC.

MaL. Follow road opposite Hare and Hounds public house in Levens village downhill. Turn left at end of road and continue downhill to bridge over drainage ditch at edge of moss. Cave entrance in small cliff to right of road just beyond bridge. Crawl along single passage. Possible to exit through tight northern entrance at right angles to main passage.

LYTH VALLEY CAVE   NGR SD 450897   Grade III
(Whitebeck Cave)
Alt. 38m   **Length 205m**
Explored 1966-69, OCC.

PL. Follow main road N along Lyth Valley towards Windermere. 250m beyond Whitebeck village is a small spring below the road to the E. Cave is 55m to W of road at this point at the head of a shallow dry valley. Crawl for 90m to 61m long sump, accessible only to divers. Immediately beyond sump, climb up 6m aven, following the water. All routes are either too tight or blocked by boulders after 30m.

MERLEWOOD CAVE   NGR SD 411789   Grade I
(Windermere Wood Cave)
Alt. 53m   **Length 9m**
Excavated 1892, H.S. Cowper.

UL. Follow Windermere Road N from centre of Grange. Through gate on right hand side of road at point where hedge begins, about 200m before sharp bend in road at Slack Farm. Cross field up slope to wood. Obvious entrance 23m into wood. Boulder slope down into chamber. Two routes on, both quickly becoming too tight. Archaeological site.

MIDNIGHT HOLE 1   NGR SD 512683   Grade III
Alt. 99m   **Length 48m**   **Depth 16m**
Explored 1968, LCMRS.

UL. In N face of Dunald Mill New Quarry. Two pitches leading to phreatic passage choked in both directions, although E choke can only have been 3m from connection with Midnight Hole 2. Now quarried away.

MIDNIGHT HOLE 2   NGR SD 511683   Grade II
Alt. 85m   **Length 26m**   **Depth 9m**
Explored 1969, LCMRS.

UL. In NW face of Dunald Mill New Quarry. Largely-phreatic passage from which lead a short pitch. Now quarried away.

MILLHEAD CAVES   NGR SD **498714**

DB.   Follow road to Warton from Carnforth. Turn right immediately after crossing River Keer. Follow road for 125m to abandoned quarry on left. Obvious cave entrances in SW face of quarry.

1.   The Big Cave   Grade I
Alt. 15m   **Length 8m**
   Single chamber infilled by breakdown and rubbish.

1.   The Little Cave   Grade II
Alt. 15m   **Length 9m**
   Entrance 24m N of The Big Cave. Crawl along largely-phreatic passge.

MISERY POT   NGR SD **234727**   Grade III
Alt. 84m   **Length 76m**   Depth 15m
Explored 1959, FSG.

   In old quarry to S of Tithe Barn Cottages. Constricted cross-rift system, largely dug out. Lower series is best entered by turning right at first junction then careful descent of Eyelet in floor; dangerous boulders in one passage.

NETHER HALL CAVE   NGR SD **436845**   Grade III
Alt. 58m   **Length 12m**
Extended 1966, OCC.

DB.   Follow track through Nether Hall Farm (NGR SD 439844) from Town End-Witherslack road. Continue along path to base of wood. Cave entrance 18m beyond spring. Low passage sloping steeply downwards for 4m. Right-hand turn at base to low stream passage which becomes too tight after 8m. Cave acts as overflow for spring in wet weather.

OTTER HOLES   NGR SD **506863**   Grade III
Alt. 15m   **Length 300m**
Explored 1950, NPC.

DB.   Follow road N from Levens Bridge towards Kendal. Take first road on right towards Sedgwick. Follow for 0.8km to first track on right, leading down to River Kent. Large main entrance just out of sight under bank. Cave is under-cut subterranean course of River Kent, and the main passage reappears in the river bank 260m downstream. Only accessible under drought conditions.

OWL TREE HOLE   NGR SD **562777**   Grade II
Alt. 213m   **Length 6m**   Depth 7m
Explored 1973, P.T. Mellars.

UL.   Follow track W from Hutton Roof village (NGR SD 570783). The track bends S, following the wall at the base of Hutton Roof Crags. Follow this wall for 1km, keeping above Park Wood, until the wall turns SW downhill at the end of the wood. At this point, cross the wall. Cave entrance in top of limestone knoll about 10m from the wall. 8m entrance pitch can be free-climbed, or belay ladder to tree. Small, domed chamber at bottom, but all routes on choked.

Tackle – 8m ladder; 3m belay; 12m lifeline.

PAPER MILL CAVE   NGR SD 496798   Grade I
Alt. 18m   **Length 87m**
Explored c 1774; rediscovered 1976, RRCPC.

PL.   Entrance beneath manhole cover in grounds of Paper Mill, Beetham. 2m drop leads down rubble slope to 1774 Hall, from where several small, interlinking passages lead off.
Permission – Cooke's Paper Mill, Beetham.

PLUMPTON SHORE CAVE   NGR SD 313781   Grade II
Alt. 3m   **Length 9m**
   A sinuous phreatic tube intersected by the sea cliff. One section enterable as low crawl to a small chamber with a tight branch passage; other sections perhaps enterable but very constricted.

POAKA BECK CAVE   NGR SD 232749   Grade I
Alt. 55m   **Length 6m**
Explored FSG.

   In obvious gully on W bank of Poaka Beck, 9m from stream. Low entrance into short mud-choked passage: uninspiring.

POOL BANK CAVE   NGR SD 433877   Grade I
(Fairies' Cave)
Alt. 58m   **Length 37m**
Extended 1969, OCC; and 1979, CDG.

DB.   Follow road N from Witherslack village to Pool Bank Farm (NGR SD 430878). From farmhouse, cross fields to base of Whitbarrow Scar to E. Follow base of scar S to spring at head of Coppy Beck. Cave entrance just inside wood at head of small gorge. Wide rift passage to small chamber, from which the cave descends steeply to the sump, accessible only to divers. 18m long sump descends steeply to a maximum depth of 5-6m. Ascend tight rift to airbell with water cascading out of small holes in roof. Beyond airbell, a tight rift upwards rapidly becomes too tight. No further passages yet found.
Permission – Pool Bank Farm.

RAVEN'S CAVE   NGR SD 457851   Grade I
Alt. 137m   **Length 5m**
PL.   Proceed SW through quarry workings from White Scar Quarry (NGR

SD 460852) for 0.4km to base of steep, narrow gully. Cave entrance is in scar at top of gully. Single high, narrow rift.

ROUDSEA WOOD CAVE (NORTH)   Grade III
NGR SD 331826
Alt. 8m   **Length 140m**
Explored 1964, A. Greening.

RHB.   Follow road from Cark towards Haverthwaite. Turn left immediately before bridge over River Leven and follow road for 2.5km to Roudsea Wood National Nature Reserve. Caving only with permission of English Nature. Cave found in low hillock within Nature Reserve. Several entrances to main system on E side of hillock, some very tight. These join a crawl running parallel to the hillside, leading to a network. From here one low passage continues through the hill to emerge on the W side as a very tight exit.
Permission – English Nature, Blackwell, Bowness-on-Windermere, Cumbria, LA2 3JR.

ROUDSEA WOOD CAVE (SOUTH)   Grade I
NGR SD 332825
Alt. 8m   **Length 490m**
Explored 1892, BNFC.   ,

RHB.   Main entrance in limestone hillock 150m SSW of entrance to Roudsea Wood Cave (North). Caving only with permission of English Nature. Main passage is large, walking and, occasionally, crawling-sized conduit, intersected at intervals by the edge of the hill. Three sets of smaller passages lead off the main passage, each leading to tight crawls and some network development.
Permission – English Nature, Blackwell, Bowness-on-Windermere, Cumbria, LA2 3JR.

SHALE CAVE   NGR SD 434826   Grade I
Alt. 9m   **Length 15m**
MaL.   Turn off Witherslack-High Newton road at NGR SD 426840 along track to Slate Hill Farm. Turn left at 'T'-junction and right at base of hill. Follow path for 1.3km. Cave entrance visible in cliffs: Shale Cave is first entrance. Short passage which soon chokes.

SHATTER CAVE   NGR SD 512683
Alt. 102m
Explored 1968, LCMRS.

UL.   In face of Dunald Mill New Quarry. Shaft leading to phreatic passage. Now quarried away.

SILVERDALE SHORE CAVE   NGR SD 456754   Grade I
Alt. 8m   Length 7m

PL.   Obvious entrance in marine cliff on N side of Silverdale Cove. Phreatic tube soon becomes too tight. Climb into aven.

SPIDER HOLES   NGR SD 219757   Grade II
Alt. 69m   Depth 9m

Slip rifts in Coniston Limestone (Ordovician) on edge of old clay pit, some very narrow.

Tackle – 15m lifeline.

STAINTON QUARRY CAVES NGR SD 24-72- Grade I-II

The large limestone quarry immediately N of Stainton village is divided into two sections; the western, now out of use and bounded to the S and W by a disused railway line, is here termed the Crown Quarry, whilst the working quarry to the E is the Devonshire Quarry.

Permission for all caves from The Manager, Stainton Quarry, Stainton, Dalton-in-Furness.

1.   Barnowl Cave   NGR SD 245727   Grade II
Alt. 70m   Length 7.6m

Entrance to N end of E side of Crown Quarry, reached by 4.6m climb.

2.   Braithwaite's Hole   NGR SD 242728   Grade I
Alt. 53m   Length 6m   Depth 3m

Obvious entrance at foot of cliff to NE of Pint Pot. May be flooded.

3.   Crown Caves   NGR SD 243728   Grade I
Alt. 61m

Entrances close together at foot of cliff below old railway track, at S end of deepest section of disused quarry. Largely excavated.

i.   Length 15m
S entrance. Tubular crawl to choke.

ii.   Length 11m
Central entrance. Crawl to choke.

iii.   Length 6m
N entrance. Muddy slope up to squeeze.

4.   Elder Tree Pot   NGR SD 242728   Grade II
Alt. 61m

Entrance at foot of quarry wall behind massive fallen block immediately SW of Pint pot. Pitch in circular shaft.

Tackle – 7.6m ladder; stake & sling belay; 9m lifeline.

5. King's Hole   NGR SD 245726   Grade I
Alt. 70m   **Length 7.6m**

Twin entrances on S side of old railway cutting. Short choked cave with some formations.

6. Pint Pot   NGR SD 242728   Grade II
Alt. 53m   **Depth 18m**

In bottom of Crown Quarry, inconspicuous entrance may be covered by slab. May contain water; the whole quarry floods at times.

Tackle – 18m ladder; stake & sling belay; 21m lifeline.

7. Rumbling Hole   NGR SD 248728   Grade II
Alt. 69m   **Length 61m**

Entrance on N side of track down into Devonshire Quarry, reached by 4.6m climb. Series of tight crawls alternating with low chambers.

8. Stainton Cavern   NGR SD 245727   Grade II
Alt. 61m   **Length 244m**   **Depth 43m**
Explored 1871.

Extensive cave system terminating in a series of steeply descending chambers. First 46m of passage quarried away prior to 1911. Since 1915 the entrance has been sealed by quarry overburden.

SWANTLEY POT   NGR SD 522679   Grade II
Alt. 107m   **Depth 8m**
UL.   Follow road E from entrance to Dunald Mill Hole. Take first turning on the left and follow track for 270m to limestone scar. Follow top of scar on left-hand side of road to entrance now infilled by sandstone boulders.

WAKEBARROW POT   NGR SD 447870   Grade II
Alt. 150m   **Length 85m**   **Depth 32m**
Explored 1964, RRCPC; extended 1982, BACC.

UL.   Follow path S from Joe Hole. After approximately 100m, take first turning on right and continue along muddy path around the base of Wakebarrow Scar. Cave entrance is obvious hole immediately to left of path after 1km. The entrance is just beyond a large expanse of deeply-gryked limestone pavement to the left of the path. Tightish descent down rift between jammed boulders. Small chamber at bottom from which a low crawl leads off. Follow this straight ahead for 6m to top of 15m pitch leading to ledge with several short routes off. A further 5m pitch leads to a large chamber. Several routes lead off this, but all choke quickly.

Tackle – 20m ladder; 5m belay; 23m lifeline.

Permission – Forestry Commission, Grizedale, Hawkshead, Cumbria.

WALL END CAVE   NGR SD 454756   Grade I
Alt. 8m   **Length 11m**

PL.   Follow marine cliff N from Silverdale Cove for 250m to small promontory. Cave entrance in base of cliffs in N corner of promontory. Easy passage, including crawl beneath stalagmite floor at one point, soon becomes too tight.

WASH DUB CAVE   NGR SD 560751   Grade II
Alt. 53m   **Length 12m**
Explored 1965, RRCPC.

RM.   Follow E bank of River Keer S from bridge at NGR SD 561752. Obvious cave entrance in bank of river just below larger waterfall. Muddy crawl in passage developed along minor anticlinal fold in Upper Carboniferous shales.

WELL HOUSE RISING   NGR SD 298741   Grade I
Alt. 9m   **Length 6m**

Strong rising from low bedding cave almost directly beneath end of house. Crawl to partial blockage.

WITHERS LANE CAVE   NGR SD 506695   Grade I
Alt. 60m   **Length 10m**
Explored 197–, LCMRS.

PL.   In Back Lane Quarry. Easy, horizontal phreatic passage. Now quarried away.

YEW TREE CAVE   NGR SD 434824   Grade II
Alt. 11m   **Length 80m**
Explored 1977, D. Baldwin.

MaL.   Main entrance in base of cliffs 170m S of entrance to Fairy Cave. Breakdown Chamber leads into short, meandering streamway and thence to second entrance. Further fragments of the same cave system can be found in the cliffs 15m to the N.

OTHER AREAS

For location of these caves see key map on front endpaper.

DIGGLE WIGGLEPIT   NGR SE 017076   Grade III
Alt. 375m   Length 61m   Vertical range 20m
Explored 1957.

Grit. Two entrances in SW side of the largest of Running Hill Pits, old quarries on the edge of the scarp above Diggle. Lower Entrance is slide down mud slope into Main Rift. At far end of Main Rift, floor steps up into the Catwalk, very narrow crawl. Before Catwalk, hole at floor level on right is narrow crawl, which must be done feet first, opening onto Stemple Rift. Climb down to foot of rift, then hole down into Lower Chamber, with many loose boulders. Awkward 9m climb up Stemple Rift leads to short passage to traverse on wedged boulders high in Main Rift, and Upper Entrance.

DOVE'S NEST CAVES   NGR NY 253114   Grade III
Alt. 457m   Length 91m   Vertical range 30m

On E side of head of Comb Gill below Glaramara in Borrowdale, 2.4km S of road. The whole front of Dove's Nest Crag has slipped down to create a unique complex of underground chimneys. N and S caves are at foot of N Gully and S Chimney respectively. Rat Hole entrance is 11m up N Chimney and Central Entrance is 27m up Central Chimney, which rises from the daylight chasm beyond the Pinnacle. N and Central Chimneys unite at Attic Cave (the highest entrance) and the Belfry is a way out 15m above the S Cave. All these are linked underground by climbs of about Difficult standard.
(See FRCC Climbing Guide – Borrowdale.)

GOOSEY TYSON'S CAVE   NGR NY 051112   Grade I
Alt. 255m   Length 55m   Depth 5.5m
Explored 1955.

Cave in stream sink 0.8km E of Wilton in deep hollow near Mousegill Quarry. Two entrances lead into descending passage and 1.5m drop into lower gallery where upper level fissure on left chokes in a short distance. Lower passage continues past crawl on right which becomes too tight then down into bedding plane leading to narrow climb up into small passage which connects back to top of 1.5m drop.

GRAYRIGG CAVE   NGR SD 576977   Grade I
Alt. 136m   **Length 6m**
Explored 1971, YURT.

On S side of beck about 365m WNW of Grayrigg Hall at edge of a small wood is a powerful rising. The water emerges from narrow fissures but a few metres to the left is a flood rising with a low cave opening above. This was enlarged for 6m but became too tight.

FAIRY HOLES   NGR SE 015047   Grade II
Alt. 427m   **Length 46m**   **Depth 11m**
Explored 1816, W.M. Robinson.

Grit.   At N end of line of depressions running along centre of ridge connecting Alderman Head with moors to N. Easy crawl to scramble down sloping ledge and 3.6m climb into larger rift passage, ending too tight. A lower series of passages was reached by a descending rift from foot of 3.6m climb, blocked by a rock fall in the 19th century.

MEARLEY QUARRY CAVE   NGR SD 774410   Grade I
Alt. 230m   **Length 13m**
Explored 1986, UBSS.

Pendleside Lmst.   Entrance in wall of small abandoned quarry on NW slope of Pendle Hill. Short crawl to junction. Both branches end after 4m.

SKULL POT   NGR NY 636115   Grade II
Alt. 290m   **Length 8m**   **Depth 4m**
Explored 1979, GC.

In shallow dry valley SE of Blasterfield Farm, c300m from Orton-Appleby road. Short pitch into roomy phreatic passage choked at both ends.

Tackle – 6m ladder; stake & sling belay; 10m lifeline.

TWIN SHAFTS   NGR SE 015046   Grade II
Alt. 427m   **Length 15m**   **Depth 11m**
Grit.   Obvious open rift about 91m SW of Fairy Holes, near edge of scarp. Northern shaft can be free-climbed, ends choked, southern shaft entered by short crawl to pitch, ends too tight.

Tackle – 9m ladder; 3m belay; 12m lifeline.

INDEX

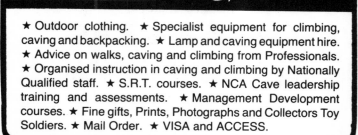

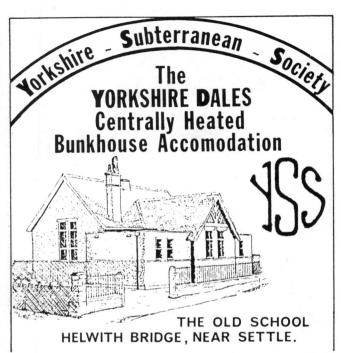

The leading publisher
on the caves of northern England

In addition to this comprehensive and definitive guide, *Dalesman* has three other titles available within the same series. They are all produced in similar format and well established as leading guides for their respective areas.

NORTHERN CAVES VOLUME I
Wharfedale and the North East
by D. Brook, G.M. Davies, M.H. Long, P.F. Ryder
(ISBN 0 85206 927 8)

NORTHERN CAVES VOLUME II
The Three Peaks
by A. Brook, D. Brook, J. Griffiths, M.H. Long
(ISBN 1 85568 033 5)

CAVES OF THE PEAK DISTRICT
by D.W. Gill, J.S. Beck
(ISBN 1 85568 034 3)

(All can be obtained directly from our offices)

In addition to caving the *Dalesman* book range covers many other outdoor subjects, such as walking, ornithology, flora/fauna, map reading, etc.

*To obtain your copy of the **Dalesman** Book Catalogue please send your name and address details to:*

Dalesman Publishing Co. Ltd.
FREEPOST
Clapham, via Lancaster, LA2 8BR
Tel: 05242 51225

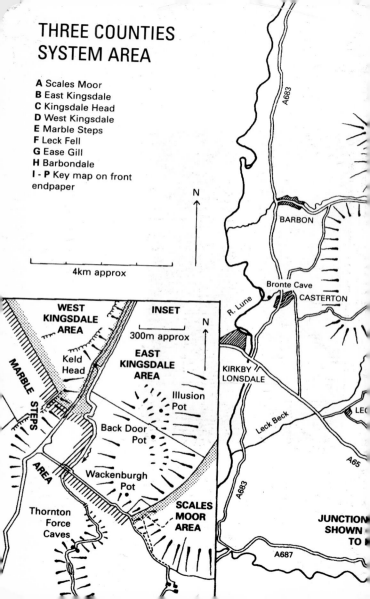

THREE COUNTIES
SYSTEM AREA

A Scales Moor
B East Kingsdale
C Kingsdale Head
D West Kingsdale
E Marble Steps
F Leck Fell
G Ease Gill
H Barbondale
I - P Key map on front
endpaper

N

4km approx

A683

BARBON

Bronte Cave

CASTERTON

R. Lune

WEST
KINGSDALE
AREA

INSET

N

300m approx

KIRKBY
LONSDALE

EAST
KINGSDALE
AREA

Keld
Head

MARBLE STEPS

Illusion
Pot

Leck Beck

LEC

Back Door
Pot

A65

Wackenburgh
Pot

AREA

A683

SCALES
MOOR
AREA

Thornton
Force
Caves

JUNCTION
SHOWN
TO

A687